The NEW Reading Teacher's BOOK OF LISTS

Edward Bernard Fry, Ph.D.
Dona Lee Fountoukidis, Ed.D.
Jacqueline Kress Polk, M.A.

Prentice-Hall, Inc.   Englewood Cliffs, New Jersey

Prentice-Hall International, Inc., *London*
Prentice-Hall of Australia, Pty. Ltd., *Sydney*
Prentice-Hall Canada Inc., *Toronto*
Prentice-Hall of India Private Ltd., *New Delhi*
Prentice-Hall of Japan, Inc., *Tokyo*
Prentice-Hall of Southeast Asia Pte. Ltd., *Singapore*
Whitehall Books, Ltd., *Wellington, New Zealand*
Editora Prentice-Hall do Brasil Ltda., *Rio de Janeiro*
Prentice-Hall Hispanoamericana, S.A., *Mexico*

© 1985 *by*

PRENTICE-HALL, INC.

Englewood Cliffs, N.J.

Library of Congress Cataloging in Publication Data

Fry, Edward Bernard
  The new reading teacher's book of lists.

  Rev. ed. of: The reading teacher's book of
lists. c.1984.
  Includes index.
  1. Reading—Miscellanea.   2. Curriculum planning—
Miscellanea.   3. Tutors and tutoring—Miscellanea.
4. Handbooks, vade-mecums, etc.   I. Fountoukidis,
Dona Lee.   II. Polk, Jacqueline K.
III. Fry, Edward Bernard   Reading teacher's
book of lists.   IV. Title.
LB1050.2.F79   1985   428.4   85-9260
ISBN 0-13-615543-X

Printed in the United States of America

About the Authors

Edward Bernard Fry, Ph.D., is director of the Reading Center and Professor of Education at Rutgers University in New Brunswick, New Jersey. Dr. Fry teaches courses for graduate and undergraduate students and serves on dissertation committees. As the Reading Center director, he provides instruction for children with reading problems, conducts statewide reading conferences, and provides teacher-training reading courses.

Dr. Fry has authored a number of practical guides for reading teachers, including *Elementary Reading Instruction* (McGraw-Hill, 1977), *Reading for Classroom and Clinic* (McGraw-Hill, 1972), *Teaching Faster Reading* (Cambridge University Press, 1963), and *The Emergency Reading Teacher's Manual* (Dreier, 1969). He also has developed a variety of curriculum materials, including typing courses for children, filmstrips, overhead transparencies, card reader programs on phonics and basic vocabulary, reading improvement drill books, criterion-referenced tests, and videotape reading improvement programs for industries and universities.

Dona Lee Fountoukidis, Ed.D., has held a variety of teaching positions. In Japan, she taught English to Japanese junior and senior high-school students. In the United States, she has taught, primarily at the college level, courses ranging from basic reading and writing to teacher training in areas such as content area reading and educational psychology.

Jacqueline Kress Polk, M.A., has had a wide range of teaching experiences in reading. She has served as a classroom teacher, a remedial reading specialist, and a reading coordinator at the elementary school level; has taught developmental reading and study skills at the college level; and has trained reading teachers. Ms. Polk also has conducted numerous workshops for teachers in decoding, comprehension, grammar, and gifted education, and she has developed curricula at the elementary and high-school levels in reading and other content areas in gifted education. She soon will complete her doctoral degree in reading at Rutgers University.

Preface to the Second Edition

We have been more than pleased with the reception the first edition of the *Reading Teacher's Book of Lists* has received from classroom teachers, reading specialists, writers of educational materials, professors of education, and college students preparing for teaching careers.

Not too many years ago, some developers of curriculum materials were talking about "teacher-proofing." The inference was that texts and supplementary tools could be developed that would provide all the instruction needed for students to learn, and that these materials would not require much of the teacher—in fact, they would ensure learning "despite" the teacher. The philosophy behind this book is just the opposite. We believe teachers are creative individuals who know how to develop lessons. The *Reading Teacher's Book of Lists* simply supplies a handy reference for some of the content. For example, one sixth-grade teacher doing a unit on propaganda techniques found that our list of thirteen was more comprehensive and useful than the list found in the basal reading series she was using. A basic skills teacher doing remedial work with third graders needed a list of contractions and found that we had one ready to go. In undergraduate teacher training courses, the book was used as a supplement to a reading methods text and supplied the content for the development of games, worksheets, and lessons.

These lists have been used by test makers, writers of children's television programs, and editors in major publishing houses. Because of their wide use and the positive response we have received about them, we were determined to make them even better. We have added a number of new sections: traditional and not-so-traditional comprehension terms; word lists for adult and basic literacy education; and expanded study skills ideas such as time planning, skimming, and memory aids. There is now a section devoted to language arts, reflecting the blend of writing and reading in instruction. Book lists—including children's classics, old-time readers, hi/lo books, modern basal reading series, and large type and Braille readers—have been added.

Significant improvement has been made in the list of homophones. The collection of Greek and Latin roots and affixes has been greatly expanded to help you teach vocabulary.

For those of you who bought the first edition, we apologize that the table of contents and page headings were somewhat confusing; we have labored to correct them. The size and binding of the book also have been changed to make it easier to use. When possible, lists begin and end on the same page. This change will make it easier for those of you who would like to make a copy of a specific list for a student or a class.

A variety of teaching ideas can be found in "Games and Methods."

We have enjoyed hearing from owners of the *Reading Teacher's Book of Lists* and have tried to incorporate in this edition many of the suggestions that were made. Suggestions and comments about this edition also are welcome.

Edward Bernard Fry
Dona Lee Fountoukidis
Jacqueline Kress Polk

PREFACE TO THE FIRST EDITION

This book has one main idea—to provide useful and occasionally amusing information for teachers of reading.

However, it is a "nonbook" in that it does not have a beginning, a conclusion, or a plot. It basically has very little prose and consists primarily of lists of words, phonetic elements, meanings, symbols, and miscellaneous ideas.

This book provides, under one cover, diverse types of information needed in developing reading lessons, preparing curriculum materials, and tutoring. The level of material ranges from beginning readers in elementary schools, through developmental materials for secondary schools, to an interesting section aimed at illiterate or semiliterate adults.

The nonlist content of the book is composed primarily of information for teachers, such as teaching suggestions, testing tips and terms, and some ideas tinged with a bit of humor.

So, make your way through this nonbook and get acquainted with it. Glance at the table of contents if you want an overview, or just open to the middle and start browsing. You can start from the back and go forward or from the front and move toward the back. On another day, you can start in the middle and move either way. This book is nonlinear. But that doesn't mean it's not organized; the structure can be seen in the table of contents or in the headings on each page.

We have made a few teaching suggestions for most lists, but this is basically an information source. It challenges you to be creative and gives you the raw information to be creative with.

We think that we have provided the largest list of phonograms anywhere, the most useful list of high-frequency words, and a whole lot more; but we will let you be the final judge of the value of this material. Without bragging or complaining too much, we will tell you that it was a lot harder to develop, gather, edit, and organize this material than we ever anticipated. We hope our efforts pay off in your classroom. We also would be pleased to receive additional suggestions from you.

Edward Bernard Fry
Dona Lee Fountoukidis
Jacqueline Kress Polk

Contents

SECTION I

Words

1. HOMOPHONES

Homophones are words that sound the same but have different meanings and usually different spellings. This list was combined from many teachers' lists and secretaries' spelling wordbooks. Homophones are used in many reading and spelling games, jokes, and workbook drills.

ad (advertisement)
add (addition)

ads (advertisements)
adz (axlike tool)

ail (be sick)
ale (beverage)

air (oxygen)
heir (successor)

aisle (path)
I'll (I will)
isle (island)

all (everything)
awl (tool)

allowed (permitted)
aloud (audible)

altar (in a church)
alter (change)

ant (insect)
aunt (relative)

arc (part of a circle)
ark (boat)

ascent (climb)
assent (agree)

assistance (help)
assistants (those who help)

ate (did eat)
eight (number)

attendance (presence)
attendants (escorts)

aural (by ear)
oral (by mouth)

away (gone)
aweigh (clear anchor)

awful (terrible)
offal (entrails)

aye (yes)
eye (organ of sight)
I (pronoun)

bail (throw water out)
bale (bundle)

bait (lure)
bate (to decrease)

ball (round object)
bawl (cry)

band (plays music)
banned (forbidden)

bard (poet)
barred (having bars)

bare (nude)
bear (animal)

bark (dog's sound)
barque (ship)

base (lower part)
bass (deep tone)

bases (plural of *base*)
basis (foundation)

be (exist)
bee (insect)

beach (shore)
beech (tree)

bearing (manner)
baring (uncovering)

beat (whip)
beet (vegetable)

beau (boyfriend)
bow (decorative knot)

been (past participle of *be*)
bin (box)

beer (drink)
bier (coffin)

bell (something you ring)
belle (pretty woman)
berry (fruit)
bury (put in ground)
berth (bunk)
birth (born)
better (more good)
bettor (one who bets)
bight (slack part of rope)
bite (chew)
byte (computer unit)
billed (did bill)
build (construct)
blew (did blow)
blue (color)
board (lumber)
bored (uninterested)
boarder (one who boards)
border (boundary)
boll (cotton pod)
bowl (dish; game)
bolder (more bold)
boulder (big stone)
born (delivered at birth)
borne (carried)
borough (town)
burro (donkey)
burrow (dig)
bough (of a tree)
bow (of a ship)
bouillon (clear broth)
bullion (uncoined gold
 or silver)
boy (male child)
bouy (floating object)
brake (stop)
break (smash)
bread (food)
bred (cultivated)
brewed (steeped)
brood (flock)

brews (steeps)
bruise (bump)
bridal (relating to bride)
bridle (headgear for horse)
but (except)
butt (end)
buy (purchase)
by (near)
bye (farewell)
cache (hiding place)
cash (money)
callous (unfeeling)
callus (hard tissue)
cannon (big gun)
canon (law)
canvas (cloth)
canvass (survey)
capital (money; city)
capitol (building of U.S. Congress)
carat (weight of precious stones)
caret (proofreader's mark)
carrot (vegetable)
carol (song)
carrel (study space in library)
cast (throw; actors in a play)
caste (social class)
cede (grant)
seed (part of a plant)
ceiling (top of room)
sealing (closing)
cell (prison room)
sell (exchange for money)
cellar (basement)
seller (one who sells)
censor (ban)
sensor (detection device)
cent (penny)
scent (odor)
sent (did send)
cereal (relating to grain)
serial (of a series)

The NEW Reading Teacher's Book of Lists, © 1985 Prentice-Hall, Inc., Englewood Cliffs, NJ 07632. By E. Fry, D. Fountoukidis, and J. Polk.

cession (yielding)
session (meeting)

chased (did chase)
chaste (modest)

cheap (inexpensive)
cheep (bird call)

chews (bites)
choose (select)

chic (style)
sheik (Arab chief)

chilly (cold)
chili (hot pepper)

choral (music)
coral (reef)

chorale (chorus)
corral (pen for livestock)

chord (musical notes)
cord (string)

chute (slide)
shoot (discharge gun)

cite (summon to court)
sight (see)
site (location)

claws (nails on animal's feet)
clause (part of a sentence)

click (small sound)
clique (group of friends)

climb (ascend)
clime (climate)

close (shut)
clothes (clothing)

coal (fuel)
cole (cabbage)

coarse (rough)
course (path; school subject)

colonel (military rank)
kernel (grain of corn)

complement (complete set)
compliment (praise)

coop (chicken pen)
coupe (car)

core (center)
corps (army group)

council (legislative body)
counsel (advise)

cousin (relative)
cozen (deceive)

creak (grating noise)
creek (stream)

crews (groups of workers)
cruise (sail)
cruse (small pot)

cue (prompt)
queue (line up)

currant (small raisin)
current (recent; fast part of a stream)

curser (one who curses)
cursor (moving pointer)

cymbal (percussion instrument)
symbol (sign)

die (expire)
dye (color)

dine (eat)
dyne (unit of force)

disburse (pay out)
disperse (scatter)

discreet (unobtrusive)
discrete (noncontinuous)

doe (female deer)
dough (bread mixture)
do (musical note)

done (finished)
dun (demand for payment; dull color)

dual (two)
duel (formal combat)

duct (tube)
ducked (did duck)

earn (work for)
urn (container)

ewe (female sheep)
yew (shrub)
you (personal pronoun)

eyelet (small hole)
islet (small island)

fain (gladly)
feign (pretend)

faint (weak)
feint (pretend attack)

fair (honest; bazaar)
fare (cost of transportation)

faze (upset)
phase (stage)

feat (accomplishment)
feet (plural of *foot*)

find (discover)
fined (penalty of money)

fir (tree)
fur (animal covering)

flair (talent)
flare (flaming signal)

flea (insect)
flee (run away)

flew (did fly)
flu (influenza)
flue (shaft)

flour (milled grain)
flower (bloom)

for (in favor of)
fore (front part)
four (number)

foreword (preface)
forward (front part)

forth (forward)
fourth (after third)

foul (bad)
fowl (bird)

franc (French money)
frank (honest)

friar (brother in religious
    order)
fryer (frying chicken)

gilt (golden)
guilt (opposite of innocence)

gnu (antelope)
knew (did know)
new (opposite of *old*)

gorilla (animal)
guerrilla (irregular soldier)

grate (grind)
great (large)

groan (moan)
grown (cultivated)

guessed (surmised)
guest (company)

hail (ice; salute)
hale (healthy)

hair (on head)
hare (rabbit)

hall (passage)
haul (carry)

hangar (storage building)
hanger (to hang things on)

halve (cut in half)
have (possess)

hart (deer)
heart (body organ)

hay (dried grass)
hey (expression to get attention)

heal (make well)
heel (bottom of foot)
he'll (he will)

hear (listen)
here (this place)

heard (listened)
herd (group of animals)

heed (pay attention)
he'd (he would)

hertz (unit of wave frequency)
hurts (pain)

hew (carve)
hue (color)

hi (hello)
hie (hasten)
high (opposite of low)

The NEW Reading Teacher's Book of Lists, © 1985 Prentice-Hall, Inc., Englewood Cliffs, NJ 07632. By E. Fry, D. Fountoukidis, and J. Polk.

higher (above)
hire (employ)

him (pronoun)
hymn (religious song)

hoarse (husky voice)
horse (animal)

hole (opening)
whole (complete)

holey (full of holes)
holy (sacred)
wholly (all)

horde (crowd)
hoard (hidden supply)

hostel (lodging for youth)
hostile (unfriendly)

hour (sixty minutes)
our (possessive pronoun)

hurdle (jump over)
hurtle (throw)

idle (lazy)
idol (god)

in (opposite of *out*)
inn (hotel)

instance (example)
instants (short periods of time)

intense (extreme)
intents (aims)

its (possessive pronoun)
it's (it is)

jam (fruit jelly)
jamb (window part)

knead (mix with hands)
need (require)

knight (feudal military servant)
night (evening)

knit (weave with yarn)
nit (louse egg)

knot (tangle)
not (in no manner)

know (familiar with)
no (negative)

lam (escape)
lamb (baby sheep)

lain (past participle of *lie*)
lane (narrow way)

lay (recline)
lei (necklace of flowers)

lead (metal)
led (guided)

leak (crack)
leek (vegetable)

lean (slender; incline)
lien (claim)

leased (rented)
least (smallest)

lessen (make less)
lesson (instruction)

levee (embankment)
levy (impose by legal authority)

lichen (fungus)
liken (compare)

lie (falsehood)
lye (alkaline solution)

lieu (instead of)
Lou (name)

lightening (becoming light)
lightning (occurs with thunder)

load (burden)
lode (vein of ore)

loan (something borrowed)
lone (single)

locks (plural of lock)
lox (smoked salmon)

loot (steal)
lute (musical instrument)

made (manufactured)
maid (servant)

mail (send by post)
male (masculine)

main (most imporant)
Maine (state)
mane (hair)

maize (Indian corn)
maze (confusing network
  of passages)

mall (courtyard)
maul (attack)

manner (style)
manor (estate)

mantel (over fireplace)
mantle (cloak)

marshal (escort)
martial (militant)

massed (grouped)
mast (support)

meat (beef)
meet (greet)
mete (measure)

medal (award)
meddle (interfere)

might (may; strength)
mite (small insect)

miner (coal digger)
minor (juvenile)

missed (failed to attain)
mist (fog)

moan (groan)
mown (cut down)

mode (fashion)
mowed (cut down)

morn (morning)
mourn (grieve)

muscle (flesh)
mussel (shellfish)

naval (nautical)
navel (depression in stomach)

nay (no)
neigh (whinny)

none (not any)
nun (religious sister)

oar (of a boat)
or (conjunction)
ore (mineral deposit)

ode (poem)
owed (did owe)

oh (exclamation)
owe (be indebted)

one (number)
won (triumphed)

overdo (go to extremes)
overdue (past due)

overseas (abroad)
oversees (supervises)

pail (bucket)
pale (white)

pain (discomfort)
pane (window glass)

pair (two of a kind)
pare (peel)
pear (fruit)

palate (roof of mouth)
palette (board for paint)
pallet (tool)

passed (went by)
past (former)

patience (composure)
patients (sick persons)

pause (brief stop)
paws (feet of animals)

peace (tranquility)
piece (part)

peak (mountaintop)
peek (look)
pique (offense)

peal (ring)
peel (pare)

pearl (jewel)
purl (knitting stitch)

pedal (ride a bike)
peddle (sell)

peer (equal)
pier (dock)

per (for each)
purr (cat sound)

The NEW Reading Teacher's Book of Lists, © 1985 Prentice-Hall, Inc., Englewood Cliffs, NJ 07632. By E. Fry, D. Fountoukidis, and J. Polk.

pi (Greek letter)
pie (kind of pastry)

plain (simple)
plane (flat surface)

plait (braid)
plate (dish)

pleas (plural of *plea*)
please (to be agreeable)

plum (fruit)
plumb (lead weight)

pole (stick)
poll (vote)

pore (ponder)
pour (flow freely)

pray (worship)
prey (victim)

principal (chief)
principle (rule)

profit (benefit)
prophet (seer)

rack (framework; torture)
wrack (ruin)

rain (precipitation)
reign (royal authority)
rein (harness)

raise (put up)
raze (tear down)
rays (of sun)

rap (hit)
wrap (cover)

read (peruse)
reed (plant)

read (perused)
red (color)

real (genuine)
reel (spool)

reek (give off strong odor)
wreak (inflict)

rest (relax)
wrest (take from)

right (correct)
rite (ceremony)
write (inscribe)

ring (circular band)
wring (squeeze)

road (street)
rode (transported)
rowed (used oars)

roe (fish eggs)
row (line; use oars)

role (character)
roll (turn over; bread)

root (part of a plant)
route (highway)

rose (flower)
rows (lines)

rote (by memory)
wrote (did write)

rude (impolite)
rued (was sorry)

rung (step on a ladder; past of *ring*)
wrung (squeezed)

rye (grain)
wry (twisted)

sail (travel by boat)
sale (bargain)

scene (setting)
seen (viewed)

scent (smell)
sent (past of *send*)

scull (boat; row)
skull (head)

sea (ocean)
see (visualize)

seam (joining mark)
seem (appear to be)

sear (singe)
seer (prophet)

serf (feudal servant)
surf (waves)

sew (mend)
so (in order that)
sow (plant)

shear (cut)
sheer (transparent)

shoe (foot covering)
shoo (drive away)

shone (beamed)
shown (exhibited)

side (flank)
sighed (audible breath)

sign (signal)
sine (trigonometric function)

slay (kill)
sleigh (sled)

sleight (dexterity)
slight (slender)

slew (killed)
slue (swamp)

soar (fly)
sore (painful)

sole (only)
soul (spirit)

some (portion)
sum (total)

son (male offspring)
sun (star)

staid (proper)
stayed (remained)

stair (step)
stare (look intently)

stake (post)
steak (meat)

stationary (fixed)
stationery (paper)

steal (rob)
steel (metal)

step (walk)
steppe (prairie of Europe
          or Asia)

stile (gate)
style (fashion)

straight (not crooked)
strait (channel of water)

suite (connected rooms)
sweet (sugary)

tacks (plural of *tack*)
tax (assess; burden)

tail (animal's appendage)
tale (story)

taught (did teach)
taut (tight)

tea (drink)
tee (holder for golf ball)

teas (plural of *tea*)
tease (mock)

team (crew)
teem (be full)

tear (cry)
tier (level)

tern (sea bird)
turn (rotate)

their (possessive pronoun)
there (at that place)
they're (they are)

theirs (possessive pronoun)
there's (there is)

threw (tossed)
through (finished)

throne (king's seat)
thrown (tossed)

thyme (herb)
time (duration)

tic (twitch)
tick (insect; sound of clock)

tide (ebb and flow)
tied (bound)

to (toward)
too (also)
two (number)

toad (frog)
towed (pulled)

toe (digit on foot)
tow (pull)

The NEW Reading Teacher's Book of Lists, © 1985 Prentice-Hall, Inc., Englewood Cliffs, NJ 07632. By E. Fry, D. Fountoukidis, and J. Polk.

The NEW Reading Teacher's Book of Lists, © 1985 Prentice-Hall, Inc., Englewood Cliffs, NJ 07632. By E. Fry, D. Fountoukidis, and J. Polk.

told (informed)
tolled (rang)

trussed (tied)
trust (confidence)

vain (conceited)
vane (wind indicator)
vein (blood vessel)

vale (valley)
veil (face cover)

vary (change)
very (absolutely)

vice (bad habit)
vise (clamp)

wade (walk in water)
weighed (measured heaviness)

wail (cry)
whale (sea mammal)

waist (middle)
waste (trash)

wait (linger)
weight (heaviness)

waive (forgive)
wave (swell)

want (desire)
wont (custom)

ware (pottery)
wear (have on)
where (what place)

way (road)
weigh (measure heaviness)
whey (watery part of milk)

we (pronoun)
wee (small)

weak (not strong)
week (seven days)

weal (prosperity)
we'll (we will)
wheel (circular frame)

weather (climate)
whether (if)

weave (interlace)
we've (we have)

we'd (we would)
weed (plant)

weir (dam)
we're (we are)

wet (moist)
whet (sharpen)

which (what one)
witch (sorceress)

while (during)
wile (trick)

whine (complaining sound)
wine (drink)

who's (who is)
whose (possessive of *who*)

wood (of a tree)
would (is willing to)

worst (most bad)
wurst (sausage)

yoke (harness)
yolk (egg center)

you'll (you will)
yule (Christmas)

your (possessive pronoun)
you're (you are)

See Also List 2, Homographs,
and List 3, Near Misses.

2. HOMOGRAPHS

Homographs are words that are spelled the same but have different meanings and different origins. Many other words have multiple meanings, but according to dictionary authorities, what makes these words homographs is that they have different origins as well.

affect (influence)
affect (pretend)

alight (get down from)
alight (on fire)

angle (shape formed by two
    connected lines)
angle (to fish with hook and line)

arch (curved structure)
arch (chief)

arms (body parts)
arms (weapons)

august (majestic)
August (eighth month of the year)

axes (plural of *ax*)
axes (plural of *axis*)

bail (money for release)
bail (handle of a pail)
bail (throw water out)

ball (round object)
ball (formal dance)

band (group of musicians)
band (thin strip for binding)

bank (mound)
bank (place of financial business)
bank (row of things)
bank (land along a river)

bark (tree covering)
bark (sound a dog makes)
bark (sailboat)

base (bottom)
base (morally low)

bass (low male voice)
bass (kind of fish)

baste (pour liquid on while roasting)
baste (sew with long stitches)

bat (club)
bat (flying mammal)
bat (wink)

batter (hit repeatedly)
batter (liquid mixture
    used for cakes)
batter (baseball player)

bay (part of a sea)
bay (aromatic leaf used in cooking)
bay (reddish brown)
bay (alcove between columns)
bay (howl)

bear (large animal)
bear (support; carry)

bill (statement of money owed)
bill (beak)

bit (small piece)
bit (tool for drilling)
bit (did bite)

blaze (fire)
blaze (mark a trail or a tree)
blaze (make known)

blow (hard hit)
blow (send forth a stream of air)

bluff (steep bank or cliff)
bluff (fool or mislead)

bob (weight at the end of a line)
bob (move up and down)
Bob (nickname for Robert)

boil (bubbling of hot liquid)
boil (red swelling on the skin)

boom (deep sound)
boom (long beam)
boom (sudden increase in size)

boon (benefit)
boon (merry)

The NEW Reading Teacher's Book of Lists, © 1985 Prentice-Hall, Inc., Englewood Cliffs, NJ 07632. By E. Fry, D. Fountoukidis, and J. Polk.

bore (make a hole)
bore (make weary)
bore (did bear)

bound (limit)
bound (obliged)
bound (spring back)
bound (on the way)

bow (weapon for shooting arrows)
bow (forward part of a ship)
bow (bend in greeting or respect)

bowl (rounded dish)
bowl (play the game of bowling)

box (four-sided container)
box (kind of evergreen shrub)
box (strike with the hand)

bridge (way over an obstacle)
bridge (card game)

brush (tool for sweeping)
brush (bushes)

buck (male deer)
buck (slang for *dollar*)

buffer (something that softens)
buffer (pad for polishing)

buffet (cabinet for dishes and linens)
buffet (self-serve meal)
buffet (strike)

butt (thicker end of a tool)
butt (object of ridicule)

can (able to)
can (metal container)

capital (money)
capital (punishable by death)

carp (complain)
carp (kind of fish)

case (condition)
case (box or container)

chap (crack or become rough)
chap (boy or man)

chop (cut with something sharp)
chop (jaw)
chop (irregular motion)
chop (cut of meat)

chord (two or more musical notes)
chord (together)
chord (an emotional response)

chow (breed of dog)
chow (slang for *food*)

chuck (throw or toss)
chuck (cut of beef)

cleave (cut)
cleave (hold on to)

clip (cut)
clip (fasten)

close (shut)
close (near)

clove (fragrant spice)
clove (section of a bulb)

cobbler (one who mends shoes)
cobbler (fruit pie with one crust)

cock (rooster)
cock (tilt upward)

colon (mark of punctuation)
colon (lower part of the
    large intestine)

commune (talk intimately)
commune (group of people living
    together)

compact (firmly packed together)
compact (agreement)

compound (having more than
    one part)
compound (enclosed yard)

con (swindle)
con (against)

console (cabinet)
console (ease grief)

content (all things inside)
content (satisfied)

converse (talk)
converse (opposite)

corporal (of the body)
corporal (low-ranking officer)

count (name numbers in order)
count (nobleman)

counter (long table in a store or
     restaurant)
counter (one who counts)
counter (opposite)

crow (loud cry of a rooster)
crow (large black bird)
Crow (tribe of American Indians)

cue (signal)
cue (long stick used in a game
     of pool)

curry (rub and clean a horse)
curry (spicy seasoning)

date (day, month, and year)
date (sweet dark fruit)

defer (put off)
defer (yield to another)

demean (lower in dignity)
demean (humble oneself)

desert (dry barren region)
desert (go away from)
desert (suitable reward or
     punishment)

die (stop living)
die (tool)

do (act; perform)
do (first tone on the musical scale)

dock (wharf)
dock (cut some off)

does (plural of *doe*)
does (present tense of *to do*)

dove (pigeon)
dove (did dive)

down (from a higher to a lower place)
down (soft feathers)
down (grassy land)

dredge (dig up)
dredge (sprinkle with flour or sugar)

dresser (one who dresses)
dresser (bureau)

drove (did drive)
drove (flock; herd; crowd)

dub (give a title)
dub (add voice or music to a film)

duck (large wild bird)
duck (lower suddenly)
duck (type of cotton cloth)

ear (organ of hearing)
ear (part of certain plants)

egg (oval or round body laid by a bird)
egg (encourage)

elder (older)
elder (small tree)

entrance (going in)
entrance (delight; charm)

excise (tax)
excise (remove)

fair (beautiful; lovely)
fair (just; honest)
fair (showing of farm goods)
fair (bazaar)

fan (device to stir up the air)
fan (admirer)

fast (speedy)
fast (go without food)

fawn (young deer)
fawn (try to get favor by slavish acts)

fell (did fall)
fell (cut down a tree)
fell (deadly)

felt (did feel)
felt (type of cloth)

file (drawer; folder)
file (steel tool to smooth material)
file (material)

fine (high quality)
fine (money paid as punishment)

firm (solid; hard)
firm (business; company)

fit (suitable)
fit (sudden attack)

flag (banner)
flag (get tired)

flat (smooth)
flat (apartment)

fleet (group of ships)
fleet (rapid)

The NEW Reading Teacher's Book of Lists, © 1985 Prentice-Hall, Inc., Englewood Cliffs, NJ 07632. By E. Fry, D. Fountoukidis, and J. Polk.

The NEW Reading Teacher's Book of Lists, © 1985 Prentice-Hall, Inc., Englewood Cliffs, NJ 07632. By E. Fry, D. Fountoukidis, and J. Polk.

flight (act of flying)
flight (act of fleeing)

flounder (struggle)
flounder (kind of fish)

fluke (lucky stroke in games)
fluke (kind of fish)

fly (insect)
fly (move through the air
    with wings)

foil (prevent carrying out plans)
foil (metal sheet)
foil (long narrow sword)

fold (bend over on itself)
fold (pen for sheep)

forearm (part of the body)
forearm (prepare for trouble ahead)

forge (blacksmith shop)
forge (move ahead)

forte (strong point)
forte (loud)

found (did find)
found (set up; establish)

founder (sink)
founder (one who establishes)

fray (become ragged)
fray (fight)

fresh (newly made; not stale)
fresh (impudent; bold)

fret (worry)
fret (ridges on a guitar)

fry (cook in shallow pan)
fry (young fish)

fuse (slow-burning wick)
fuse (melt together)

gall (bile)
gall (annoy)

game (pastime)
game (lame)

gauntlet (challenge)
gauntlet (protective glove)

gill (breathing organ of a fish)
gill (small liquid measure)

gin (alcoholic beverage)
gin (apparatus for separating seeds
    from cotton)
gin (card game)

gore (blood)
gore (wound from a horn)
gore (three-sided insert of cloth)

grate (framework for burning fuel in
    a fireplace)
grate (have an annoying effect)

grave (place of burial)
grave (important; serious)
grave (carve)

graze (feed on grass)
graze (touch lightly in passing)

ground (soil)
ground (did grind)

grouse (game bird)
grouse (grumble; complain)

gull (water bird)
gull (cheat; deceive)

gum (sticky substance from certain
    trees)
gum (tissue around teeth)

guy (rope; chain)
guy (fellow)

hack (cut roughly)
hack (carriage or car for hire)

hail (pieces of ice that fall like rain)
hail (shout of welcome)

hamper (hold back)
hamper (large container or basket)

hatch (bring forth young from an egg)
hatch (opening in a ship's deck)

hawk (bird of prey)
hawk (peddle goods)

haze (mist; smoke)
haze (bully)

heel (back of the foot)
heel (tip over to one side)

hide (conceal; keep out of sight)
hide (animal skin)

hinder (stop)
hinder (rear)

hold (grasp and keep)
hold (part of ship or plane for cargo)

husky (big and strong)
husky (sled dog)

impress (have a strong effect on)
impress (take by force)

incense (substance with a sweet smell
    when burned)
incense (make very angry)

intern (force to stay)
intern (doctor in training at a hospital)

intimate (very familiar)
intimate (suggest)

invalid (disabled person)
invalid (not valid)

jam (fruit preserve)
jam (press or squeeze)

jar (container of glass)
jar (rattle; vibrate)

jerky (with sudden starts and stops)
jerky (strips of dried meat)

jet (stream of water, steam, or air)
jet (hard black coal)
jet (type of airplane)

jig (dance)
jig (fishing lure)

job (work)
Job (Biblical man of patience)

jumper (person or thing that jumps)
jumper (type of dress)

junk (trash)
junk (Chinese sailing ship)

key (instrument for locking and
    unlocking)
key (low island)

kind (friendly; helpful)
kind (same class)

lap (body part formed when sitting)
lap (drink)
lap (one course traveled)

lark (small songbird)
lark (good fun)

lash (cord part of a whip)
lash (tie or fasten)

last (at the end)
last (continue; endure)

launch (start out)
launch (type of boat)

lead (show the way)
lead (metallic element)

league (measure of distance)
league (group of persons or
    nations)

lean (stand slanting)
lean (not fat)

leave (go away)
leave (permission)

left (direction)
left (did leave)

lie (falsehood)
lie (place oneself in a flat position;
    rest)

light (not heavy)
light (not dark)

like (similar to)
like (be pleased with)

lime (citrus fruit)
lime (chemical substance)

limp (lame walk)
limp (not stiff)

line (piece of cord)
line (place paper or fabric inside)

list (series of words)
list (tilt to one side)

live (exist)
live (having life)

loaf (be idle)
loaf (shaped as bread)

lock (fasten door)
lock (curl of hair)

long (great measure)
long (wish for)

The NEW Reading Teacher's Book of Lists, © 1985 Prentice-Hall, Inc., Englewood Cliffs, NJ 07632. By E. Fry, D. Fountoukidis, and J. Polk.

The NEW Reading Teacher's Book of Lists, © 1985 Prentice-Hall, Inc., Englewood Cliffs, NJ 07632. By E. Fry, D. Fountoukidis, and J. Polk.

loom (frame for weaving)
loom (threaten)

lumber (timber)
lumber (move along heavily)

mace (club; weapon)
mace (spice)

mail (letters) .
mail (flexible metal armor)

maroon (brownish red color)
maroon (leave helpless)

mat (woven floor covering)
mat (border for picture)

match (stick used to light fires)
match (equal)

meal (food served at a certain time)
meal (ground grain)

mean (signify; intend)
mean (unkind)
mean (average)

meter (unit of length)
meter (poetic rhythm)
meter (device that measures flow)

might (past of may)
might (power)

mine (belonging to me)
mine (hole in the earth to get ores)

minute (sixty seconds)
minute (very small)

miss (fail to hit)
miss (unmarried woman or girl)

mold (form; shape)
mold (fungus)

mole (brown spot on the skin)
mole (small underground animal)

mortar (cement mixture)
mortar (short cannon)

mount (high hill)
mount (go up)

mow (cut down)
mow (pile of hay or grain in a barn)

mule (cross between donkey and horse)
mule (type of slipper)

mum (silent)
mum (chrysanthemum)

nag (scold)
nag (old horse)

nap (short sleep)
nap (rug fuzz)

net (open-weave fabric)
net (remaining after deductions)

nip (small drink)
nip (pinch)

pad (cushion)
pad (walk softly)

page (one side of a sheet of paper)
page (youth who runs errands)

palm (inside of hand)
palm (kind of tree)

patent (right or privilege)
patent (type of leather)

patter (rapid taps)
patter (light, easy walk)

pawn (leave as security for loan)
pawn (chess piece)

peaked (having a point)
peaked (looking ill)

peck (dry measure)
peck (strike at)

pen (instrument for writing)
pen (enclosed yard)

pile (heap or stack)
pile (nap on fabrics)

pine (type of evergreen)
pine (yearn or long for)

pitch (throw)
pitch (tar)

pitcher (container for pouring liquid)
pitcher (baseball player)

poach (tresspass)
poach (cook an egg)

poker (card game)
poker (rod for stirring a fire)

pole (long piece of wood)
pole (either end of the earth's axis)

policy (plan of action)
policy (written agreement)

pool (tank with water)
pool (game played with balls on a table)

pop (short, quick sound)
pop (dad)
pop (popular)

post (support)
post (job or position)
post (system for mail delivery)

pound (unit of weight)
pound (hit hard again and again)
pound (pen)

present (not absent)
present (gift)

press (squeeze)
press (force into service)

prime (chief)
prime (prepare)

primer (first book)
primer (something used to prepare another)

prune (fruit)
prune (cut; trim)

pry (look with curiosity)
pry (lift with force)

pump (type of shoe)
pump (machine that forces liquid out)

punch (hit)
punch (beverage)

pupil (student)
pupil (part of the eye)

quack (sound of a duck)
quack (phony doctor)

racket (noise)
racket (paddle used in tennis)

rail (bar of wood or metal)
rail (complain bitterly)

rank (row or line)
rank (having a bad odor)

rare (unusual)
rare (not cooked much)

rash (hasty)
rash (small red spots on the skin)

rear (the back part)
rear (bring up)

ream (500 sheets of paper)
ream (clean a hole)

recount (count again)
recount (tell in detail)

reel (spool for winding)
reel (sway under a blow)
reel (lively dance)

refrain (hold back)
refrain (part repeated)

refuse (say no)
refuse (waste; trash)

rest (sleep)
rest (what is left)

rifle (gun with a long barrel)
rifle (ransack; search through)

ring (circle)
ring (bell sound)

root (underground part of a plant)
root (cheer for someone)

row (line)
row (use oars to move a boat)
row (noisy fight)

sage (wise person)
sage (herb)

sap (liquid in a plant)
sap (weaken)

sash (cloth worn around the waist)
sash (frame of a window)

saw (did see)
saw (tool for cutting)
saw (wise saying)

scale (balance)
scale (outer layer of fish and snakes)
scale (series of steps)

school (place for learning)
school (group of fish)

scour (clean)
scour (move quickly over)

The NEW Reading Teacher's Book of Lists, © 1985 Prentice-Hall, Inc., Englewood Cliffs, NJ 07632. By E. Fry, D. Fountoukidis, and J. Polk.

The NEW Reading Teacher's Book of Lists, © 1985 Prentice-Hall, Inc., Englewood Cliffs, NJ 07632. By E. Fry, D. Fountoukidis, and J. Polk.

scrap (small bits)
scrap (quarrel)

seal (mark of ownership)
seal (sea mammal)

second (after the first)
second (one-sixtieth of a minute)

sewer (one who sews)
sewer (underground pipe for wastes)

shark (large meat-eating fish)
shark (dishonest person)

shed (small shelter)
shed (get rid of)

shingles (roofing materials)
shingles (viral disease)

shock (sudden violent disturbance)
shock (thick busy mass)

shore (land near water's edge)
shore (support)

shot (fired a gun)
shot (worn out)

size (amount)
size (preparation of glue)

slaver (dealer in slaves)
slaver (salivate)

sledge (heavy sled)
sledge (large hammer)

slip (go easily)
slip (small strip of paper)

slough (swamp)
slough (shed old skin)

slug (small slow-moving animal)
slug (hit hard)

smack (slight taste)
smack (open lips quickly)
smack (small boat)

snare (trap)
snare (strings on bottom of
a drum)

snarl (growl)
snarl (tangle)

sock (covering for foot)
sock (hit hard)

soil (ground; dirt)
soil (make dirty)

sole (type of fish)
sole (only)

sow (scatter seeds)
sow (female pig)

spar (mast of a ship)
spar (argue)
spar (mineral)

spell (say the letters of a word)
spell (magic influence)
spell (period of work)

spray (sprinkle liquid)
spray (small branch with leaves
and flowers)

spruce (type of evergreen)
spruce (neat or trim)

squash (press flat)
squash (vegetable)

stable (building for horses)
stable (unchanging)

stake (stick or post)
stake (risk or prize)

stalk (main stem of a plant)
stalk (follow secretly)

stall (place in a stable for
one animal)
stall (delay)

staple (metal fastener for paper)
staple (principal element)

stay (remain)
stay (support)

steep (having a sharp slope)
steep (soak)

steer (guide)
steer (young male cattle)

stem (part of a plant)
stem (stop; dam up)

stern (rear part of a ship)
stern (harsh; strict)

stick (thin piece of wood)
stick (pierce)

still (not moving)
still (apparatus for making alcohol)
stoop (bend down)
stoop (porch)
story (account of a happening)
story (floor of a building)
strain (pull tight)
strain (group of individuals with an inherited quality)
strand (leave helpless)
strand (thread or string)
strip (narrow piece of cloth)
strip (remove)
stroke (hit)
stroke (pet; soothe)
stunt (stop growth)
stunt (bold action)
sty (pen for pigs)
sty (swelling on eyelid)
swallow (take in)
swallow (small bird)
tap (strike lightly)
tap (faucet)
tarry (delay)
tarry (covered with tar)
tart (sour but agreeable)
tart (small fruit-filled pie)
tear (drop of liquid from the eye)
tear (pull apart)
temple (building for worship)
temple (side of forehead)
tend (incline to)
tend (take care of)
tender (not tough)
tender (offer)
tender (one who cares for)
tick (sound of a clock)
tick (small insect)
tick (pillow covering)
till (until)
till (plow the land)
till (drawer for money)

tip (end point)
tip (slant)
tip (present of money for services)
tire (become weary)
tire (rubber around a wheel)
toast (browned bread slices)
toast (wish for good luck)
toll (sound of a bell)
toll (fee paid for a privilege)
top (highest point)
top (toy that spins)
troll (ugly dwarf)
troll (method of fishing)
unaffected (not influenced)
unaffected (innocent)
vault (storehouse for valuables)
vault (jump over)
vice (habit)
vice (clamp)
wake (stop sleeping)
wake (trail left behind a ship)
wax (substance made by bees)
wax (grow bigger)
well (satisfactory)
well (hole dug for water)
whale (large sea mammal)
whale (whip)
will (statement of desire for distribution of property after one's death)
will (is going to)
will (deliberate intention or wish)
wind (air in motion)
wind (turn)
yak (long-haired ox)
yak (talk endlessly)
yard (enclosed space around a house)
yard (thirty-six inches)
yen (strong desire)
yen (unit of money in Japan)

See Also List 1, Homophones,
and List 3, Near Misses.

The NEW Reading Teacher's Book of Lists, © 1985 Prentice-Hall, Inc., Englewood Cliffs, NJ 07632. By E. Fry, D. Fountoukidis, and J. Polk.

FORECLOS

ORIGINALL
TIME

NOW

3. NEAR MISSES

Near Misses are words that sound similar or have other confusing characteristics. They have different meanings and their misuse can cause embarrassing errors.

accede (v.)—to comply with
exceed (v.)—to surpass

accent (n.)—stress in speech or writing
ascent (n.)—act of going up
assent (v., n.)—consent

accept (v.)—to agree or take what is offered
except (prep.)—leaving out or excluding

access (n.)—admittance
excess (n., adj.)—surplus

adapt (v.)—to adjust
adept (adj.)—proficient
adopt (v.)—to take by choice

adverse (adj.)—opposing
averse (adj.)—disinclined

affect (v.)—to influence
affect (n.)—feeling
effect (n.)—result of a cause
effect (v.)—to make happen

alley (n.)—narrow street
ally (n.)—supporter

allusion (n.)—indirect reference
delusion (n.)—mistaken belief
illusion (n.)—mistaken vision

all ready (adj.)—completely ready
already (adv.)—even now or by this time

all together (pron. and adj.)—everything or everyone in one place
altogether (adv.)—entirely

anecdote (n.)—short amusing story
antidote (n.)—something to counter the effect of poison

angel (n.)—heavenly body
angle (n.)—space between two lines that meet in a point

annul (v.)—to make void
annual (adj.)—yearly

any way (adj. and n.)—in whatever manner
anyway (adv.)—regardless

The *NEW Reading Teacher's Book of Lists*, © 1985 Prentice-Hall, Inc., Englewood Cliffs, NJ 07632. By E. Fry, D. Fountoukidis, and J. Polk.

appraise (v.)—to set a value on
apprise (v.)—to inform

area (n.)—surface
aria (n.)—melody

biannual (adj.)—occurring twice per year
biennial (adj.)—occurring every other year

bibliography (n.)—list of writings on a particular topic
biography (n.)—written history of a person's life

bizarre (adj.)—odd
bazaar (n.)—market, fair

breadth (n.)—width
breath (n.)—respiration
breathe (v.)—to inhale and exhale

calendar (n.)—a chart of days and months
colander (n.)—a strainer

casual (adj.)—informal
causal (adj.)—relating to cause

cease (v.)—to stop
seize (v.)—to grasp

click (n.)—short, sharp sound
clique (n.)—small exclusive subgroup

collision (n.)—a clashing
collusion (n.)—a scheme to cheat

coma (n.)—an unconscious state
comma (n.)—a punctuation mark

command (n., v.)—an order, to order
commend (v.)—to praise, to entrust

comprehensible (adj.)—understandable
comprehensive (adj.)—extensive

confidant (n.)—friend or advisor
confident (adj.)—sure

confidentially (adv.)—privately
confidently (adv.)—certainly

conscience (n.)—sense of right and wrong
conscious (adj.)—aware

contagious (adj.)—spread by contact
contiguous (adj.)—touching or nearby

continual (adj.)—repeated, happening again and again
continuous (adj.)—uninterrupted, without stopping

cooperation (n.)—the art of working together
corporation (n.)—a business organization

The NEW Reading Teacher's Book of Lists, © 1985 Prentice-Hall, Inc., Englewood Cliffs, NJ 07632. By E. Fry, D. Fountoukidis, and J. Polk.

costume (n.)—special way of dressing
custom (n.)—usual practice or habit

credible (adj.)—believable
creditable (adj.)—deserving praise

deceased (adj.)—dead
diseased (adj.)—ill

decent (adj.)—proper
descent (n.)—way down
dissent (n., v.)—disagreement, to disagree

deference (n.)—respect
difference (n.)—dissimilarity

deposition (n.)—a formal written statement
disposition (n.)—temperament

depraved (adj.)—morally corrupt
deprived (adj.)—taken away from

deprecate (v.)—to disapprove
depreciate (v.)—to lessen in value

desert (n.)—arid land
desert (v.)—to abandon
dessert (n.)—course served at the end of a meal

desolate (adj.)—lonely, sad
dissolute (adj.)—loose in morals

detract (v.)—to take away from
distract (v.)—to divert attention away from

device (n.)—a contrivance
devise (v.)—to plan

disapprove (v.)—to withhold approval
disprove (v.)—to prove something to be false

disassemble (v.)—to take something apart
dissemble (v.)—to disguise

disburse (v.)—to pay out
disperse (v.)—to scatter

discomfort (n.)—distress
discomfit (v.)—to frustrate or embarrass

disinterested (adj.)—impartial
uninterested (adj.)—not interested

elapse (v.)—to pass
lapse (v.)—to become void
relapse (v.)—to fall back to previous condition

elicit (v.)—to draw out
illicit (adj.)—unlawful

elusive (adj.)—hard to catch
illusive (adj.)—misleading

eminent (adj.)—well known
imminent (adj.)—impending

emerge (v.)—rise out of
immerge (v.)—plunge into

emigrate (v.)—to leave a country and take up residence elsewhere
immigrate (v.)—to enter a country for the purpose of taking up residence

envelop (v.)—to surround
envelope (n.)—a wrapper for a letter

erasable (adj.)—capable of being erased
irascible (adj.)—easily provoked to anger

expand (v.)—to increase in size
expend (v.)—to spend

expect (v.)—to suppose; to look forward
suspect (v.)—to mistrust

extant (adj.)—still existing
extent (adj.)—amount

facility (n.)—ease
felicity (n.)—happiness

farther (adj.)—more distant (refers to space)
further (adj.)—extending beyond a point (refers to time, quantity, or degree)

finale (n.)—the end
finally (adv.)—at the end
finely (adv.)—in a fine manner

fiscal (adj.)—relating to finance
physical (adj.)—relating to the body

formally (adv.)—with rigid ceremony
formerly (adv.)—previously

human (adj.)—relating to mankind
humane (adv.)—kind

hypercritical (adj.)—very critical
hypocritical (adj.)—pretending to be virtuous

imitate (v.)—to mimic
intimate (v.)—to hint or make known; familiar, close

incredible (adj.)—too extraordinary to be believed
incredulous (adj.)—unbelieving, skeptical

indigenous (adj.)—native
indigent (adj.)—needy
indignant (adj.)—angry

The NEW Reading Teacher's Book of Lists, © 1985 Prentice-Hall, Inc., Englewood Cliffs, NJ 07632. By E. Fry, D. Fountoukidis, and J. Polk.

ingenious (adj.)—clever
ingenuous (adj.)—straightforward

later (adj.)—more late
latter (adj.)—second in a series of two

lay (v.)—to set something down or place something
lie (v.)—to recline

least (adj.)—at the minimum
lest (conj.)—for fear that

loose (adj.)—not tight
lose (v.)—not win; misplace

magnet (n.)—iron bar with power to attract iron
magnate (n.)—person in prominent position in large industry

moral (n., adj.)—lesson; ethic
morale (n.)—mental condition

morality (n.)—virtue
mortality (n.)—the state of being mortal; death rate

of (prep.)—having to do with; indicating possession
off (adv.)—not on

official (adj.)—authorized
officious (adj.)—offering services where they are neither wanted nor needed

perfect (adj.)—without fault
prefect (n.)—an official

perpetrate (v.)—to be guilty of; to commit
perpetuate (v.)—to make perpetual

perquisite (n.)—a privilege or profit in addition to salary
prerequisite (n.)—a preliminary requirement

persecute (v.)—to harass, annoy, or injure
prosecute (v.)—to press for punishment of a crime

personal (adj.)—private
personnel (n.)—a body of people, usually employed in some organization

peruse (v.)—to read
pursue (v.)—to follow in order to overtake

picture (n.)—drawing or photograph
pitcher (n.)—container for liquid; baseball player

precede (v.)—to go before
proceed (v.)—to advance

preposition (n.)—a part of speech
proposition (n.)—a proposal or suggestion

pretend (v.)—to make believe
portend (v.)—to give a sign of something that will happen

quiet (adj.)—not noisy
quit (v.)—to stop
quite (adv.)—very

recent (adj.)—not long ago
resent (v.)—to feel indignant

respectably (adv.)—in a respectable manner
respectively (adv.)—in order indicated
respectfully (adv.)—in a respectful manner

restless (adj.)—constantly moving, uneasy
restive (adj.)—contrary, resisting control

suppose (v.)—assume or imagine
supposed (adj.)—expected

than (conj.)—used in comparison
then (adv.)—at that time; next in order of time

through (prep.)—by means of; from beginning to end
thorough (adj.)—complete

use (v.)—employ something
used (adj.)—secondhand

veracious (adj.)—truthful
voracious (adj.)—greedy

See Also List 1, Homophones,
and List 2, Homographs.

The NEW Reading Teacher's Book of Lists, © 1985 Prentice-Hall, Inc., Englewood Cliffs, NJ 07632. By E. Fry, D. Fountoukidis, and J. Polk.

4. INSTANT WORDS

These are the most common words in English, ranked in frequency order. The first 25 make up about a third of all printed material. The first 100 make up about half of all written material. Is it any wonder that all students must learn to recognize these words instantly and to spell them correctly also?

The Instant Words*
First Hundred

Words 1–25	Words 26–50	Words 51–75	Words 76–100
the	or	will	number
of	one	up	no
and	had	other	way
a	by	about	could
to	word	out	people
in	but	many	my
is	not	then	than
you	what	them	first
that	all	these	water
it	were	so	been
he	we	some	call
was	when	her	who
for	your	would	oil
on	can	make	now
are	said	like	find
as	there	him	long
with	use	into	down
his	an	time	day
they	each	has	did
I	which	look	get
at	she	two	come
be	do	more	made
this	how	write	may
have	their	go	part
from	if	see	over

Common suffixes: -s, -ing, -ed

*For additional instant words, see *3,000 Instant Words, 2nd Ed.,* by Elizabeth Sakiey and Edward Fry, Jamestown Publications, Providence, RI, 1984.

The NEW Reading Teacher's Book of Lists, © 1985 Prentice-Hall, Inc., Englewood Cliffs, NJ 07632. By E. Fry, D. Fountoukidis, and J. Polk.

Second Hundred

Words 101–125	*Words 126–150*	*Words 151–175*	*Words 176–200*
new	great	put	kind
sound	where	end	hand
take	help	does	picture
only	through	another	again
little	much	well	change
work	before	large	off
know	line	must	play
place	right	big	spell
year	too	even	air
live	mean	such	away
me	old	because	animal
back	any	turn	house
give	same	here	point
most	tell	why	page
very	boy	ask	letter
after	follow	went	mother
thing	came	men	answer
our	want	read	found
just	show	need	study
name	also	land	still
good	around	different	learn
sentence	form	home	should
man	three	us	America
think	small	move	world
say	set	try	high

Common suffixes: *-s, -ing, -ed, -er, -ly, -est*

The NEW Reading Teacher's Book of Lists, © 1985 Prentice-Hall, Inc., Englewood Cliffs, NJ 07632. By E. Fry, D. Fountoukidis, and J. Polk.

Third Hundred

The NEW Reading Teacher's Book of Lists, © 1985 Prentice-Hall, Inc., Englewood Cliffs, NJ 07632. By E. Fry, D. Fountoukidis, and J. Polk.

Words 201–225	*Words 226–250*	*Words 251–275*	*Words 276–300*
every	left	until	idea
near	don't	children	enough
add	few	side	eat
food	while	feet	face
between	along	car	watch
own	might	mile	far
below	close	night	Indian
country	something	walk	real
plant	seem	white	almost
last	next	sea	let
school	hard	began	above
father	open	grow	girl
keep	example	took	sometimes
tree	begin	river	mountain
never	life	four	cut
start	always	carry	young
city	those	state	talk
earth	both	once	soon
eye	paper	book	list
light	together	hear	song
thought	got	stop	leave
head	group	without	family
under	often	second	body
story	run	late	music
saw	important	miss	color

Common suffixes: *-s, -ing, -ed, -er, -ly, -est*

Fourth Hundred

Words 301–325	*Words 326–350*	*Words 351–375*	*Words 376–400*
body	order	listen	farm
music	red	wind	pulled
color	door	rock	draw
stand	sure	space	voice
sun	become	covered	seen
questions	top	fast	cold
fish	ship	several	cried
area	across	hold	plan
mark	today	himself	notice
dog	during	toward	south
horse	short	five	sing
birds	better	step	war
problem	best	morning	ground
complete	however	passed	fall
room	low	vowel	king
knew	hours	true	town
since	black	hundred	I'll
ever	products	against	unit
piece	happened	pattern	figure
told	whole	numeral	certain
usually	measure	table	field
didn't	remember	north	travel
friends	early	slowly	wood
easy	waves	money	fire
heard	reached	map	upon

The NEW Reading Teacher's Book of Lists, © 1985 Prentice-Hall, Inc., Englewood Cliffs, NJ 07632. By E. Fry, D. Fountoukidis, and J. Polk.

Fifth Hundred

The NEW Reading Teacher's Book of Lists, © 1985 Prentice-Hall, Inc., Englewood Cliffs, NJ 07632. By E. Fry, D. Fountoukidis, and J. Polk.

Words 401–425	*Words 426–450*	*Words 451–475*	*Words 476–500*
done	decided	plane	filled
English	contain	system	heat
road	course	behind	full
half	surface	ran	hot
ten	produce	round	check
fly	building	boat	object
gave	ocean	game	am
box	class	force	rule
finally	note	brought	among
wait	nothing	understand	noun
correct	rest	warm	power
oh	carefully	common	cannot
quickly	scientists	bring	able
person	inside	explain	six
became	wheels	dry	size
shown	stay	though	dark
minutes	green	language	ball
strong	known	shape	material
verb	island	deep	special
stars	week	thousands	heavy
front	less	yes	fine
feel	machine	clear	pair
fact	base	equation	circle
inches	ago	yet	include
street	stood	government	built

Sixth Hundred

Words 501–525	*Words 526–550*	*Words 551–575*	*Words 576–600*
can't	picked	legs	beside
matter	simple	sat	gone
square	cells	main	sky
syllables	paint	winter	glass
perhaps	mind	wide	million
bill	love	written	west
felt	cause	length	lay
suddenly	rain	reason	weather
test	exercise	kept	root
direction	eggs	interest	instruments
center	train	arms	meet
farmers	blue	brother	third
ready	wish	race	months
anything	drop	present	paragraph
divided	developed	beautiful	raised
general	window	store	represent
energy	difference	job	soft
subject	distance	edge	whether
Europe	heart	past	clothes
moon	sit	sign	flowers
region	sum	record	shall
return	summer	finished	teacher
believe	wall	discovered	held
dance	forest	wild	describe
members	probably	happy	drive

The NEW Reading Teacher's Book of Lists, © 1985 Prentice-Hall, Inc., Englewood Cliffs, NJ 07632. By E. Fry, D. Fountoukidis, and J. Polk.

Seventh Hundred

Words 601–625	*Words 626–650*	*Words 651–675*	*Words 676–700*
cross	already	hair	rolled
speak	instead	age	bear
solve	phrase	amount	wonder
appear	soil	scale	smiled
metal	bed	pounds	angle
son	copy	although	fraction
either	free	per	Africa
ice	hope	broken	killed
sleep	spring	moment	melody
village	case	tiny	bottom
factors	laughed	possible	trip
result	nation	gold	hole
jumped	quite	milk	poor
snow	type	quiet	let's
ride	themselves	natural	fight
care	temperature	lot	surprise
floor	bright	stone	French
hill	lead	act	died
pushed	everyone	build	beat
baby	method	middle	exactly
buy	section	speed	remain
century	lake	count	dress
outside	consonant	cat	iron
everything	within	someone	couldn't
tall	dictionary	sail	fingers

The NEW Reading Teacher's Book of Lists, © 1985 Prentice-Hall, Inc., Englewood Cliffs, NJ 07632. By E. Fry, D. Fountoukidis, and J. Polk.

Eighth Hundred

Words 701–725	Words 726–750	Words 751–775	Words 776–800
row	president	yourself	caught
least	brown	control	fell
catch	trouble	practice	team
climbed	cool	report	God
wrote	cloud	straight	captain
shouted	lost	rise	direct
continued	sent	statement	ring
itself	symbols	stick	serve
else	wear	party	child
plains	bad	seeds	desert
gas	save	suppose	increase
England	experiment	woman	history
burning	engine	coast	cost
design	alone	bank	maybe
joined	drawing	period	business
foot	east	wire	separate
law	pay	choose	break
ears	single	clean	uncle
grass	touch	visit	hunting
you're	information	bit	flow
grew	express	whose	lady
skin	mouth	received	students
valley	yard	garden	human
cents	equal	please	art
key	decimal	strange	feeling

The NEW Reading Teacher's Book of Lists, © 1985 Prentice-Hall, Inc., Englewood Cliffs, NJ 07632. By E. Fry, D. Fountoukidis, and J. Polk.

Ninth Hundred

Words 801–825	*Words 826–850*	*Words 851–875*	*Words 876–900*
supply	guess	thick	major
corner	silent	blood	observe
electric	trade	lie	tube
insects	rather	spot	necessary
crops	compare	bell	weight
tone	crowd	fun	meat
hit	poem	loud	lifted
sand	enjoy	consider	process
doctor	elements	suggested	army
provide	indicate	thin	hat
thus	except	position	property
won't	expect	entered	particular
cook	flat	fruit	swim
bones	seven	tied	terms
tail	interesting	rich	current
board	sense	dollars	park
modern	string	send	sell
compound	blow	sight	shoulder
mine	famous	chief	industry
wasn't	value	Japanese	wash
fit	wings	stream	block
addition	movement	planets	spread
belong	pole	rhythm	cattle
safe	exciting	eight	wife
soldiers	branches	science	sharp

The NEW Reading Teacher's Book of Lists, © 1985 Prentice-Hall, Inc., Englewood Cliffs, NJ 07632. By E. Fry, D. Fountoukidis, and J. Polk.

Tenth Hundred

Words 901–925	*Words 926–950*	*Words 951–975*	*Words 976–1000*
company	sister	gun	total
radio	oxygen	similar	deal
we'll	plural	death	determine
action	various	score	evening
capital	agreed	forward	nor
factories	opposite	stretched	rope
settled	wrong	experience	cotton
yellow	chart	rose	apple
isn't	prepared	allow	details
southern	pretty	fear	entire
truck	solution	workers	corn
fair	fresh	Washington	substances
printed	shop	Greek	smell
wouldn't	suffix	women	tools
ahead	especially	bought	conditions
chance	shoes	led	cows
born	actually	march	track
level	nose	northern	arrived
triangle	afraid	create	located
molecules	dead	British	sir
France	sugar	difficult	seat
repeated	adjective	match	division
column	fig	win	effect
western	office	doesn't	underline
church	huge	steel	view

The NEW Reading Teacher's Book of Lists, © 1985 Prentice-Hall, Inc., Englewood Cliffs, NJ 07632. By E. Fry, D. Fountoukidis, and J. Polk.

See Also List 8, Survival Words.

5. COMPUTER TERMS

The NEW Reading Teacher's Book of Lists, © 1985 Prentice-Hall, Inc., Englewood Cliffs, NJ 07632. By E. Fry, D. Fountoukidis, and J. Polk.

This is a list of terms commonly known by computer users. Since most students and workers in all fields are increasing their use of computers, or will be, this list is a good place to start for "computer literacy."

Address. A name or number that designates the location of data in internal memory or some other memory device.

Alphanumeric. A set of symbols that consists of letters (A-Z), numbers (0-9), and sometimes other special symbols.

ASCII. American Standard Code for Information Interchange. Pronounced "ASK EE." This code has been accepted as standard by the computer industry. It specifies the binary numbers that will represent letters, numbers, symbols, and special characters.

Assembly Language. A computer language that uses names to stand for machine language instructions. Assembly language instructions are more directly interpretable by the computer and thus can be executed faster than higher level languages such as BASIC.

BASIC. Beginner's All-Purpose Symbolic Instruction Code. A computer language that is widely used in schools, businesses, and in personal-use programming.

Baud. The rate in bits per second (bps) at which data can be transferred between two devices. One baud is one bit per second and 10 baud is approximately 1 character per second. Thus, 300 baud would be approximately 30 characters per second.

Binary Code. Code using 0s and 1s to represent data. The binary number system is based on the number 2, with each place representing a power of 2.

Bit. Binary digit. The smallest unit of data. It has a value of either 0 or 1, and represents whether a circuit is open or closed.

Boot. The use of a short program to load a larger program (e.g., DOS) into the main memory of a system.

Bug. Error, usually in the software or its use.

Byte. The fundamental unit of data that can be processed by a computer. In most microcomputers, a byte consists of eight binary bits. This is approximately one character.

CAI. Computer Assisted Instruction. The direct use of computers in the instructional process for drill and practice, tutorials, dialogue, games, and simulations.

Chip. A small rectangle of silicon material on which thousands of electronic circuits have been implanted. This microprocessor contains all the circuits necessary to carry out computer operations.

CMI. Computer Managed Instruction for recordkeeping of individuals and suggested teaching and diagnosis.

COBOL. Common Business-Oriented Language. A higher level computer language used for business applications.

Command. A single instruction to the computer that is executed as soon as it is received.

Computer Language. An organized set of rules, codes, and procedures used to communicate with the computer. Examples are: BASIC, FORTRAN, and COBAL.

CPU. Central Processing Unit. The central unit of the computer that contains the memory, logic, and arithmetic procedures necessary to process data and perform computations. The CPU also directs functions of input, output, and memory devices.

CRT. Cathode Ray Tube. Display screen like that of a TV. Also called a monitor.

Cursor. Movable indicator appearing on the monitor (often flashing) that shows where the next character to be typed will appear.

Daisy Wheel Printer. A printer that has a wheel mechanism with characters on the perimeter of the wheel. Unlike the Dot Matrix printer, the Daisy Wheel printer forms a solid character on the paper.

Database. A collection of data files that are organized for efficient access and use.

Debug. Process of locating and correcting errors.

Disk Drive. A mechanical device that transfers information to and from a diskette.

Diskette (Disk). A recordlike magnetic-coated disc that can store information in a manner similar to storing music on a magnetic tape.

Documentation. The written description of software or hardware.

DOS. Disk Operating System. A collection of programs that allows communications with the disk drive.

Dot Matrix Printer. A printer that generates characters that are composed of small dots.

Drill and Practice. A common type of CAI which gives the student practice and enrichment, but not initial instruction in an area.

Execute. The carrying out of an instruction or set of instructions by the computer.

Floppy Disk. See *Diskette.*

FORTRAN. Formula Translation. A higher-level computer language used in scientific applications.

GIGO. Garbage In, Garbage Out. The information you get out of a computer can't be any better than what you put in.

Hard Copy. Computer output produced on paper by a printer.

Hardware. The physical components of a computer system.

Initialize. The use of DOS to create a structure on a blank diskette in order to store data on it.

I/O. Input/Output. The use of peripheral devices (e.g., keyboard, printer, or disk drive) to enter, store, or retrieve information.

The NEW Reading Teacher's Book of Lists, © 1985 Prentice-Hall, Inc., Englewood Cliffs, NJ 07632. By E. Fry, D. Fountoukidis, and J. Polk.

Joystick. A hand control device that allows the user to control input to the computer without a keyboard. Frequently used in games.

Keyboarding. Using the keyboard to input information into the computer; typing skill. This should be taught to all students.

K. Kilobyte. It represents 2^{10} or 1024 bytes and is used to describe a computer's memory capacity. For example, a computer with 48K has 48×1024, or 49,152 bytes of memory.

LOGO. A higher level language that permits easy interaction and problem solving with a computer. Often used as a first computer language for children.

Memory. That part of the computer that stores information and instructions. Memory capacity is described in K (see, above).

Menu. A list of options such as a choice of programs on a diskette, or a choice of routines in a program. The menu is usually displayed on the monitor.

Modem. Modulator/Demodulator. A device that permits computers to transmit information over regular telephone lines.

Monitor. A kind of TV screen that provides a video display of computer input and output.

Mouse. A hand-held device that, when moved over a flat surface such as a table top, can move the cursor on the screen.

Pascal. A higher level computer language that is useful for scientific applications.

Peripheral. A device, such as a printer or disk drive that is used to transfer information to and from the central processing unit.

Program. A sequential set of instructions in a computer language that a computer can execute.

RAM. Random Access Memory. Computer memory that holds information put there by the user. This information can be erased and changed as frequently as necessary.

ROM. Read-Only Memory. Computer memory that cannot be altered by the user. It usually contains the operating system and sometimes a computer language such as BASIC.

Software. Computer programs and accompanying documentation.

Terminal. A device that allows the user to communicate with a computer. It usually consists of a keyboard and a monitor.

Tutorial. CAI lessons that provide initial instruction as opposed to drill and practice.

Syntax. Rules about how to write instructions to the computer. If these rules are not followed, instructions cannot be executed.

Write-Protect. Use of a small label placed over the cutout edge of a diskette to prevent writing additional information onto the diskette. Information may still be read from the diskette and, if the label is removed, information can once again be written onto the diskette.

See Also List 10, Measurement Terms, and Lists 17 and 18, Science Vocabulary.

6. APPLICATION FORM WORDS

These words are valuable for adult literacy students or secondary students who will be entering the job market. The words were all taken from actual application forms that job seekers are expected to fill out accurately.

ability	credit	indicate	reconcile
above	creditor	information	recruiter
absentee ballot	date	last	referred
account	day	lease	registration
address	deed	liability	relationship
adjusted	denied	license	renewal
amount	department	line	restriction
annual	depositor	list	revoked
annulment	dues	marital status	school
applicant	duplicate	military	security
application	each	mortgage	service
available	earned	month	service charge
ballot	education	name	signature
baptismal certificate	eligible	no.	social
beneficiary	employment	number	spouse
birth	enlistment	office	state
birth certificate	enter	only	street
Blue Cross	equal opportunity	other	suspended
Blue Shield	ever	outstanding	tax
bonded	exempt	passbook	total
car	felony	passport	trustee
certificate	first	person	type
check	following	personnel	under
citizen	form	phone	U.S.
city	full	place	use
company	give	please	waived
compensation	health	polling place	when
complete	home	position	witness
confidential	impairment	previous	write
consent	income	print	year
code	indebtedness	qualifications	zip code

See Also List 7, Government Form Words.

The NEW Reading Teacher's Book of Lists, © 1985 Prentice-Hall, Inc., Englewood Cliffs, NJ 07632. By E. Fry, D. Fountoukidis, and J. Polk.

7. GOVERNMENT FORM WORDS

The NEW Reading Teacher's Book of Lists, © 1985 Prentice-Hall, Inc., Englewood Cliffs, NJ 07632. By E. Fry, D. Fountoukidis, and J. Polk.

All citizens must fill out numerous government forms for income tax, change of address, driver's license, etc. If you do not know these words, you can get penalized, and not just by poor grades.

additional	employee	limit	require
administration	employer	maiden	section
agency	employment	married	self-employed
alien	enrolled	medicaid	self-employment
allowance	enrollment	medical	separately
amount	enter	medicare	sign
applicant	estate	middle	signature
application	exemption	minor	specific
apply	expense	mortgage	spouse
arrangement	federal	notice	standard
assistance	filing	notify	statement
attached	first	obtain	status
authorize	furnish	organization	substantial
balance	head of house	pension	supplemental
benefits	household	performed	support
both	include	period	surname
certificate	income	permanent	table
certification	income tax	physician	tax
check	indicate	policy	temporary
claim	individual	premium	total
compensation	information	previous	type
complete	initial	program	union
coupons	institution	property	veteran
deduct	insurance	protection	visa
deduction	interest	provide	wages
dependent	item	remarks	widow
disabled	itemize	residence	widower
disability	joint return	resources	withholding
dividends	jury	retirement	witness
earnings	larger	request	zip code
eligible			

See Also List 6, Application Form Words.

8. SURVIVAL WORDS

These words can save your life, or at least keep you from making some bad mistakes. They are necessary for survival in any civilized place.

acid	drugs	insert coins	receipt
admission	due	installment	refund
alarm	east	keep off	repair service
appetizer	electrical	keep out	reserved
bakery	elevator	keep refrigerated	reservations
bank	emergency	ladies	restaurant
beauty shop	enclose	laundry	rest rooms
blasting-keep away	enter	license number	rinse
breakfast	entrance	lights	sale
break glass	entree	local	sales tax
bus	exit	manager	schedule
bus stop	explosives	M.D.	school
cab	fire escape	money order	seafood
cabstand	fire exit	no admittance	self-service
cafeteria	fire hose	north	size
cancel	first aid	northbound	smoking
cash	first class	no smoking	prohibited
caution	flammable	no trespassing	south
charge	flight	notice	southbound
checks	follow signs	nurse	stairway
cleaners	for fire use	one way	stop
C.O.D.	fragile	open	storeroom
cold	free	operator	straight ahead
cold drinks	fuel	out	subway
collect	garage	out of order	taxi
combustible	gas	oxygen	telephone
coupon	general admission	passengers	this end up
credit cards	gentlemen	pedestrians	this way
customer service	glass	per couple	timetable
danger	ground	perishable	tobacco
delicatessan	transportation	phone	toll
delivery	hamburger	pick-up	total
dentist	handle with care	poison	tow away zone
deposit	hardware	press	use other door
destination	harmful if swallowed	private	walk
dimes	help wanted	private property	warm
discount	home game	proceed at	warning
dispensary	hospital	your own risk	wash
do not bend	hospital zone	public parking	water
do not drink	hot	pull	watch your step
don't walk	hot dog	push	weekday
down	inch	quiet	west
drinking water	information	railroad	women

See Also List 4, Instant Words.

The NEW Reading Teacher's Book of Lists, © 1985 Prentice-Hall, Inc., Englewood Cliffs, NJ 07632. By E. Fry, D. Fountoukidis, and J. Polk.

9. TRANSPORTATION WORDS

We all have to travel around and some of us can earn a good living as part of the transportation industry. For the traveler or worker, these words are basic. They also are of special interest to students studying for a driver's license test.

The NEW Reading Teacher's Book of Lists, © 1985 Prentice-Hall, Inc., Englewood Cliffs, NJ 07632. By E. Fry, D. Fountoukidis, and J. Polk.

alternate route
bike route
bridge freezes before road
bridge may be slippery
bridge out
camping
cattle Xing (crossing)
caution
children crossing
congested area ahead
construction ahead
curve
danger
dangerous curve
dangerous intersection
dead end
deer Xing (crossing)
detour ahead
dip
divided highway
do not block entrance
do not enter
do not pass
emergency parking only
end construction
entrance
exit
exit only
express lane
expressway
falling rock
farm machinery
fine for littering
food
four-way stop
freeway
gasoline
go slow
hidden driveway
highway ends
hill—trucks use lowest gear
hospital zone
information center

intersection
interstate
junction
keep right
left lane ends
left lane must turn left
left turn on signal only
local traffic only
low clearance
low shoulder
maximum speed ____
mechanic on duty
men working
merge
merge left/merge right
merging traffic
minimum speed ____
narrow bridge
next gas ____ miles
next right/next left
no dumping
no left turn
no parking this side
no passing zone
no right turn on red
no thoroughfare
no trucks
no turns
no turn on red
north
not a through street
no U turn
one way
one way—do not enter
parking ahead
parkway
pavement ends
pedestrian crossing
pedestrians prohibited
ped Xing (pedestrian crossing)
plant entrance
private road—keep out
railroad crossing

ramp speed ____
reduce speed ahead
restricted lane ahead
resume speed
right lane must turn right
right turn only
right turn on red after stop
road closed
road construction
    next ____ miles
roadside table
route
runaway truck ramp
school bus crossing
school zone when flashing
signal ahead
slippery when wet
slow
slower traffic keep right
soft shoulder
south
speed checked by radar
speed limit ____
speed zone ahead
steep grade
stop
stop ahead
towaway zone
trail
truck route
turnpike
two-way traffic
use low gear
walk
watch for fallen rocks
wayside park
weigh station
weight limit ____ tons
west
winding road
wrong way
yield
yield right of way

See Also List 101, Traffic Signs.

10. MEASUREMENT TERMS

We all use measurement to know distance, to make things, or to purchase things. This list of measurement terms gives meanings and shows relationships for many common and some less common terms.

The NEW Reading Teacher's Book of Lists, © 1985 Prentice-Hall, Inc., Englewood Cliffs, NJ 07632. By E. Fry, D. Fountoukidis, and J. Polk.

METRIC			
length			
millimeter	mm	.001	
centimeter	cm	.01	(10 mm)
decimeter	dm	.1	(10 cm)
meter	m	1.	(10 dm)
decameter	dkm	10.	(10 m)
hectometer	hm	100.	(10 dkm)
kilometer	km	1000.	(10 hm)
myriameter		10,000.	(10 km)
capacity			
milliliter	ml	.001	
centiliter	cl	.01	(10 ml)
deciliter	dl	.1	(10 cl)
liter	l	1.	(10 dl)
decaliter	dkl	10.	(10 l)
hectoliter	hl	100.	(10 dkl)
kiloliter	kl	1000.	(10 hl)
weight			
milligram	mg	.001	
centigram	cg	.01	(10 mg)
decigram	dg	.1	(10 cg)
gram	g	1.	(10 dg)
decagram	dkg	10.	(10 g)
hectogram	hg	100.	(10 dkg)
kilogram	km	1000.	(10 hg)
temperature			
centigrade	C		
celsius	C		

area

square kilometer = 1,000,000 square meters

hectare = 10,000 square meters

STANDARD (U.S.)		
length		
inch	in.	
foot	ft.	(12 in.)
yard	yd.	(3 ft.)
rod	r.	(16½ ft.)
furlong	fur.	(220 yd. or ⅛ mi.)
mile	mi.	(5280 ft.)
capacity liquid		
ounce	oz.	
pint	pt.	(12 oz.)
quart	qt.	(2 pt.)
gallon	gal.	(4 qt.)
barrel	bb.	(31 to 42 gal.)
capacity dry		
pint	pt.	(12 oz.)
quart	qt.	(2 pt.)
peck	pk.	(8 qt.)
bushel	bu.	(4 pk.)
weight		
dram	dr.	(1/16 oz.)
ounce	oz.	(16 dr.)
pound	lb.	(16 oz.)
hundredweight	hwt.	(100 lb.)
ton	t.	(net—2000 lb.)
(gross or long ton 2240 lb.)		
temperature		
fahrenheit F		

area

square mile (640 acres)

acre (43,560 square feet or 4,840 square yards)

Some Conversions

1 meter	= 3.3 feet or 1.1 yards	1 inch	= 2.5 centimeters
1 kilometer	= 0.6 miles (1000 m)	1 foot	= 30 centimeters
1 hectare	= 2.5 acres	1 yard	= 0.9 meters
1 centimeter	= 0.4 inches (1/100 m)	1 mile	= 1.6 kilometers
1 liter	= 1.06 quarts or 0.26 gallons	1 acre	= 0.4 hectares
1 gram	= 0.035 ounces	1 ounce	= 28 grams (weight)
1 kilogram	= 2.2 pounds (1000 g)	1 pound	= 0.45 kilograms
		1 quart	= 0.95 liters
		1 gallon	= 3.8 liters

See Also Lists 11 and 12, Mathematics Vocabulary.

11. MATHEMATICS VOCABULARY—ELEMENTARY

Believe it or not, all of these terms have been used in mathematics books of the first three grades, although all of us might want to place some of them in higher grades. If you wonder why some students have trouble with "word problems," it is sometimes because of these words.

A
add
addend
addition
alike
all
amount
angle
Arabic numerals
area
array
associative property
average

B
base
base ten
between
both

C
calendar
cent
center
centimeter
change
circle
circumference
column
combine
common factor
common multiple
commutative property
compare
compass
composite number
compute
cone
congruent
connect
contain

corner
cost
count
counting numbers
cube
curve
cylinder

D
decimal
degree
denominator
diagonal
diameter
difference
digit
dime
distance
distributive property
divide
dividend
divisor
dollar
double
dozen

E
each
element
empty set
end point
equal
equation
equivalent
estimate
even number
expanded numeral

F
fact
factor
fewer

figure
foot, feet
fraction

G
gallon
geometry
gram
graph
greater than
grid
group

H
half
height
hexagon
horizontal
hour

I
identify
inch
inequality
infinite set
inside
instead
intersect

J
join

K
kilogram
kilometer

L
least
length
less
line
liter

M
many
match
mathematics
measure
median
member
metric
middle
mile
minuend
minus
minute
missing
mixed
model
money
more
most
multiple
multiplication

N
name
natural order
negative
nickel
number
number line
numerator

O
object
octagon
odd
one-to-one
open
operation
opposite
order
ordinal
ounce

The NEW Reading Teacher's Book of Lists, © 1985 Prentice-Hall, Inc., Englewood Cliffs, NJ 07632. By E. Fry, D. Fountoukidis, and J. Polk.

P
pair
parallel
parallelogram
parenthesis, parentheses
pattern
penny
pentagon
percent
perimeter
perpendicular
place holder
place value
plane
plus
point
polygon
positive
pound
prime number
principle
problem
product
property
probability
protractor
pyramid

Q
quadrilateral
quart
quotient

R
radius
range
ratio
ray
reciprocal
rectangle
regroup
related facts
remainder
rename
rhombus
right angle
Roman numeral
round
row

S
same
score
second
segment
sequence

set
shaded
shape
short form
side
sign
similar
simple
single
size
solution
solve
some
space
sphere
square
standard numeral
straight
subset
subtract
subtrahend
sum
symbol
symmetrical

T
table
temperature

thermometer
time
times
ton
total
triangle

U
unequal
union
unit
unknown
unnamed

V
value
vertex
vertical
volume

W
week
weight
whole number
width

Y
yard

Z
zero

The NEW Reading Teacher's Book of Lists, © 1985 Prentice-Hall, Inc., Englewood Cliffs, NJ 07632. By E. Fry, D. Fountoukidis, and J. Polk.

See Also List 5, Computer Terms, and List 10, Measurement Terms.

12. MATHEMATICS VOCABULARY—INTERMEDIATE

These words have all been used in mathematics texts of the upper elementary school. Many of them are found more frequently in secondary mathematics texts. If you can define all of these words, you do indeed know something about mathematics. It may be best to be selective in teaching and learning these.

The NEW Reading Teacher's Book of Lists, © 1985 Prentice-Hall, Inc., Englewood Cliffs, NJ 07632. By E. Fry, D. Fountoukidis, and J. Polk.

A
abscissa
absolute value
acre
actual
acute angle
acute triangle
additive
additive inverse
adjacent
alternate
altitude
approximately
arc
arithmetic mean
avoirdupois
axis

B
baker's dozen
bar graph
base five
base two
basic facts
billion
binary operation
bisect
broken-line
    graph

C
calculate
capacity
cardinal
caret
cast out
Celsius
centigrade
centigram
centiliter
central angle

century
circle graph
circumscribe
clock arithmetic
closed curve
closure
commission
common
    denominator
comparison
complex
computation
concentric
consecutive
constant
construct
convert
coordinate axis
corresponding
cross-product
cross-section
cubed
cubic
currency

D
data
decade
decimal point
decrease
deposit
depth
derive
determine
diagram
dimension
discount
denominator
diagonal
diameter

divisibility
division
dot graph
dry measure
duplicate

E
equality
equiangular triangle
equilateral triangle
error of
    measurement
estimation
exact
expanded
experiment
exponent
exponential notation
express
extend
exterior

F
face
face value
factor tree
factorial
Fahrenheit
family of facts
finite
fixed
fluid ounce
foci
foot-pound
formula
frequency
frequency table

G
generalization
given
graduated scale

graph of the equation
greatest common
    factor
greatest possible
    multiple
gross
gross weight

H
hemisphere
histogram

I
identity property
imply
improper fraction
include
inclusion
increase
inference
input
integer
interest rate
interior
interpret
intersection
interval
inverse
isosceles triangle

K
kiloliter

L
lateral
least common
    denominator
least common factor
least common
    multiple
leg of a triangle
linear
line graph

line of symmetry
line segment
lowest terms

M
magic square
markup
matching
maximum
mean
meter stick
micron
midway
minimum
mixed numeral
mode
month
multiplicand
multiplier

N
natural number
negative number
notation
numeral
numeration
numeration system

O
obtuse angle
odd number
open equation
open figure
open sentence
ordered pairs
origin
outcome
output

P
partial
per
perfect number
period
pi
pictograph
plane figure
plot
power
precision
predict
prime factor
procedure
profit
progression
proper fraction
proportion
Pythagorean
    theorem

Q
quadrant
quantity

R
radian
radii
ranking
rate
rational number
reduce
reflexive property
regular
repeating decimal
restriction

reverse
right triangle

S
satisfies
scale drawing
scalene triangle
scientific notation
sector
semicircle
short division
simplest terms
simplify
skew lines
skip counting
solid
squared
square feet
square inches
square meter
square mile
square root
standard
statute mile
story problem
straight angle
straight edge
subscript
substitute
subtraction
successive
super set
supplementary
    angle
surface area
system

T
tablespoon
tally
tangent
teaspoon
terminate
terms
theorem
transitive property
trapezoid
trial
triple
two-dimensional

U
undivided
union of sets
universal set
unlimited
unmatched
upper limit

V
variable
vertical angle
vertical axis

W
word problem

X
x-axis

Y
yardstick
y-axis
yearly

The NEW Reading Teacher's Book of Lists, © 1985 Prentice-Hall, Inc., Englewood Cliffs, NJ 07632. By E. Fry, D. Fountoukidis, and J. Polk.

See Also List 5, Computer Terms; and List 10, Measurement Terms.

13. SOCIAL STUDIES VOCABULARY—INTERMEDIATE

These terms are from textbooks used in teaching social studies in the upper elementary and middle schools, however, many of the terms are also used in advanced courses in secondary schools.

The NEW Reading Teacher's Book of Lists, © 1985 Prentice-Hall, Inc., Englewood Cliffs, NJ 07632. By E. Fry, D. Fountoukidis, and J. Polk.

A
abolish
abolitionist
aborigine
absolute power
administration
alien
alliance
ally
amnesty
amendment
ancestor
ancient
anthropology
archaeology
aristocracy
artifact
assembly
authority
autocracy
automation
average

B
balance of
    power
barbarian
barter
bill
bloc
blockade
bourgeois
boycott
bureaucracy

C
cabinet
candidate
capitalism
charter
city
civil
civilization
civil war
colony
communist
compromise
confederation
Congress
Constitution

D
debate
declaration
delegate
demarcation
democracy
depression
dictator
diplomat
disarmament
discrimination
divine right

E
ecology
ecosystem
election
emancipate
embargo
emigration
emperor
executive
    branch
exile
expedition
explorer

F
fact
federal
feudal
foreign
freedom
frontier

G
generation
government
governor
group

H
heritage
history
homestead
humanitarian

I
immigrant
impeach
imperialism
inaugurate
indentured
    servant
independence
Industrial
    Revolution
invention

J
judicial branch
jury
justice

L
labor union
law
legal
legislative
    branch

M
majority
mandate
manufacturing
mayor
medieval
mercantilism
migrant
military
minority

missionary
monarchy
monopoly
monotheism

N
nationalism
neutrality
nobility
nomination

O
official
oligarchy
oligopoly
oppression
oracle
organization

P
Parliament
patriot
peasant
per capita
    income
persecute
petition
pharaoh
pilgrim
pioneer
planned
    economic
    system
political
political
    process
politics
policy
polytheism
pope
possession
prehistoric
prejudice
president

primary
prime minister
primitive
proclamation
prohibit
propaganda
public opinion
puritan

R
radical
ratify
Reconstruction
referendum
reform
Reformation
refugee
renaissance
represent
representative
republic
republican
reservation
residential
resolution
revenue
revolt
revolution
Revolutionary
    War
royalist
rule

S
sanction
secession
segregation
senator
serf
settlement
sharecropper
shogun
siege

slavery
socialist
social scientist
society
sociology
sovereignty
state
strike
system

T
tariff
taxation
technology
territories
theory
time line
tolerance
totalitarian
trade
traditional
trait
traitor
treason
treaty
truce
tyranny
tyrant

U
unanimous
unconstitutional
union
unite

V
vassal
veteran
veto
viceroy
volunteer

W
warfare
worship

See Also List 7, Government Form Words,
and List 14, Social Studies Vocabulary—Secondary.

14. SOCIAL STUDIES VOCABULARY—SECONDARY

Social studies students in grades 9 through 12 will benefit from a review of key terms before reading assignments. These words frequently occur in texts and related materials.

A
acculturation
acre
affluent
agriculture
alluvial
altitude
Antarctic Circle
anthracite
apartheid
aqueduct
arable
archipelago
Arctic Circle
artesian well
atmosphere
atomic energy
axis

B
basin
bay
bazaar
Bedouins
birth rate
bituminous
boundary

C
canal
canneries
capital
cartographer
cash crop
Caucasian
cellulose
century
chaparral
climate
cistern
citrus fruit
civil rights
coast

code
cold war
collective farm
colonialism
colonization
commercial
    farming
Common Market
commonwealth
commune
communism
competition
condensation level
coniferous
conquistador
conservation
consumer goods
continent
continental divide
convection process
cooperative
country
craftsmen
crop rotation
crude oil
culture
current
czar

D
dam
death rate
deciduous
degree
delta
demographer
density of
    population
desalinization
desert
dew point
dictatorship

dike
doldrums
dust storm
dynasty

E
earth
earthquake
electricity
elevation
empire
environment
equal-area map
equator
equinox
erosion
erratics
estuary
evaporation
export

F
fiord
flash flood
flood plain
flow resources
foreign policy
fossil
fossil fuels
freeway
Free World
fund resources

G
gaucho
geography
geologist
ghetto
glacier
globe
grassland
greenhouse effect
grid

gross national
    product
growing season
gulf
Gulf Stream

H
harbor
heavy industry
hemisphere
herbicide
herdsman
highland
high latitude
highrise apartment
horticulture
humidity
hydroelectric

I
ice cap
Ice Age
illiteracy
industrial region
insecticide
International
    Date Line
investment
Iron Curtain
irrigation
island
isthmus

J
jet stream
jungle

K
kibbutz

L
lake
landlocked
leaching

The NEW Reading Teacher's Book of Lists, © 1985 Prentice-Hall, Inc., Englewood Cliffs, NJ 07632. By E. Fry, D. Fountoukidis, and J. Polk.

legend
legislature
life expectancy
light industry
lines of latitude
lines of longitude
literacy
lowland
low latitudes

M
magistrate
marine climate
market
maritime
mass production
megalopolis
Mercator map
merchant
meridian
meteorologist
metropolis
metropolitan area
middle class
Middle East
middle latitudes
migratory farming
migratory workers
mineral
minority groups
missile
Mongoloid
monsoon
moraine
Moslem
mosque
mother country

N
natural resources
Near East
nomad
North Atlantic Treaty
    Organization
North Pole

O
oasis
ocean
ocean current
open-housing laws
orbit
Orient
outback

P
papyrus
parallel
party line
peninsula
peon
petrified
physical
pilgrimage
plain
plantation
plateau
polar map
pollution
population density
prairie
precipitation
Prime Meridian

R
rainfall

rain forest
ration
raw materials
reclamation
refine
reincarnation
relief map
renewable resource
reserves
reservoir
river
river mouth
river source
rotation
rural

S
satellite country
savannah
scale of miles
sea level
sediment
seismograph
sheik
Shinto
slum
smelting
smog
South Pole
Soviet
statistics
steppe
strait
subsistence farming
subtropical
suburb
surplus

T
tableland
temperature
tenant
tenement
textile
tidal wave
topography
topsoil
tributary
Tropic of Cancer
Tropic of Capricorn
tsetse fly
tundra
typhoon

U
underdeveloped
United Nations
urban
urban blight
urban revolution

V
valley
vertical climate
volcano

W
warm front
water power
watershed
water vapor
weather

Z
zone
zoologist

See Also List 7, Government Form Words;
List 13, Social Studies Vocabulary—Intermediate;
and List 15, Geography Vocabulary—Intermediate.

15. GEOGRAPHY VOCABULARY—INTERMEDIATE

This list of key words that often appear in middle grade geography books lends itself well to crossword puzzles, search-a-words, and even a classroom version of popular trivia games (see List 104 for other ideas).

A
acre
adapt
agriculture
altitude
antarctic
arable
archipelago
arctic
area
arid
Asia
atmosphere
autonomy
axis

B
balance
barren
barter
basin
bay
bayou
beliefs
belt
Bering Strait
blizzard
boundary
branch
broadleaf
burgher

C
canal
canyons
cape
capital
census
central
cliff
climate
coast
commercial

communal
community
compass
continent
continental divide
contour
cottage industry
country
county
crater
crops
crust
cultivation
cultural region
culture
current
customs
cyclone

D
data
death rate
deciduous
degree
delta
density
desert
developing nation
diagram
dialect
direction
distance
diversity
domestic
drought
dust bowl

E
earthquake
east
eastern hemisphere
eclipse
ecology

economy
elevation
emigration
empire
environment
epidemic
equator
equinox
erosion
estuary
ethnic
Europe
evergreen
export

F
famine
fathom
fault
fertile
fiord
fishery
foliage
fossil
freight
fuel

G
geography
geyser
glacier
globe
goods
grain
graph
grasslands
gravity
great circle
Great Plains
grid
gross national
    product
gulf

H
harbor
harvest
hemisphere
hinterland
horizon
humidity
hurricane
hydroelectric

I
iceberg
ice cap
import
income
industry
inland
inlet
international waters
irrigation
island
isolated
isthmus

J
jet stream
jungle

K
kilometer
knot

L
lake
lagoon
latitude
lava
legend
levee
level
life expectancy
literacy
longitude
lowlands

M
mainland
manufacture
map
marine
marsh
mass
meadow
Mediterranean
megalopolis
meridian
mesa
meters
metropolitan area
migrant
moderate
monarchy
monsoon
mountain
mouth of a river

N
nation
nationalism
nationality
native
natural
natural resources
navigable
navigation
neighborhood
neutral
nomad
nonrenewable
    resource
North Pole

O
oasis
occidental
ocean
oceanography
orbit
ore
oriental
overpopulation

P
parallel
pasture
peak
peninsula
petroleum
physical map
plain
planet
plateau
polar
pollution
population density
port
prairie
precipice
precipitation

R
rainfall
rain forest
range
rapids
raw materials
reef
refinery
region

relief
religion
renewable
    resource
resources
reservoir
residential area
resort
river
rotation
route
rural

S
savannah
scale
sea
season
semiarid
silt
smog
solar
South Pole
sphere
standard of living
steppe
strait
suburb
supply
surplus
survey
swamp

T
technology
temperature
terracing

tidal wave
tide
tidewater
timberline
time line
trade
tributary
tropic
tundra

U
universal
urban

V
valley
vast
vegetation
vernacular
vertical
vital statistics
volcano
voyage

W
waterpower
weather
Western
    Hemisphere
wharf
whirlpool
wilderness
windmill

Z
zone

See Also List 13, Social Studies Vocabulary—Intermediate, and List 14, Social Studies Vocabulary—Secondary.

16. HISTORY VOCABULARY—SECONDARY

In secondary schools, history is usually a major subject for all students. These terms come from secondary history texts.

A
abolitionist
absolute
   monarchy
AFL-CIO
age
aggressor
alien
alliance
Allied Powers
ally
amendment
American
   Federation
   of Labor
American
   Revolution
ancestors
annex
appointed
armistice
arsenal
Articles of
   Confederation
artifact
assassinate
assembly
automation
average
Axis Powers

B
balance
bill
Bill of Rights
birth rate
blockade
bonds
boom
bootleg
boundaries
boycott

C
cabinet
campaign

capitalism
captains of
   industry
carpetbaggers
caucus
cede
census
Central Powers
century
charter
checks and
   balances
civilization
civil rights
civil war
cold war
collective
   bargaining
colony
commerce
communism
communities
compromise
concentration
   camps
confederacy
conflicts
Congress
Congress of
   Industrial
   Organizations
conquer
conquistador
conservation
conservative
Constitution
consumer
continents
contraband
convention
convert
corporation
crisis
Crusades
culture

currency
customs

D
Dark Ages
debts
declare
defense
delegates
democracy
density of
   population
deposits
depression
desegregation
dictators
discovery
discrimination
dissent
divorce
document
draft
duty

E
ecology
economy
effigy
elastic clause
elector
electoral vote
emancipation
embargo
emigration
empire
energy
enforced
environment
equality
ethnic
excise
executive
expedition
exploration
export

F
factory
Far East
fascism
favored
federal
Federalist
Federal Reserve
   System
feminist
filibuster
fleet
foreign
founded
freed
free enterprise
frontier

G
gangsters
generation
geography
ghetto
glacier
government
granges
greenbacks
growth

H
habeas corpus
harvesting
heritage
homestead
House of
   Representatives
housing
hypothesis

I
illegal
immigration
impeach
import
inaugurate
income

income tax
indentured servant
independence
industrial
Industrial
   Revolution
inflation
influenced
injunction
integration
invasion
invention
invested
investigation
Iron Curtain
irrigate
Islam
isolationism

J
judiciary
jury
justice

K
kidnapped
knowledge
Ku Klux Klan

L
labor
labor union
lack
laissez faire
Latin America
legislature
League of Nations
leisure
liberal
life expectancy
limits
local
lockout
loyalist
lynching

M
Manifest Destiny
manufacture
martial law
mass production
materials
Mayflower
    Compact
megalopolis
merchant
metropolitan area
migrant
migration
military
militia
mineral
minimum
minority
minutemen
missile
missionary
moderates
modern
monopoly
Monroe Doctrine
Moslems
movement
muckrakers
museum

N
nationalism
Nazism
negotiate
neutral
nobles
nomad
nominate
nonviolence
North Atlantic
    Treaty
    Organization

nuclear weapons
null and void

O
occupied
officials
opinion
opportunity
opposed
organization

P
pacifists
Parliament
passage
patent
patriot
patriotism
peasant
petition
pilgrim
pioneer
plantation
platform
pocket veto
political party
politician
poll tax
pollution
population
possessions
postwar
poverty
practices
preamble
precedent
prehistory
prejudice
primary
profit
progressive
prohibition

promotion
propaganda
property
prospector
protest
Protestant
provision
public works
Puritans

R
radicals
ratify
ration
raw materials
reapportionment
rebellion
rebels
recession
reconstruction
recovery
recreation
referendum
refineries
reform
regions
regulation
religion
relocation centers
remains
repeal
representatives
republic
reservations
reservoirs
resign
resources
retreat
revolution
riots
ruins
rural

S
sabotage
satellite
scandal
secede
secession
segregate
Selective Service
    Act
Senate
seniority
separation of
    powers
serf
settlements
sharecropper
shortage
slavery
smuggling
socialists
social security
spoils system
standard of living
stock
stockade
stock market
strategy
strike
suburbs
surrender
survive
sweatshops

T
tariff
taxation
technology
telegraph
tenant
tenement
territory

tolerate
town meeting
traditional
trails
traitors
transcontinental
treason
treaty
trend
trial
tribes
troops
truce

U
unanimous
underdeveloped
underground
    railroad
union
United Nations
unskilled worker
urban revolution

V
veteran
veto
violence
vocational
voyage

W
wages
war hawks
warrant
welfare
wilderness
worship
worker's
    compensation

See Also List 13, Social Studies Vocabulary—
Intermediate, and List 14, Social
Studies Vocabulary—Secondary.

17. SCIENCE VOCABULARY—ELEMENTARY

These terms are from elementary grade science textbooks. The ability to read a science-based article is an increasingly important part of every citizen's reading needs.

A
abdomen
absorb
accurate
adaptation
air current
air pressure
algae
amoeba
amphibian
ancestor
apply
astronaut
astronomer
atmosphere

B
backbone
bacteria
balance
barometer
battery
behavior
blood vessels
boil
breathe

C
calcium
capillary
carbohydrate
carbon dioxide
cartilage
cell
Celsius
census
centimeter
chemical
chlorine
chlorophyll
circuit
circulation

classify
climate
cloud
community
compass
compound
concave
condense
conductor
constant
constellation
continent
contract
control
convection
convex
core
crust
current

D
decay
decompose
degree
density
desert
dew
diaphragm
diatom
digestion
dinosaur
disease
dissolve
distance

E
ear
eardrum
earth
earthworm
echo
eclipse

egg
electricity
embryo
energy
environment
equator
erosion
esophagus
evaporate
evidence
expand
extinct

F
Fahrenheit
fat
fern
fertile
fertilizer
filament
flood
flow
flower
focus
fog
food chain
force
fossil
friction
frost
fruit
fuel
funnel

G
gas
geyser
gills
glacier
grain
gravity

H
habitat
hail
hatch
heat
hemisphere
hibernate
horizon
humus
hurricane

I
iceberg
image
incisor
infection
insect
instinct
insulate

J
jet
joint

L
larva
lava
leaf
length
lens
liquid
lungs

M
magnet
mammal
mantle
marble
marine
  biologist
mass
matter
melting point

membrane
mercury
meteor
meter
metric
microscope
mineral
model
moisture
molar
mold
molecule
moon
motion
muscle

N
natural
  resource
nerves
nucleus

O
optical
orbit
organ
organism
outlet
ovary
oxygen

P
paramecium
parasite
pendulum
periodic
pesticide
phase
physical
pitch
planet
plankton
pollen

pollute
population
power
predator
predict
prescribe
preserve
prey
produce
property
protein
protozoan
prove
pulse
pupa
pupil
pure

R
radiant
rainfall
range
rate
recycle
red blood cell
reflection
reproduction
reptile
response
retina
revolve
rib
ridge
root

S
saliva
satellite
scale
season
sediment
sedimentary

seed
senses
series
skeleton
skin
smog
solid
solution
sound
space
sperm
spinal
spore
starch
stem
stimulus
stomach
surface
survive
switch
system

T
taste
temperature
tendon
terrarium
thermometer
thunder
tides
transparent
treatment

V
variable
vein
vibration
vitamin
volcano

W
water vapor
wave
weight

The NEW Reading Teacher's Book of Lists, © 1985 Prentice-Hall, Inc., Englewood Cliffs, NJ 07632. By E. Fry, D. Fountoukidis, and J. Polk.

See Also List 5, Computer Terms; List 10, Measurement Terms; and List 18, Science Vocabulary—Intermediate.

18. SCIENCE VOCABULARY—INTERMEDIATE

As technology advances, students need to broaden their understanding of scientific concepts. This is a basic list from texts in grades 4 through 8. Many of these terms are also important in secondary science classes.

A
accelerate
acid
addictive
adrenal glands
alcohol
alimentary canal
alloy
alternating current
altitude
amino acid
ampere
amphetamine
anatomy
angle of incidence
angle of reflection
annual
anthropology
antibiotic
aorta
approximate
archeologist
artery
artifact
asexual
asteroid
astrology
atom
atomic
automatic
autonomic
average

B
ball-and-socket joint
barbiturates
base
biceps
bifocal
bile
binocular
biological clock
biologist
biome
biosphere

blood type
brain
bronchial tubes

C
caffeine
calculate
calorie
cancer
carbon
carbon monoxide
carcinogen
cardiac
carrier
central nervous
    system
cerebrum
characteristics
charge
chemotherapy
chromosome
cilia
circulatory
circumference
cirrus
classification
cocaine
cocoon
colony
color blindness
condensation
conditioned response
conservation
consumer
crystal
culture
cumulus
cycle

D
data
deaf
deficiency
demographer
deoxyribonucleic
    acid (DNA)

depressant
desalinization
dew point
diet
diffuse
dig
digestive tract
direct current
discharge
disinfectant
dissect
distillation
dominant trait
dormant
drug
dry-cell battery

E
earthquake
ecology
electrodes
electrolyte
electromagnetic
electron
element
elevation
ellipse
endocrine
enzyme
epidemic
epidermis
evolution
excretion
experimental
extraterrestrial
eye

F
facet
farsightedness
fault
fauna
ferment
fetus
fever
filtration

fission
flora
focal point
formula
fossil fuels
fungus
fuse
fusion

G
galaxy
galvanometer
gene
generation
generator
genetics
geologist
geothermal
    energy
germ
gestation
gland
glucose
granite
graph
graphite
growth

H
hallucinatory
heart
hemoglobin
hemophilia
heredity
heroin
hormone
host
humidity
hybrid
hydrocarbon
hypothesis

I
identical twins
igneous
immunity

impulse
inertia
infrared
inherit
inoculate
insoluble
interaction
intestine
intoxication
invertebrate
involuntary muscle

K
kidney
kinetic energy

L
large intestine
lifespan
limestone
ligament
liter
litmus
liver
lymph node

M
magma
magnetic field
marijuana
marine
marrow
maturity
medium
medulla
metabolism
metamorphic
metamorphosis
mitosis
mixture
morphine
moss
mutation

N
narcotic
natural selection

nearsightedness
negative
nervous system
neuron
neutral
neutron
nicotine
nitrate
nitrogen
noise
nuclear energy
nutrient
nutrition

O
observe
olfactory
opaque
orbital
ore
organic
osmosis
ossification
ovulation
oxidation
oxide
ozone

P
pancreas
pasteurization
perennial
periodic table
peripheral
petrified
pH
photosynthesis
pigment
pituitary
plasma
poliomyelitis
pollination
pollution
porous
potential energy
precipitation

primate
probability
pulley
pulmonary

Q
qualitative
quantitative
quarantine

R
reaction
recessive trait
recharge
refine
reflex
refraction
relative humidity
resistance
respiration
Rh factor
ribonucleic
    acid (RNA)
rickets
rod
roughage

S
saturate
scurvy
self-preservation
sensory
small intestine
smooth muscle
solar energy
solar system
species
sphere
spinal cord
static electricity
sterilization
stimulant
symbiosis
symbol
symmetry
synapse

T
taxonomy
telescope
technology
theory
thermostat
tissue
tolerance
trace elements
transfer
translucent
turbine

U
ultraviolet
universe
uvula

V
vaccination
vacuum
valve
vapor
vertebrate
vertical
virus
viscosity
vocal cords
voltage
volume
voluntary muscles

W
warm-blooded
water pressure
wave length
withdrawal

Y
yeast culture

Z
zoologist
zygote

The NEW Reading Teacher's Book of Lists, © 1985 Prentice-Hall, Inc., Englewood Cliffs, NJ 07632. By E. Fry, D. Fountoukidis, and J. Polk.

See Also List 5, Computer Terms; List 10, Measurement Terms;
and List 17, Science Vocabulary—Elementary.

19. SPELLING DEMONS—ELEMENTARY

Those who study children's spelling errors and writing difficulties have repeatedly found that a relatively small number of words make up a large percentage of all spelling errors. Many commonly misspelled words are presented in this Spelling Demons list. Other lists in this book, such as Homophones, Instant Words, and Subject Matter Words, can also be used as spelling lists.

about	could	Halloween	off	shoes	tomorrow
address	couldn't	handkerchief	often	since	tonight
advise	country	haven't	once	skiing	too
again	cousin	having	outside	skis	toys
all right	cupboard	hear	party	some	train
along	dairy	heard	peace	something	traveling
already	dear	height	people	sometime	trouble
although	decorate	hello	piece	soon	truly
always	didn't	here	played	store	Tuesday
among	doctor	hospital	plays	straight	two
April	does	hour	please	studying	until
arithmetic	early	house	poison	sugar	used
aunt	Easter	instead	practice	summer	vacation
awhile	easy	knew	pretty	Sunday	very
balloon	enough	know	principal	suppose	wear
because	every	laid	quarter	sure	weather
been	everybody	latter	quit	surely	weigh
before	favorite	lessons	quite	surprise	were
birthday	February	letter	raise	surrounded	we're
blue	fierce	little	read	swimming	when
bought	first	loose	receive	teacher	where
built	football	loving	received	tear	which
busy	forty	making	remember	terrible	white
buy	fourth	many	right	Thanksgiving	whole
children	Friday	maybe	rough	their	women
chocolate	friend	minute	route	there	would
choose	fuel	morning	said	they	write
Christmas	getting	mother	Santa Claus	though	writing
close	goes	name	Saturday	thought	wrote
color	grade	neither	says	through	you
come	guard	nice	school	tired	your
coming	guess	none	schoolhouse	together	you're
cough	half	o'clock	several		

See Also List 20, Spelling Demons—Secondary.

The NEW Reading Teacher's Book of Lists, © 1985 Prentice-Hall, Inc., Englewood Cliffs, NJ 07632. By E. Fry, D. Fountoukidis, and J. Polk.

20. SPELLING DEMONS—SECONDARY

Secondary students may misspell words on the elementary list of Demons, and since their writing is more advanced than the younger students they may also have trouble with these Demons.

absence	concede	gaiety	occurrence	repetition
acceptable	conceive	gauge	occurring	restaurant
accommodate	condemn	grammar	opinion	rhythm
accustom	conscience	guarantee	opportunity	saucer
ache	conscientious	guidance	paid	seize
achievement	conscious	height	parallel	sense
acquire	controversial	heroes	paralyzed	separate
across	controversy	hypocrite	particular	sergeant
adolescent	council	incredible	performance	shining
advantageous	criticize	interest	personal	similar
advertisement	definitely	interrupt	personnel	sincerely
advice	definition	irrelevant	pleasant	sophomore
against	descendant	its	politician	stationary
aisle	describe	jealousy	portrayed	studying
amateur	description	led	possession	substantial
analyze	desert	leisurely	possible	subtle
annually	dilemma	license	practical	succeed
anticipated	diligence	lieutenant	preferred	succession
apparent	dining	listener	prejudice	supersede
appreciate	disastrous	lose	prepare	surprise
arctic	discipline	luxury	prescription	susceptible
arguing	disease	magnificent	prestige	technique
argument	dissatisfied	maneuver	prevalent	thorough
arrangement	endeavor	marriage	principal	tragedy
athlete	effect	mathematics	principle	transferred
bargain	embarrass	medicine	privilege	tremendous
belief	emigrate	mere	probably	unnecessary
beneficial	environment	miniature	procedure	vacuum
benefited	especially	miscellaneous	proceed	valuable
breathe	exaggerate	mischief	profession	vegetable
Britain	exceed	moral	professor	vengeance
bury	except	muscle	prominent	villain
business	exercise	mysterious	pursue	visible
calendar	exhausted	necessary	quiet	waive
category	existence	niece	receipt	woman
cemetery	experience	noticeable	receive	wrench
certainly	explanation	numerous	recommend	write
cite	fascinate	occasion	referring	writing
comparative	formerly	occurred	renowned	yacht

See Also List 19, Spelling Demons—Elementary.

The NEW Reading Teacher's Book of Lists, © 1985 Prentice-Hall, Inc., Englewood Cliffs, NJ 07632. By E. Fry, D. Fountoukidis, and J. Polk.

21. SPELLING DEMONS—WISE GUYS

Try using these as tie-breakers in a spelling bee, or as examples of the utility of syllabication for pronouncing new words.

Antidisestablishmentarianism: State support of the church.

Supercalifragilisticexpialidocious: Mary Poppins says it means "good."

Pneumonoultramicroscopicsilicovolcanoconiosis: Lung disease caused by inhaling silica dust.

Floccinaucinihilipilification: Action of estimating as worthless.

Llanfairpwllgwyngyllgogerychwyrndrobwllllandysiliogogogoch: Name of a town in Wales.

22. SYNONYMS

Synonyms are words that have similar meanings. Dictionaries often use synonyms in their definitions. There are whole books of synonyms and special reference works, such as the thesaurus, that have clusters of words or phrases, all with similar meanings. These are particularly useful in finding just the "right" word when writing.

The NEW Reading Teacher's Book of Lists, © 1985 Prentice-Hall, Inc., Englewood Cliffs, NJ 07632. By E. Fry, D. Fountoukidis, and J. Polk.

have, own, possess
one, single, unit
word, term, expression
all, every, entire
say, state, remark
use, operate, employ
many, several, numerous
make, do, construct
like, enjoy, be fond of
time, period, season
look, glance, see
write, record, draft
people, public, individuals
call, shout, summon
find, locate, retrieve
long, lengthy, drawn-out
day, date, occasion
come, arrive, reach
make, build, construct
part, portion, piece
new, fresh, recent
sound, noise, note
take, grab, seize
little, small, short
work, labor, toil
place, put, arrange
give, grant, hand over
after, following, behind
name, title, designation
good, suitable, just
man, mankind, homo sapiens
think, consider, believe
great, grand, large

help, aid, assist
before, prior to, in front of
line, mark, stripe
right, correct, proper
mean, stand for, denote
old, aged, ancient
boy, lad, youth
want, desire, crave
show, demonstrate, display
form, shape, make up
end, finish, complete
large, big, enormous
turn, revolve, twist
ask, question, probe
go, leave, depart
need, require, want
different, varied, unique
move, transport, budge
try, attempt, endeavor
kind, benign, humane
picture, photo, painting
change, vary, alter
play, frolic, romp
point, peak, apex
page, sheet, leaf
answer, response, reply
find, locate, recover
study, consider, reflect
still, unmoving, silent
learn, acquire, understand
world, globe, earth
high, tall, lofty
near, close by, convenient

add, increase, sum
food, nourishment, edibles
below, under, beneath
country, nation, state
keep, hold, retain
start, begin, commence
city, borough, town
story, tale, account
while, during, at the same time
might, may, perhaps
close, shut, seal
seem, appear, look
hard, difficult, troublesome
open, unlock, unseal
beginning, starting, initial
group, arrange, gather
often, frequently, repeatedly
run, gallop, trot
important, needed, necessary
children, youngsters, tots
car, auto, vehicle
night, evening, dark
walk, stroll, saunter
sea, ocean, waters
grow, increase, accumulate
take, grab, steal
carry, tote, lug
state, claim, announce
stop, halt, end
idea, thought, concept
enough, sufficient, ample
eat, devour, dine

See Also List 1, Homophones;
List 2, Homographs; and List
23, Antonyms.

23. ANTONYMS

Antonyms are words that mean the opposite or nearly the opposite of each other. Both synonyms and antonyms are often used in tests and language drills.

The NEW Reading Teacher's Book of Lists, © 1985 Prentice-Hall, Inc., Englewood Cliffs, NJ 07632. By E. Fry, D. Fountoukidis, and J. Polk.

to–from
in–out
that–this
he–she
on–off
with–without
his–her
one–several
all–none
there–here
him–her
up–down
other–same
many–few
then–now
make–destroy
like–dislike
more–less
go–come
no–yes
same–different
boy–girl
following–preceding
small–large
end–begin
well–badly
even–odd
asked–told

move–stay
kind–cruel
change–remain
off–on
away–toward
mother–father
answer–question
found–lost
high–low
near–far
add–subtract
below–above
never–always
started–finished
light–dark
left–right
close–open
hard–soft
life–death
together–apart
group–individual
often–seldom
child–adult
white–black
stop–start
allow–prohibit
leave–arrive
problem–solution

friend–enemy
first–last
find–lose
long–short
down–up
day–night
get–give
part–whole
over–under
new–old
sound–silence
take–give
little–big
work–play
alive–dead
back–front
most–least
after–before
something–nothing
good–bad
man–woman
great–small
help–hurt
much–little
right–wrong
mean–kind
old–young

See Also List 22, Synonyms.

SECTION II
Word Groups

24. ANALOGIES

Analogies are used for teaching and testing. The key is to determine the relationship between two words; then find other pairs of words that have a similar relationship. To interpret the notation used below, say "*in* is to *out* as *hot* is to ——." Since the relationship is one of opposites, the answer is *cold*. Other relationships used in analogies are: synonyms, object-to-action (ear : hear :: mouth : speak), action-to-object (hear : ear :: talk : mouth), part-whole, purpose (chair : sit :: bed : sleep), cause and effect, numerical (5 : 10 :: 3 : 6), sequence, degree (pretty : beautiful :: warm : hot), characteristics (snow : cold :: sun : hot), grammatical (she : her :: he : him), place (bear : den :: bee : hive), and association (soap : clean :: mud : dirty).

in : out :: hot :

mother : aunt :: father :

ear : hear :: mouth :

dog : barks :: bird :

one : two :: three :

she : her :: he :

snow : cold :: sun :

finger : hand :: toe :

brother : boy :: sister :

bear : den :: bee :

girl : mother :: boy :

left : right :: top :

car : driver :: plane :

bird : sky :: fish :

rich : wealth :: sick :

green : color :: cinnamon :

coffee : drink :: hamburger :

arrow : bow :: bullet :

ceiling : room :: lid :

page : book :: Ohio :

small : tiny :: large :

glove : hand :: boot :

swim : pool :: jog :

easy : simple :: hard :

breakfast : lunch :: morning :

blue : color :: round :

meat : beef :: fruit :

date : calendar :: time :

cells : skin :: bricks :

win : lose :: stop :

try : attempt :: avoid :

minute : hour :: day :

help : aid :: gentle :

paw : dog :: fin :

kettle : soup :: griddle :

moon : earth :: earth :

tree : lumber :: wheat :

library : books :: cupboard :

three : six :: four :

princess : queen :: prince :

story : read :: song :

length : weight :: inches :

one : three :: single :

blind : deaf :: see :

pen : write :: broom :

wrist : hand :: ankle :

water : ship :: air :

engine : go :: brake :

glass : break :: paper :

soap : clean :: mud :

book : character :: recipe :

silk : smooth :: sandpaper :

sing : pleased :: shout :

much : little :: early :

penny : dollar :: foot :

runner : sled :: wheel :

cabin : build :: well :

temperature : humidity :: thermometer :

Suggested Answers to List 24

in : out :: hot : cold
mother : aunt :: father : uncle
ear : hear :: mouth : speak
dog : barks :: bird : chirps
one : two :: three : four
she : her :: he : him
snow : cold :: sun : hot
finger : hand :: toe : foot
brother : boy :: sister : girl
bear : den :: bee : hive
girl : mother :: boy : father
left : right :: top : bottom
car : driver :: plane : pilot
bird : sky :: fish : sea
rich : wealth :: sick : disease
green : color :: cinnamon : spice
coffee : drink :: hamburger : eat
arrow : bow :: bullet : gun
ceiling : room :: lid : pan
page : book :: Ohio : U.S.
small : tiny :: large : huge
glove : hand :: boot : foot
swim : pool :: jog : road
easy : simple :: hard : difficult
breakfast : lunch :: morning : afternoon
blue : color :: round : shape
meat : beef :: fruit : apple
date : calendar :: time : clock
cells : skin :: bricks : wall

win : lose :: stop : go
try : attempt :: avoid : escape
minute : hour :: day : year
help : aid :: gentle : soft
paw : dog :: fin : fish
kettle : soup :: griddle : pancake
moon : earth :: earth : sun
tree : lumber :: wheat : flour
library : books :: cupboard : dishes
three : six :: four : eight
princess : queen :: prince : king
story : read :: song : sing
length : weight :: inches : pounds
one : three :: single : triple
blind : deaf :: see : hear
pen : write :: broom : sweep
wrist : hand :: ankle : foot
water : ship :: air : airplane
engine : go :: brake : stop
glass : break :: paper : tear
soap : clean :: mud : dirty
book : character :: recipe : ingredient
silk : smooth :: sandpaper : rough
sing : pleased :: shout : angry
much : little :: early : late
penny : dollar :: foot : yard
runner : sled :: wheel : wagon
cabin : build :: well : dig
temperature : humidity ::
    thermometer : hygrometer

The NEW Reading Teacher's Book of Lists, © 1985 Prentice-Hall, Inc., Englewood Cliffs, NJ 07632. By E. Fry, D. Fountoukidis, and J. Polk.

25. SIMILES

A simile is a figure of speech that uses the words "as" or "like." Figures of speech are used like adjectives or adverbs. They modify or describe a person, place, thing, or action with a colorful and often visual term or phrase. Creative writers and poets make good use of these.

The NEW Reading Teacher's Book of Lists, © 1985 Prentice-Hall, Inc., Englewood Cliffs, NJ 07632. By E. Fry, D. Fountoukidis, and J. Polk.

as fat as a pig
as light as a feather
as cold as ice
as lovely as a rose
as green as grass
as smooth as glass
as hard as a rock
as soft as old leather
as fresh as dew
as strong as steel
as strong as an ox
as cute as a button
as cuddly as a baby
as worn as an old shoe
as dark as night
as final as death
as busy as a bee
as happy as a lark
as hungry as a bear
as sly as a fox
as sweet as honey
as quick as a wink
as quiet as a mouse
as deaf as a post
as stubborn as a mule

as dry as a bone
as soft as silk
as meek as a lamb
as thin as a rail
as blue as a mountain lake
as deep as the ocean
as quiet as an empty church
as loud as thunder
as harsh as the clang of a fire engine
as clear as day
as musical as a flute
as bright as the sun
as white as snow
as rough as sandpaper
felt like two cents
cheeks like roses
eyes like stars
laughed like a hyena
drank like a fish
spoke like an orator
walked like an elephant
waddled like a duck
worked like a horse
sparkled like diamonds

See Also List 28, Common Word Idioms,
and List 74, Descriptive Words.

26. METAPHORS

Metaphors are figures of speech that compare two things, but do not use the words "like" and "as." These colorful phrases are used like adverbs or adjectives to describe persons, places, things, or actions. Students must learn not to take them literally but to enjoy their use. This is not an exhaustive list, but it might be just enough to get a lesson or an essay started. See List 27, Idiomatic Expressions, for additional metaphors.

Ann is a walking encyclopedia.
John's head is a computer.
A rocket of a man shot past me at the finish line.
The arthritic car squeaked, rattled, and moaned down the road.
Her porcelain skin is flawless.
She's a regular adding machine.
A fossil of a man greeted us at the door.
His sandpaper hand scratched her cheek.
Skip is a clown.
Her heart is a fountain of kindness.
The mountain of paper work seemed to grow.
Carla was a mermaid slipping through the water.
His heart is an iceberg.
The army of ants attacked the fallen lollipop.
Tom is a marionette; his brother Bill works the strings.
She is the shining star in his dark, dreary life.
He is a snail when it comes to getting his work done.
Mr. Mather's bark is worse than his bite.
The toddler was a clinging vine near his mother.
His books were steamships and starships taking him to new worlds.
His new car turned out to be a lemon.
She was thunderstruck when she learned she had won.
He's top banana where he works.
The police were determined to get to the bottom of the mystery.
When her mother died, she shouldered the burden of raising the children.
I'm a real chicken when it comes to getting an injection.
At night my bedroom is a real icebox.
When my mother saw how poor my grades were, she gave me a real tongue
      lashing.
When I was lost in the woods, the branches of the trees became hands
      reaching out to grab me.
By the time she finished her first day at work, she was dead tired.
His stomach was a bottomless pit.
The night was growing old and there was still so much to be done.
My grandmother is very broad-minded about most things.
He turned thumbs down at the idea of moving to a new town.

The NEW Reading Teacher's Book of Lists, © 1985 Prentice-Hall, Inc., Englewood Cliffs, NJ 07632. By E. Fry, D. Fountoukidis, and J. Polk.

27. IDIOMATIC EXPRESSIONS

Idiomatic expressions cannot be understood from their literal definitions. For example, *break the news* has little to do with breaking. Rather, it is used as a more colorful way of saying that someone is informing another. Some idiomatic expressions are considered slang (*blow the whistle*), but the majority are well accepted in all but very formal communication. For students who are learning the English language, idiomatic expressions are particularly troublesome. Teach these expressions just as you would a single vocabulary word because they must be comprehended that way.

The NEW Reading Teacher's Book of Lists, © 1985 Prentice-Hall, Inc., Englewood Cliffs, NJ 07632. By E. Fry, D. Fountoukidis, and J. Polk.

Stop pulling my leg.
It looks like a record snow.
It's raining cats and dogs.
It's a dog's life.
We're all in the same boat.
You'll catch a cold that way.
He's a cracker-jack mechanic.
The boss just gave him the ax.
You could have knocked me over with a feather.
By the skin of your teeth you won the game.
Tom caught the train at eight.
You really put your foot in your mouth this time.
Expensive? Naw, it's just chicken feed.
Get off my back!
She's always a ball of fire.
The criminal tried to beat the rap.
The manager's over a barrel on this one.
Somebody might blow the whistle on your plan.
We're up a creek.
Stop bugging me!
The boys had a bull session Friday night.
You've hit it on the button.
The judge threw the book at him.
This car can stop on a dime.
I'll put this one in the circular file.
The boys were just shooting the breeze.
He quit cold turkey.
The way he got the job was dirty pool.
That's the way the cookie crumbles.

He's out on his ear.
She's over the hill.
He got in by the seat of his pants.
I'm hung up on this problem.
He's out in left field.
I gave up the rat race.
He's got rocks in his head.
It's in the bag.
Take the tiger by the tail.
I got it straight from the horse's mouth.
We're in hot water.
Drop me a line.
I'll do it when the cows come home.
Go fly a kite.
That's a sharp tie.
I'd really like to catch her eye.
We have to straighten up the house.
Go jump in the lake.
Button your lip.
Can you dig it?
Cat got your tongue?
You're off your rocker.
Get out of my hair.
Time flies.
You're out of sight.
He has a green thumb.
Keep a stiff upper lip.
Lend a hand.
She let the cat out of the bag.
Cut it out.
She gave him a dirty look.
The traffic was heavy.
We don't see eye to eye on this.

See Also List 74, Descriptive Words.

71

28. COMMON WORD IDIOMS

Many idioms are formed around key words that are very common. Use this list as a starter for exploring English idioms.

Back: back down, back out, back up

Blow: blow a fuse, blow hot and cold, blow your own trumpet, blow out, blow over, blow the whistle, blow up

Break: break down, break in, break into, break your word, break out, break the ice, break the news, break up, break with

Bring: bring about, bring around, bring down the house, bring (something) home to one, bring in, bring off, bring on, bring one to do something, bring out, bring around, bring up

Call: call a halt, call a spade a spade, call attention to, call for, call forth, call in, call names, call on, call out, call up

Come: come about, come across, come around, come by, come clean, come down on, come in, come in for, come into, come into your own, come off, come off it, come out, come to pass, come up, come up to, come upon

Cut: cut in, cut it out, cut someone out, cut out for, cut up

Do: do away with, do for, do in, do someone proud, do out of, do up, do well (badly) by someone, do without

Eat: eat humble pie, eat crow, eat dirt, eat someone out of house and home, eat your heart out, eat your words, eat your hat, eat out of your hand, eat their heads off

Fall: fall by the wayside, fall down, fall flat, fall for, fall in with, fall out, fall over each other, fall short, fall through

Get: get along, get at, get away with, get back at, get by, get carried away by, get even with, get in with, get into, get on, get on someone's nerves, get your back up, get someone's goat, get out of, get over, get the better of, get the hang of, get up, get wind of

Give: give a damn, give away, give in, give off, give out, give up

Go: go all out, go by, go down, go easy, go far, go for, go in for, go into, go off the deep end, go on, go one better, go out, go over, go to the dogs, go with, go with the crowd, go without

Hang: hang around, hang on, hang out, hang up

Have: have it both ways, have it coming, have it in for someone, have it out with someone

Hit: hit it off, hit your stride, hit the books, hit the ceiling, hit the roof, hit the hay, hit the sack, hit the headlines, hit the high points (spots), hit the nail on the head, hit upon

Hold: hold a candle to, hold forth, hold on, hold your own

The NEW Reading Teacher's Book of Lists, © 1985 Prentice-Hall, Inc., Englewood Cliffs, NJ 07632. By E. Fry, D. Fountoukidis, and J. Polk.

Keep: keep a straight face, keep company, keep on, keep your head, keep your head above water, keep your temper, keep your word, keep open house, keep the pot boiling, keep the wolf from the door, keep to (a plan, a promise, your word, etc.), keep up, keep up appearances, keep up with

Knock: knock about, knock around, knock dead, knock down, knock for a loop, knock off, knock out

Lay: lay a finger on someone, lay aside, lay down one's life, lay down the law, lay hands on, lay it on, lay off, lay your hand on something, lay yourself open to, lay out, lay up

Let: let off steam, let on, let your hair down, let sleeping dogs lie, let the cat out of the bag, let up

Look: look down on, look down your nose, look for, look into, look out, look up, look up to someone

Make: make a move, make a play for, make certain, make something do, make ends meet, make fun of, make good, make haste, make head or tail of something, make it, make out, make over, make shift with, make sure, make the fur fly, make the grade, make up, make up for, make up your mind, make up to

Play: play at something, play down, play fast and loose, play havoc with, play hell, play hooky, play into someone's hands, play on, play second fiddle, play the devil, play the fool, play the game

Pull: pull a fast one, pull in your belt, pull off, pull up your socks, pull your weight, pull strings, pull through, pull to pieces, pull together, pull up, pull the wool over your eyes, pull up stakes

Put: put down, put forward, put in for, put off, put on, put your cards on the table, put your foot down, put out, put right, put two and two together, put up, put up with

Run: run across, run into, run away, run down, run afoul of, run in, run out of, run over, run ragged, run rings around, run through

See: see about, see eye to eye, see into, see through, see to

Sit: sit on, sit on the fence, sit out, sit pretty, sit tight, sit up

Take: take a back seat, take a powder, take after, take care, take it easy, take someone or something for, take for granted, take heart, take ill, take in, take issue, take it easy, take it from me, take it hard, take it into your head, take it out on someone, take something lying down, take note of, take off, take on, take your time, take out, take over, take the cake, take to heart, take the trouble, take it upon yourself

Throw: throw a fit, throw a party, throw in the sponge, throw light on, throw off, throw one's weight around, throw out, throw up

Turn: turn a cold shoulder to, turn a deaf ear, turn down, turn in, turn loose, turn on, turn your head, turn out, turn over (money), turn over a new leaf, turn the tables on someone, turn to, turn turtle, turn up

See Also List 27, Idiomatic Expressions, and List 74, Descriptive Words.

29. PROVERBS

Proverbs are common, wise, or thoughtful sayings that are short and often applicable to different situations. Every culture and language has its own, from the ancient Chinese Confucious "A picture is worth a thousand words" to the American "A stitch in time saves nine." Here are just a few; you and your students might enjoy adding to the collection.

Animals

Birds of a feather flock together.
When the cat's away the mice will play.
He who lies down with dogs gets up with fleas.
Don't count your chickens until they're hatched.
A bird in the hand is worth two in the bush.
You can lead a horse to water, but you can't make it drink.
The early bird catches the worm.
Curiosity killed the cat.
You can't teach an old dog new tricks.
Don't change horses in the middle of the stream.
Let sleeping dogs lie.

Food

Don't cry over spilt milk.
The proof of the pudding is in the eating.
Too many cooks spoil the broth.
You can't have your cake and eat it too.
An apple a day keeps the doctor away.
Half a loaf is better than none.

Money

A penny saved is a penny earned.
Time is money.
Lend your money and lose your friend.
Money burns a hole in your pocket.
All that glitters is not gold.
A fool and his money are soon parted.
Early to bed, early to rise makes a man healthy, wealthy, and wise.

Nature

It never rains but it pours.
A rolling stone gathers no moss.
Make hay while the sun shines.
Every cloud has a silver lining.
Leave no stone unturned.
The grass always looks greener on the other side.
One tree doesn't make a forest.
Still waters run deep.

The NEW Reading Teacher's Book of Lists, © 1985 Prentice-Hall, Inc., Englewood Cliffs, NJ 07632. By E. Fry, D. Fountoukidis, and J. Polk.

Relationships

Marry in haste, repent at leisure.
If you can't beat them, join them.
Familiarity breeds contempt.
Short visits make long friends.
A faint heart never won a fair lady.
Like father, like son.
Absence makes the heart grow fonder.
Good fences make good neighbors.
A friend in need is a friend indeed.

Miscellaneous

If the shoe fits wear it.
People who live in glass houses shouldn't throw stones.
Two wrongs don't make a right.
The pen is mightier than the sword.
Necessity is the mother of invention.
Actions speak louder than words.
Haste makes waste.
He who hesitates is lost.
Look before you leap.
Beggars can't be choosers.
A stitch in time saves nine.
Two heads are better than one.
Many hands make light work.
Fool me once, shame on you. Fool me twice, shame on me.
Strike while the iron is hot.
Where there's smoke there's fire.
Out of the frying pan and into the fire.
A watched pot never boils.

See Also List 112, Murphy's Law and Others.

The NEW Reading Teacher's Book of Lists, © 1985 Prentice-Hall, Inc., Englewood Cliffs, NJ 07632. By E. Fry, D. Fountoukidis, and J. Polk.

SECTION III
Word Origins

30. CLIPPED WORDS—WORDS SHORTENED BY COMMON USAGE

These are words that have been shortened or clipped by common use, as in *sub* for *submarine*. This shortening is called Zipf's Principle and is well known in the study of languages.

The NEW Reading Teacher's Book of Lists, © 1985 Prentice-Hall, Inc., Englewood Cliffs, NJ 07632. By E. Fry, D. Fountoukidis, and J. Polk.

ad	advertisement	memo	memorandum
auto	automobile	miss	mistress
bike	bicycle	mod	modern
burger	hamburger	movie	moving picture
bus	omnibus	mum	chrysanthemum
bust	burst	pants	pantaloons
cab	cabriolet	pen	penitentiary
canter	Canterbury gallop	pep	pepper
cent	centum	perk	percolate
champ	champion	perk	perquisite
chemist	alchemist	phone	telephone
clerk	cleric	pike	turnpike
coed	coeducational student	plane	airplane
con	convict	pop	popular
cop	copper	prof	professor
cuke	cucumber	prom	promenade
curio	curiosity	ref	referee
deb	debutante	scram	scramble
doc	doctor	specs	spectacles
dorm	dormitory	sport	disport
drape	drapery	still	distill
exam	examination	sub	submarine
fan	fanatic	tails	coattails
flu	influenza	taxi	taxicab
fridge	refrigerator	teen	teenager
gab	gabble	tie	necktie
gas	gasoline	trig	trigonometry
grad	graduate	trump	triumph
gym	gymnasium	tux	tuxedo
hack	hackney	typo	typographical error
lab	laboratory	van	caravan
limo	limousine	varsity	university
lube	lubricate	vet	veteran
lunch	luncheon	vet	veterinarian
mart	market	wig	periwig
math	mathematics	zoo	zoological garden
mend	amend		

See Also List 31, Portmanteau Words; and List 32, Compound Words.

31. PORTMANTEAU WORDS—WORDS THAT HAVE BEEN BLENDED TOGETHER

Alice, in *Alice in Wonderland,* asks Humpty Dumpty what "slithy" (from the Jabberwocky) means. He tells her that it means "lithe" and "slimy." "You see there are two meanings packed into one word."

autobus	automobile + bus
bit	binary + digit
blimp	B + limp
blotch	blot + botch
brunch	breakfast + lunch
because	by + cause
chortle	chuckle + snort
clash	clap + crash
clump	chunk + lump
conman	confidence + man
daisy	day's + eye
farewell	fare + ye + well
flare	flame + glare
flurry	flutter + hurry
flush	flash + gush
fortnite	fourteen + nights
gerrymander	Gerry + salamander
glimmer	gleam + shimmer
goodbye	God + be (with) + ye
hifi	high + fidelity
modem	modulator + demodulator
moped	motor + pedal
motel	motor + hotel
motocross	motor + cross country
motorcade	motor + cavalcade
napalm	naphthene + palmitate
o'clock	of (the) + clock
paratroops	parachute + troops
pixel	picture + element
skylab	sky + laboratory
slosh	slop + slush
smash	smack + mash
smog	smoke + fog
sparcity	sparceness + scarcity
splatter	splash + spatter
squiggle	squirm + wriggle
taxicab	taximeter + cabriolet
telethon	television + marathon
travelogue	travel + monologue
twinight	twilight + night
twirl	twist + whirl

See Also List 30, Clipped Words; List 40, Greek Roots; and List 41, Latin Roots.

The NEW Reading Teacher's Book of Lists, © 1985 Prentice-Hall, Inc., Englewood Cliffs, NJ 07632. By E. Fry, D. Fountoukidis, and J. Polk.

32. COMPOUND WORDS—WORDS GLUED TOGETHER TO FORM NEW WORDS

Compound words do not always join the meanings of the two words used. For example, *brainstorm*. These words are great fun to illustrate the silliness of literal translations.

afternoon	copout	gentleman	notebook	ripoff	timetable
airconditioning	copperhead	goldenrod	nutcracker	rowboat	tiptoe
airline	copyright	goldfish	oatmeal	runway	toenail
airmail	cowboy	grasshopper	offbeat	sailboat	toothbrush
airport	crosswalk	haircut	outboard	sandpaper	toothpick
anchorman	cupboard	handcuff	outcome	scarecrow	touchdown
anchorwoman	cupcake	handlebar	outfield	screwball	tugboat
another	cutout	hangup	outfit	screwdriver	turntable
applesauce	daydream	hardware	outlaws	shipwreck	turtleneck
ashtray	daytime	haystack	outstanding	shoelace	undercover
backyard	dishpan	headache	overalls	shortstop	underground
bareback	doorknob	headlight	overcoat	sidewalk	understand
barefoot	doorway	headquarters	overlook	silverware	undertake
baseball	downpour	highchair	overpass	skateboard	uproot
basketball	downstairs	highrise	pancake	skyscraper	uptown
bathroom	downtown	highway	paperback	slipcover	vineyard
bedspread	dragonfly	holdup	payoff	snowdrift	volleyball
billfold	drawbridge	homemade	peanut	snowfall	washcloth
birthday	drive-in	jellyfish	peppermint	softball	wastebasket
blackbird	driveway	landlady	pigtail	splashdown	watchman
blackboard	dropout	landlord	pinball	spotlight	watercolor
blackout	drugstore	leftover	pinpoint	starfish	waterfall
bloodhound	earring	lifeboat	playmate	streetcar	waterfront
blueprint	earthquake	lifeguard	playpen	suitcase	watermelon
bookkeeper	eyeball	lipstick	ponytail	sunbeam	weatherman
breakfast	ferryboat	lookout	popcorn	sunflower	weekend
broadcast	filmstrip	loudspeaker	postcard	sunrise	whirlpool
bulldog	fireplace	midnight	postman	sunset	wholesale
buttercup	flashback	moonship	pushover	sunshine	wildcat
buttermilk	flashcube	moonwalk	quicksand	sweatshirt	windmill
campfire	flashlight	motorcycle	railroad	sweetheart	windpipe
carpool	folklore	newsboy	railway	teacup	windshield
cattail	football	newscast	rainbow	textbook	wiretapping
classmate	frogman	newspaper	rattlesnake	Thanksgiving	woodland
clipboard	frostbite	newsprint	rawhide	thumbtack	woodpecker
clothesline	fruitcake	nightgown	redwood	thunderstorm	wristwatch
clothespin					

33. CONTRACTIONS

Contractions substitute an apostrophe for a letter or letters. You will find the grouping of contractions by verb a good teaching strategy.

am	is, has	would, had	have	will	not
I'm	he's	I'd	I've	I'll	can't
	she's	you'd	you've	you'll	don't
are	it's	he'd	we've	she'll	isn't
you're	what's	she'd	they've	he'll	won't
we're	that's	we'd	could've	it'll	shouldn't
they're	who's	they'd	would've	we'll	couldn't
who're	there's	it'd	should've	they'll	wouldn't
	here's	there'd	might've	that'll	aren't
	one's	what'd	who've	these'll	doesn't
		who'd	there've	those'll	wasn't
		that'd		there'll	weren't
				this'll	hasn't
			us	what'll	haven't
			let's	who'll	hadn't
					mustn't
					didn't
					mightn't
					needn't

The NEW Reading Teacher's Book of Lists, © 1985 Prentice-Hall, Inc., Englewood Cliffs, NJ 07632. By E. Fry, D. Fountoukidis, and J. Polk.

See Also List 30, Clipped Words.

34. ACRONYMS AND INITIALIZATIONS

Everyone knows about TGIF, but what about MMB (Monday Morning Blues)? Acronyms and initializations are used frequently in media and everyday communication. This reference should keep you and your students well informed.

ABC	American Broadcasting Company
ACTION	American Council to Improve Our Neighborhoods
AID	Agency for International Development
AIDS	Acquired Immune Deficiency Syndrome
APO	Army Post Office
ASAP	As soon as possible
AWOL	Absent without leave
BASIC	Beginners All-Purpose Symbolic Instruction Code (See List 47, Computer Terms)
BASIC	British-American Scientific International Commercial English
BBC	British Broadcasting Corporation
BLT	Bacon, lettuce, and tomato
BMOC	Big man on campus
BTO	Big-time operator
CARE	Cooperative for American Relief Everywhere
CB	Citizen's Band
CBS	Columbia Broadcasting System
CETA	Comprehensive Employment and Training Act
CLASS	Computer-based Laboratory for Automated School Systems
CLASSMATE	Computer Language to Aid and Stimulate Scientific, Mathematical, and Technical Education
COBOL	Common Business-Oriented Language (see List 47, Computer Terms)
COD	Cash on delivery
CORE	Congress of Racial Equality
CPA	Certified Public Accountant
CPO	Chief petty officer
DA	District attorney
DDT	Dichlorodiphenyltrichloroethane
DEW	Distant Early Warning
DEWLINE	Distant Early Warning Line
DJ	Disc jockey
DOA	Dead on arrival
EDP	Electronic data processing
EEG	Electroencephalogram
EKG, ECG	Electrocardiogram
ERA	Equal Rights Amendment
EURAILPASS	European railway passenger
FIAT	Fabbrica Italiana Automobili Torino
FORTRAN	Formula Translation (see List 47, Computer Terms)
GASP	Group Against Smoking in Public

The NEW Reading Teacher's Book of Lists, © 1985 Prentice-Hall, Inc., Englewood Cliffs, NJ 07632. By E. Fry, D. Fountoukidis, and J. Polk.

GESTAPO	Geheime Staats Polizei
GI	Government issue
HEW	Health, Education & Welfare
HQ	Headquarters
HUD	Housing and Urban Development
ICBM	Intercontinental ballistic missile
IQ	Intelligence quotient
IRS	Internal Revenue Service
JAYCEES	U.S. Junior Chamber of Commerce
JEEP	General Purpose (vehicle)
JOBS	Job Opportunities for Better Skills
KKK	Ku Klux Klan
LASER	Light amplification by stimulated emission of radiation
LEM	Lunar Excursion Module
LIFO	Last in, first out
LP	Long playing (phonograph record)
LSD	Lysergic acid diethylamide
MIA	Missing in action
MO	Modus operandi
MYOB	Mind your own business
NAACP	National Association for the Advancement of Colored People
NABISCO	National Biscuit Company
NASA	National Aeronautics and Space Administration
NATO	North Atlantic Treaty Organization
NAZI	National Socialist German Workers' Party
NBC	National Broadcasting Company
NOW	National Organization for Women
OPEC	Organization of Petroleum Exporting Countries
PA	Public address
PAC	Pacific Athletic Conference
PBS	Public Broadcasting System
PDQ	Pretty darn quick
POW	Prisoner of war
PS	Postscript
PUSH	People United to Save Humanity
RADAR	Radio detecting and ranging
RAM	Random Access Memory (see List 47, Computer Terms)
RIP	Rest in peace
ROM	Read Only Memory (see List 47, Computer Terms)
ROTC	Reserve Officer Training Corps
RR	Railroad
RSVP	Répondez s'il vous plaît
RV	Recreational vehicle
SALT	Strategic Arms Limitation Talks
SCUBA	Self-contained underwater breathing apparatus
SNAFU	Situation normal, all fouled up
SNCC	Student Nonviolent Coordinating Committee

The NEW Reading Teacher's Book of Lists, © 1985 Prentice-Hall, Inc., Englewood Cliffs, NJ 07632. By E. Fry, D. Fountoukidis, and J. Polk.

The NEW Reading Teacher's Book of Lists, © 1985 Prentice-Hall, Inc., Englewood Cliffs, NJ 07632. By E. Fry, D. Fountoukidis, and J. Polk.

SONAR	Sound navigation ranging
SOS	Save our ship
SWAK	Sealed with a kiss
SWAT	Special weapons action team
TEFLON	Tetrafloroethylene resin
TELEX	Teletypewriter Exchange Service
TGIF	Thank God It's Friday
TLC	Tender loving care
TNT	Trinitrotoluene
TV	Television
UFO	Unidentified flying object
UNESCO	United Nations Educational, Scientific, and Cultural Organization
UNICEF	United Nations International Children's Education Fund
VEEP	Vice-president
VIP	Very important person
VISTA	Volunteers in Service to America
WAC	Women's Army Corps
WASP	White Anglo-Saxon Protestant
WAVES	Women Accepted for Volunteer Emergency Service
WHO	World Health Organization
ZIP	Zone Improvement Plan

See Also List 90, State Abbreviations;
and List 91, Common Abbreviations.

35. WORDS BORROWED FROM NAMES

Did you know that the word *bloomers* is named after feminist Amelia Bloomer, who made them popular? Or, that the word *maverick* comes from Texan rancher Samuel Maverick, who wouldn't brand his cattle? These and other words borrowed from names can be used to help stimulate an interest in word origins.

Words named after people:

ampere	Andre Ampere, a French physicist
braille	Louis Braille, a French teacher of the blind
bloomers	Amelia Bloomer, a pioneer feminist who made them popular
boycott	Charles Boycott, a British army officer and first victim
chauvinist	Nicholas Chauvin, a soldier who worshipped France and Napolean uncritically
diesel	Rudolf Diesel, a German automotive engineer
dunce	Johannes Duns Scotus, a theologian whose followers were called Dunsmen
graham crackers	Sylvester Graham, an American reformer in dietetics and a vegetarian
guillotine	Joseph Guillotin, a French physician who urged its use
maverick	Samuel Maverick, a Texan who didn't brand his cattle
mesmerize	Friedrich Mesmer, an Austrian physician who practiced hypnotism
pasteurize	Louis Pasteur, a French bacteriologist
sandwich	John Montagu, fourth Earl of Sandwich who invented it so he could gamble without stopping for a regular meal
tawdry	St. Audrey, queen of Northumbria; used to describe lace sold at her fair
teddy bear	Teddy Roosevelt, president of the U.S. who spared the life of a bear cub on a hunting trip in Mississippi
volt	Alessandro Volta, an Italian physicist
watt	James Watt, a Scottish engineer and inventor

Words named after places:

cashmere	Kashmir, India
cologne	Cologne, Germany
denim	Nimes, France—*serge de Nimes* (French for fabric of Nimes)
frankfurter	Frankfurt, Germany
hamburger	Hamburg, Germany
manila paper	Manila, Philippines
rhinestone	Rhine, river that flows from Switzerland through Germany and the Netherlands
tabasco sauce	Tabasco, Mexico
tangerine	Tangier, Morocco
vandal	Vandal, Germanic tribe that sacked Rome

The NEW Reading Teacher's Book of Lists, © 1985 Prentice-Hall, Inc., Englewood Cliffs, NJ 07632. By E. Fry, D. Fountoukidis, and J. Polk.

The NEW Reading Teacher's Book of Lists, © 1985 Prentice-Hall, Inc., Englewood Cliffs, NJ 07632. By E. Fry, D. Fountoukidis, and J. Polk.

Days of the week:

Sunday	sun's day
Monday	moon's day
Tuesday	Tiw's day—Teutonic god of war; translated from Latin for day of Mars
Wednesday	Woden's day—Norse god of the hunt; translated from Latin for day of Mercury
Thursday	Thor's day—Norse god of the sky; translated from Latin for day of Jove
Friday	Fria's day—Norse goddess of love and beauty and wife of Thor
Saturday	Saturn's day—Roman god of agriculture

Months of the year:

January	Janus—Roman god with two faces, one looking forward and one looking backward
February	*februa*—Roman feast of purification
March	Mars—Roman god of war
April	*aprilis*—Latin for opening
May	Maia—Roman goddess and mother of Mercury
June	Junius—Roman clan name
July	Julius Caesar—Roman general and statesman
August	Augustus Caesar—Roman emperor
September	*septem*—Latin for seven. September was the 7th month of the Roman calendar.
October	*octo*—Latin for eight. October was the eighth month of the Roman calendar.
November	*novem*—Latin for nine. November was the ninth month of the Roman calendar.
December	*decem*—Latin for ten. December was the tenth month of the Roman calendar.

See Also List 40, Greek Roots;
and List 41, Latin Roots.

36. FOREIGN WORDS AND PHRASES

Foreign words and phrases are used in many novels, magazines, and newspapers, and in some academic writing. Your students might enjoy learning some of the more common ones. Some will demonstrate a *penchant* for picking up foreign phrases *tout de suite* and using them to impress their friends. *N'est-ce pas?*

addenda—list of additions (Latin)
ad hoc—with respect to this condition (Latin)
ad infinitum—to infinity (Latin)
ad nauseam—to the point of disgust (Latin)
à la carte—according to the menu (French)
à la mode—in fashion (French)
alfresco—outdoors (Italian)
au contraire—on the contrary (French)
au courant—well informed (French)
au revoir—until we meet again (French)
à votre santé—to your health (French)

bona fide—in good faith (Latin)
bon jour—good day (French)
bon soir—good evening (French)
bon vivant—lover of good living (French)
bon voyage—have a good voyage (French)

carte blanche—full authority (French)
caveat emptor—let the buyer beware (Latin)
circa—about (Latin)
cogito ergo sum—I think, therefore I am (Latin)
coup d'etat—quick political change (French)
cul-de-sac—dead end (French)
de rigueur—required (French)
double entendre—double meaning (French)

emeritus—retired after long service (Latin)
en masse—in a large group (French)
en route—on the way (French)
entourage—those closely associated with a person (French)
e pluribus unum—one from many (Latin)
errata—list of errors (Latin)
esprit de corps—group spirit (French)
et cetera—and others (Latin)
eureka—I have found it (Latin)

faux pas—mistakes (French)
fiancé—man to whom one is engaged (French)
fiancée—woman to whom one is engaged (French)

hors d'oeuvre—appetizer (French)

in memoriam—in memory of (Latin)

The NEW Reading Teacher's Book of Lists, © 1985 Prentice-Hall, Inc., Englewood Cliffs, NJ 07632. By E. Fry, D. Fountoukidis, and J. Polk.

The NEW Reading Teacher's Book of Lists, © 1985 Prentice-Hall, Inc., Englewood Cliffs, NJ 07632. By E. Fry, D. Fountoukidis, and J. Polk.

in re—regarding (Latin)
in toto—totally (Latin)

je ne sais quoi—I don't know what (French)
laissez faire—noninterference (French)
mâitre d'hôtel—head waiter (French)
malapropos—out of place (French)
mañana—tomorrow (Spanish)
mardi gras—Shrove Tuesday (French)
mea culpa—my fault (Latin)
modus operandi—manner of working (Latin)

née—born (French)
n'est-ce pas?—isn't that so? (French)
noblesse oblige—rank imposes obligations (French)
Noel—Christmas (Latin)
nom de plume—pen name (French)
non sequitur—it does not follow (Latin)
nota bene—note well (Latin)
nuance—subtle distinction (French)

pardonnez-moi—excuse me (French)
penchant—strong liking or inclination (French)
persona non grata—person not accepted (Latin)
per—for (Latin)
pièce de resistance—the irresistible part (French)
prima dona—first lady (Italian)
pro forma—done as a matter of formality (Latin)
pro rata—according to a rate or proportion (Latin)
protégé—one under the guidance of another (French)

quid pro quo—one thing for another (Latin)

raconteur—story teller (French)
raison d'être—reason for existence (French)
résumé—summary (French)

savoir faire—social know-how (French)
sine qua non—indispensable (Latin)
status quo—the way things are (Latin)
stet—leave as is (Latin)
sub rosa—secret or confidential (Latin)

tempus fugit—time flies (Latin)
tout de suite—immediately (French)

vice versa—conversely (Latin)
vis-à-vis—in relation to (French)
voilà—there it is (French)

wanderlust—passion for traveling (German)

See Also List 35, Words Borrowed from Names;
List 40, Greek Roots; and List 41, Latin Roots.

37. ONOMATOPOEIA—WORDS BORROWED FROM SOUNDS

Onomatopoeic words, borrowed from sounds, resemble the real sound that they refer to. For example, a cow *moos*. These words are favorites with poets and comic-strip writers. Entertainers love them and children's authors use them regularly. Your students will enjoy them and probably add some to this list.

bang	grind
beep	hiss
blip	honk
boom	hum
bong	moo
bow wow	murmur
buzz	ping
chirp	plop
chug	quack
clang	rip
clatter	roar
click	rustle
clink	slurp
clomp	smack
cluck	smash
cuckoo	splash
crack	squeak
crash	squeal
creak	squish
crunch	tic tock
ding dong	thump
drip	twang
fizz	whack
flip flop	zip

See Also List 74,
Descriptive Words.

The NEW Reading Teacher's Book of Lists, © 1985 Prentice-Hall, Inc., Englewood Cliffs, NJ 07632. By E. Fry, D. Fountoukidis, and J. Polk.

38. -OLOGY WORD FAMILY

Many subjects that are studied in schools and colleges have *-ology* in their names. The suffix *-ology* means "the science of" or "the study of." For example, since *cardia* means "heart," *cardiology* means "the science of the heart." Moreover, since the suffix *-ist* means "one who practices" (see Suffix Lists 43 and 44), a *cardiologist* is "one who practices the science of the heart."

Anthropology	man (culture)
Archaeology	antiquities (ancient people)
Astrology	stars (divination by stars—the study of stars is referred to as astronomy)
Audiology	hearing
Bacteriology	bacteria
Biology	life
Cardiology	heart
Cosmetology	cosmetics
Cosmology	universe
Criminology	crime
Cryptology	codes and cyphers
Cytology	cells
Dermatology	skin
Ecology	relationship of organisms with their environment
Embryology	embryo
Entomology	insects
Epistemology	knowledge
Ethnology	historical development of cultures
Etymology	word origins
Genealogy	ancestors
Geology	earth
Gerontology	old age
Gynecology	women
Herpetology	reptiles
Histology	living tissue
Hydrology	water
Ideology	doctrine of a group
Meteorology	weather
Microbiology	microbes
Mineralogy	minerals
Morphology	structure of animals and plants
Musicology	music
Neurology	nerves
Ornithology	birds

Paleontology	fossils
Pathology	diseases
Pharmacology	drugs
Physiology	life processes
Pomology	fruit
Psychology	mind
Radiology	radiation
Seismology	earthquakes
Sociology	society
Technology	applied science
Theology	God
Toxicology	poisons
Typology	classification based on type
Zoology	animals

See Also List 39,
Phobia Word Family;
List 40, Greek Roots; and
List 41, Latin Roots.

The NEW Reading Teacher's Book of Lists, © 1985 Prentice-Hall, Inc., Englewood Cliffs, NJ 07632. By E. Fry, D. Fountoukidis, and J. Polk.

39. PHOBIA WORD FAMILY

The Greek word *phobos,* meaning "fear," is combined with a variety of roots to form an interesting group of phobias. Some of these, such as claustrophobia (fear of closed spaces) or acrophobia (fear of high places), are quite common; others may be new to you. Use the root words of Lists 40 and 41 to coin a few of your own. How about "bibliophobia"?

Acrophobia	fear of heights (edges)
Aerophobia	fear of flying
Agoraphobia	fear of open spaces
Ailurophobia	fear of cats
Amaxophobia	fear of vehicles, driving
Androphobia	fear of men
Anthophobia	fear of flowers
Anthropophobia	fear of people
Arachnophobia	fear of spiders
Aquaphobia	fear of water
Astraphobia	fear of lightning
Brontophobia	fear of thunder
Claustrophobia	fear of closed spaces
Cynophobia	fear of dogs
Dementophobia	fear of insanity
Gephyrophobia	fear of bridges
Gerontophobia	fear of old age
Hemophobia	fear of blood
Herpetophobia	fear of reptiles
Mikrophobia	fear of germs
Murophobia	fear of mice
Necrophobia	fear of death
Numerophobia	fear of numbers
Nyctophobia	fear of darkness
Ochlophobia	fear of crowds
Ophidiophobia	fear of snakes
Ornithophobia	fear of birds
Phonophobia	fear of speaking aloud
Pyrophobia	fear of fire
Trichophobia	fear of hair
Triskaidekaphobia	fear of the number thirteen
Xenophobia	fear of strangers

See Also List 38, Ology Word Family;
List 40, Greek Roots; and List 41,
Latin Roots.

40. GREEK ROOTS

Most modern English words originated in other languages. The study of word origins, or etymology, is a fascinating subject. The Greek roots that follow will unlock the meaning of many English words. These and the Latin roots (List 41) can form the basis for a vocabulary-building course. Roots are taught successfully in families such as *microscope, telescope, periscope* to illustrate that *scope* means "see."

Easy Greek Roots—Begin by Teaching These

Root	Meaning	Examples
ast	star	astronaut, astronomy, disaster, asterisk
cycl	circle, ring	bicycle, cyclone, cycle, encyclopedia, cyclops
gram	letter, written	telegram, diagram, grammar, epigram, monogram
graph	write	telegraph, photograph, phonograph, autograph
meter	measure	thermometer, centimeter, diameter, barometer
phon	sound	phonograph, symphony, telephone, microphone, phonics
photo	light	photograph, photography, telephoto, photosynthesis
scop	see	microscope, telescope, periscope, stethescope
therm	heat	thermometer, thermal, thermostat, thermos

More Greek Roots—Continue with These

Root	Meaning	Examples
aero	air	aerate, aerial, aerobics, aerodynamics, aeronautics
aesthet	sense perception	aesthete, aesthetic (see also esth)
andr	man	androgynous, androphobia, polyandry, philander
anthr	man	anthropology, philanthropist, anthropoid, misanthrope
arch	chief	monarch, archbishop, archenemy, oligarchy
archae, arche	primitive, ancient	archaeology, archaic, archetype, archive

The NEW Reading Teacher's Book of Lists, © 1985 Prentice-Hall, Inc., Englewood Cliffs, NJ 07632. By E. Fry, D. Fountoukidis, and J. Polk.

The NEW Reading Teacher's Book of Lists, © 1985 Prentice-Hall, Inc., Englewood Cliffs, NJ 07632. By E. Fry, D. Fountoukidis, and J. Polk.

Root	*Meaning*	*Examples*
baro	weight	barometer, barograph, isobar
biblio	book	bibliography, Bible, bibliophile
bio	life	biology, biography, biochemistry, biopsy
cardi	heart	cardiac, cardiology, cardiogram
chron	time	chronological, synchronize, anachronism, chronicle, chronic
cosm	universe	cosmonaut, cosmos, cosmopolitan, microcosm
crat	rule	democrat, aristocrat, bureacracy, theocracy, autocratic
dem	people	democracy, demography, demagogy, epidemic
dont	tooth	orthodontist
dogma	opinion	dogma, dogmatic, dogmatism
dox	belief	orthodox, unorthodox, heterodoxy
esth	feeling	anesthetist, anesthetic, esthetic (see also aesthet)
gam	marriage	polygamy, monogamy, bigamy
gen	birth, race	generation, genocide, progeny, genealogy, generate
geo	earth	geography, geometry, geology, geophysical
gnos	know	gnostic, agnostic, diagnostic, prognosis
gon	angle	pentagon, octagon, diagonal, trigonometry
gyn	woman	gynecologist, misogynist, monogyny, androgynous
hydr	water	hydroelectric, hydrogen, hydrant, dehydrate
iatr	medical care	psychiatry, podiatry, pediatrician, geriatrics
kine, cine	movement	kinetic, cinema, hyperkinesia, cinemascope
lith	stone	lithograph, monolith, paleolithic, neolithic
log	word	prologue, apology, dialogue, eulogy, monologue
lys	break down	analysis, paralysis, electrolysis, catalyst
mania	madness	maniac, pyromania, cleptomania, megalomania
mech	machine	mechanic, mechanical, mechanism, mechanize

Root	Meaning	Examples
morph	shape	amorphous, metamorphosis, morphology, polymorphous, anthropomorphic
neo	new	neoclassic, neophyte, neologism, neon, neonatal
opt	eye	optician, optometrist, optic, optical
onym	name	synonym, antonym, pseudonym, acronym, heteronym
ortho	straight, right	orthodontist, orthodox, orthopedist, orthography
paed, ped	child	encyclopedia, pediatrician, pedagogical
paleo	old	paleontology, paleolithic
path	feeling, suffer	pathology, sympathy, empathy, antipathy, pathos
phil	love	philosophy, philanthropist, philharmonic, Anglophile, philately
phob	fear	claustrophobia, (see List 39, Phobia Word Family)
phys	nature	physical, physique, metaphysical, physician
pod	foot	podiatrist, podium, tripod
poli	city	metropolis, cosmopolitan, police, political
psych	mind, soul	psychology, psyche, psychopath, psychiatrist
soph	wise	philosopher, sophomore, sophisticated, sophist
the	god	theology, atheism, monotheism, polytheism, pantheism

The NEW Reading Teacher's Book of Lists, © 1985 Prentice-Hall, Inc., Englewood Cliffs, NJ 07632. By E. Fry, D. Fountoukidis, and J. Polk.

See Also List 38, -Ology Word Family; List 39, Phobia Word Family; List 41, Latin Roots; List 42, Prefixes; and Lists 43 and 44, Suffixes.

41. LATIN ROOTS

English has an Anglo-Saxon base (like German) that was spoken by the common folk in Britain. But the learned conquerors were Roman and spoke Latin with many borrowed Greek words. Thus, the more cultured language of Britain grew from Latin. Learning these Latin roots will be a considerable advantage in determining the meaning of new words.

Easy Latin Roots—Begin by Teaching These

Root	Meaning	Examples
act	do	action, react, transact, actor, enact
ang	bend	angle, triangle, quadrangle, angular
aud	hear	auditorium, audience, audiovisual, audible, audition
credit	believe	credit, discredit, incredible, credulous
dict	speak	predict, contradict, dictate, verdict, diction
duc, duct	lead	conduct, aquaduct, duct, induct, educate
fac	make, do	factory, manufacture, benefactor, facsimile
loc	place	locate, dislocate, relocate, location, allocate
man	hand	manual, manufacture, manuscript, manipulate
migr	move	migrate, immigrant, emigrate, migratory
miss	send	missile, dismiss, missionary, mission, remiss
mob	move	automobile, mobile, mobility, mobilize
mot	move	motion, motor, promote, demote, motile
ped	foot	pedal, pedestrian, biped, pedistal
pop	people	population, popular, pop, populace
port	carry	transport, import, portable, porter
rupt	break	erupt, interrupt, rupture, bankrupt, abrupt
sign	mark	signature, signal, significant, insignia
spec	see	inspect, suspect, respect, spectator, spectacle
tract	pull, drag	tractor, subtract, attraction, traction
urb	city	urban, suburb, suburban, urbane
vac	empty	vacant, vacation, vacuum, evacuate, vacate
vid	see	video, evidence, provide, providence
volv	roll	revolve, revolver, involve, evolve, revolution

More Latin Roots—Continue with These

Root	Meaning	Examples
agri	field	agriculture, agrarian, agronomy
alt	high	altitude, altimeter, alto, altocumulus
alter	other	alternate, alternative, altercation
ambul	walk, go	ambulance, amble, circumambulate, preamble, somnambulant
amo, ami	love	amiable, amorous, amateur, amity
anim	life, spirit	animate, animosity, animal, inanimate
ann, enn	year	annual, biennial, anniversary, anuity
apt, ept	suitable	aptitude, ineptitude, adept, inept, apt
aqua	water	aquarium, aquatic, aqueous, aquamarine
art	skill	artisan, artist, artificial, artifact
belli	war	bellicose, antebellum, belligerent, rebellion
brev	short	abbreviation, brevity, breve
cad, cas	fall	cadence, cadaver, cascade, decadence
cal	hot	calorie, caldron, scald
cam	field	campus, camp, campaign, encamp
cand	glow, white	candle, candidate, candelabra, incandescent
cap	head	cap, captain, capital, decapitate, caput
cede, ceed	go, yield	proceed, exceed, antecedent, concede, succeed
ceive, cept	take, receive	receive, reception, accept, conception
center, centr	center	central, centrifugal, eccentric, egocentric
cert	sure	certain, certify, ascertain, certificate
cess	go, yield	process, recess, access, cessation
cide, cise	cut, kill	suicide, scissor, incisor, insecticide, suicide
cip	take, receive	recipient, incipient, participate, recipe
claim, clam	shout	proclaim, clamor, exclaim, acclaim, proclamation
clar	clear	clarity, declare, clarify, declaration
cline	lean	incline, recline, decline, inclination
clud	shut	include, conclude, exclude, preclude, seclude
cogn	know	recognize, cognition, cognizant, incognito
commun	common	community, communal, communism, excommunicate

The NEW Reading Teacher's Book of Lists, © 1985 Prentice-Hall, Inc., Englewood Cliffs, NJ 07632. By E. Fry, D. Fountoukidis, and J. Polk.

Root	Meaning	Examples
cord	heart	cordial, accord, concord, discord
corp	body	corporation, corpus, corpse, corps, corpuscle
cum	heap	cumulative, accumulate, cumulus
cur	run	current, occurrence, excursion, concur, recur
cur	care	manicure, pedicure, cure, curable, curative
dent	tooth	dentist, dentifrice, trident, indent, dental
div	divide	divide, dividend, division, divorce, divisible
doc	teach	doctrine, document, docile, doctor, indoctrinate
domin	master	dominate, predominate, dominion, A.D. (Anno Domini)
don, donat	give	donation, donor, pardon, donate
fer	bear, carry	transfer, ferry, conifer, infer, refer
fic	make, do	efficient, proficient, sufficient
fid	faith	fidelity, confidence, infidel, bona fide
fig	form	figure, figment, configuration, disfigure, effigy
firm	securely fixed	firmament, confirm, affirm, infirm
flect	bend	deflect, reflect, infect, reflection
flex	bend	reflex, flexible, flexor
form	shape	conform, reform, uniform, transform
fract, frag	break	fracture, fraction, fragile, fragment
frater	brother	fraternity, fraternal, fratricide
fric	rub	friction, fricative, dentifrice
fug	flee	fugitive, refugee, centrifugal, refuge
funct	perform	function, functional, malfunction, dysfunction
grad, gress	step	gradual, graduation, degrade, progress, regress
grat	pleasing	gratify, gratitude, ingrateful, congratulate
greg	gather	gregarious, congregation, segregation, aggregation
hab, hib	hold	habit, habitual, habitat, prohibit, exhibit
homo	man	homicide, Homo sapiens, hombre, homage

Root	Meaning	Examples
hosp, host	host	hospitality, hospice, hospital, hostess
imag	likeness	image, imagine, imaginative, imagery
init	beginning	initial, initiate, initiative
integ	whole	integrate, integral, integrity, integer
ject	throw	reject, inject, project, trajectory, eject
junct	join	juncture, conjunction, adjunct, injunction
jud	law	judge, judicial, judicate, judicious
jur	law, swear	jury, jurisdiction, perjury, jurisprudence
jus	law	justice, just, justify
lab	work	labor, laboratory, elaborate, collaborate
laps	slip	elapse, collapse, relapse, prolapse
lat	carry	translate, relate, prelate
lat	side	lateral, bilateral, unilateral, quadrilateral, collateral
liber	free	liberty, libertine, liberal, liberate
luc	light	lucid, elucidate, translucent
lud, lus	play	ludicrous, interlude, elude, illusion, illusive
lum	light	luminous, luminescent, illuminate
luna	moon	lunar, lunatic
lust	shine	luster, illustrate, lackluster, illustrious
mand	to order	command, demand, mandate, remand
mar	sea	maritime, marine, mariner, submarine
mater, matri	mother	maternal, maternity, matricide, matrix, matron
max	greatest	maximum, maxim, maximize
mem	mindful	memory, remember, memorial, commemorate
ment	mind	mental, demented, mention, menticide
merge, mers	dip, dive	submerge, submerse, emerge, immerse
mim	same	mime, mimeograph, pantomime, mimic
min	small, lesses	minute, mini, minor, minus, minimize
minist	servant, officer	minister, administer, administration
mit	send	submit, remit, admit, transmit
mon	advise, warn	admonish, premonition, admonition, monitor
mort	death	mortician, mortuary, mortal, immortal
mov	move	remove, movement, unmoved
mut	change, interchange	mutation, immutable, mutual, commute

The NEW Reading Teacher's Book of Lists, © 1985 Prentice-Hall, Inc., Englewood Cliffs, NJ 07632. By E. Fry, D. Fountoukidis, and J. Polk.

The NEW Reading Teacher's Book of Lists, © 1985 Prentice-Hall, Inc., Englewood Cliffs, NJ 07632. By E. Fry, D. Fountoukidis, and J. Polk.

Root	*Meaning*	*Examples*
narr	tell	narrate, narrative, narrator
nat	born	natal, native, nation, nativity, innate
nav	ship	navy, naval, navigate, circumnavigate
neg	no	negation, abnegnation, negative, renege
not	mark	notation, notable, denote, notice
noun, nunc	declare	announce, pronounce, denounce, enunciate
nov	new	novel, novelty, novice, innovate
numer	number	numeral, enumerate, numerous, enumerable
ocu	eye	oculist, binocular, monocular
opt	best	optimum, optimist, optimal, optimize
ord	row	order, ordinary, ordinal, extraordinary, ordinance
orig	beginning	origin, original, originate, aborigine
pater	father	paternity, paternal, patriarch, patricide
pel	drive	compel, propel, expel, repel
pend, pens	hang	pendulum, suspend, append, appendix, suspense
plic, plex	fold	complicated, multiplication, duplicate, implicate, complex, duplex, plexiglass, perplex
plur	more	plural, plurality, plus, pluralism
pon	place	opponent, exponent, proponent, postpone
pos	place	position, compose, deposit, composit, preposition
pug	fight	pugnacious, pugilist, repugnant, impugn
pul	urge	compulsory, expulsion, compulsion, repulse
put	think	computer, reputation, deputy, disreputable
quer, ques	ask, seek	query, inquiry, question, inquest, request
rad	ray, spoke	radius, radiology, radio, radioactive, radium
ras	scrape	erase, abrasive, rasp, razor
rect	straight	erect, rectangle, rectify, direction, correct
reg	guide, rule	regal, reign, regulate, regime, regent
rid	laugh	ridiculous, deride, ridicule, derisive
san	health	sanitary, sanitarium, sane, insanity
scend	climb	ascend, descend, descendent, transcend

Root	Meaning	Examples
sci	know	science, conscience, conscious, omniscient, scientific
scribe, script	write	scribe, inscribe, describe, script, scripture
sect	cut	dissect, intersection, sect, section, sector
sed	settle	sedative, sediment, sedentary, sedate
sens	feel	sensation, sensitive, sensible, sensory
sent	feel	consent, sentimental, dissent, assent
serv	save, keep	conserve, preserve, reservoir, reservation
serv	serve	servant, service, servile
sim	like	similar, simultaneous, simulate, simile
sist	stand	consist, resist, subsist, assist
sol	alone	solo, solitary, desolate, soliloquy
solv	loosen	dissolve, solvent, absolve, resolve, solve
son	sound	sonar, sonata, sonorous, unison, sonnet
spir	breathe	respiration, inspire, conspirator, spirit
sta	stand	status, stationary, stabile, stagnant, statue
stell	star	stellar, constellation, stellate
stimu	goad	stimulation, stimulus, stimulate, stimulant
strict	draw tight	strict, stricture, restrict, constrict
struct	build	structure, construct, instruct, destruction
sum	highest	summit, summary, sum, summon, summation
surg, surr	rise	resurrect, insurgent, insurrection, resurgent
tact, tang	touch	tactile, intact, contact, tact, tangible
tain	hold	retain, contain, container, detain, attain
temp	time	temporal, temporary, contemporary, extemporaneous, tempo
ten	hold	tenacious, tenor, tenure, detension, tenant, retentive, tennis
ten	stretch	tendon, tendency, tent, tense, tensile
term	end	terminal, termination, determine, exterminate
terr	land	terrain, terrestrial, territory, terrace
tex	weave	texture, textile, context, text
tort	twist	contort, torture, tort, tortoise, retort
trib	give	tributary, tribute, contribute, attribute
trud, trus	push	intrude, protrude, obtrusive, abstrusive
turb	confusion	disturb, turbulence, perturb, turbine, turbid

The NEW Reading Teacher's Book of Lists, © 1985 Prentice-Hall, Inc., Englewood Cliffs, NJ 07632. By E. Fry, D. Fountoukidis, and J. Polk.

Root	*Meaning*	*Examples*
vag	wander	vagrant, vague, vagabond, vagary
var	different	vary, invariable, variant, variety, variegated
ven	come	invent, convention, advent, convene, venue
ver	turn	convert, introvert, invert, reverse, versatile
ver	truth	verdict, verify, verity, veracity, aver
vict, vinc	conquer	victim, victory, convince, invincible, conviction
viv, vit	live	vivid, survive, vitality, vitamin, vivify
voc, vok	voice	vocal, advocate, evocation, convocation, invoke
void	empty	devoid, avoid, void, voided
vol	wish, will	volition, volunteer, voluntary, benevolent, malevolent
vor	eat	carnivorous, voracious, herbivorous, omnivorous

See Also List 40, Greek Roots; List 42, Prefixes;
and Lists 43 and 44, Suffixes.

42. PREFIXES

Prefixes—small but meaningful letter groups added before a base word or root—change the meaning of a word. The change in meaning can be complete as in *un + happy = unhappy* or *non + profit = nonprofit*. Or the change in meaning can clarify or make the word more specific, as in *pre + game = pregame*.

Knowing the meaning of these prefixes, together with the meaning of common base words and Greek and Latin roots, will give students the tools for unlocking the meanings of hundreds of words.

Although you will want to make a point of teaching these prefixes directly, it is a good idea to explain prefixes and their meanings when your students encounter them in new vocabulary words throughout the year.

Easy Prefixes—Begin by Teaching These

Prefix	Meaning	Example
anti-	against	antiwar, antinuclear, antisocial, antislavery
auto-	self	automobile, automatic, autograph, autobiography
bi-, bin	two	bicycle, binocular, biceps, bifocal, biplane
cent-	hundred	centigrade, century, cent, centimeter
inter-	among, between	interrupt, intermission, international, interpret, intervene
micro-	small, short	microphone, microscope, microbe, microfilm
re-	again	redo, rewrite, reappear, repaint, relive
tele-	distant	telephone, telescope, telegram, television
tri-	three	triangle, tricycle, trillion, triplet
un-	not	unhappy, unable, unbeaten, uncertain, uncomfortable
under-	below	underneath, undercover, underground, underpass

The NEW Reading Teacher's Book of Lists, © 1985 Prentice-Hall, Inc., Englewood Cliffs, NJ 07632. By E. Fry, D. Fountoukidis, and J. Polk.

More Prefixes Grouped by Meaning—Continue with These

Prefixes Expressing Number

Prefix	Meaning	Examples
demi-	half	demigod, demitasse
hemi-	half	hemisphere, hemicycle
semi-	half	semiannual, semicircle, semiclassic, semicolon, semiconscious
prot-	first	protagonist, protein, proton, prototype, protoplasm
mon-, mono-	one	monk, monarch, monocular, monogamy, monorail
uni-	one	unicorn, uniform, unify, unite, universe
di-	two	digraph, dioxide, diploma, diphthong
bi-, bin-	two	bicycle, binocular, biceps, bifocal, biplane
du-	two	dual, duet, duo, duplex, duplicate
tri-	three	triangle, tricycle, trillion, triplet
tetra-	four	tetrahedron, tetrameter
quadr-	four	quadrangle, quadrant, quart, quarter, quadruple
pent-	five	pentagon, pentathlon, Pentecost
quint-	five	quintuplet, quintessential, quintet
hex-	six	hexagon, hexameter, hexagram
sex-	six	sextet, sextant, sextuple
hept-	seven	heptagon, heptameter
sept-	seven	September, septuagenarian
oct-	eight	octet, October, octane, octopus
ennea-	nine	enneagon, enneahedron, ennead
non-	nine	nonagenarian
nove-	nine	November, novena
dec-	ten	decade, decathalon, decagram, December, decameter
deci-	ten	decimal, decimeter, decigram, decile, decimate
cent-	hundred	centigrade, century, cent, centigram, centimeter
hect-	hundred	hectogram, hectometer, hectare
milli-	thousand	millibar, milligram, millimeter, million
kilo-	thousand	kilometer, kilogram, kilowatt, kiloliter
myria-	ten thousand	myriameter, myriad

Prefixes for Super-Large Numbers

Prefix	*Meaning*	*Example*
kilo-	thousand, 10^3	kilometer
mega-	million, 10^6	megameter
giga-	billion, 10^9	gigameter
tera-	trillion, 10^{12}	terameter
peta-	quadrillion, 10^{15}	petameter
exa-	quintillion, 10^{18}	exameter

Prefixes for Super-Small Numbers

milli-	thousandth, 10^{-3}	millisecond
micro-	millionth, 10^{-6}	microsecond
nano-	billionth, 10^{-9}	nanosecond
pico-	trillionth, 10^{-12}	picosecond
femto-	quadrillionth, 10^{-15}	femtosecond
atto-	quintillionth, 10^{-18}	attosecond

Prefixes that Describe Size

macro-	large, long	macrocosm, macron, macroscopic, macrobiotic
magni-	great	magnify, magnitude, magnificent, magnanimous, magnum
mega-	large	megacycle, megalith, megalomania, megaphone, megaton
micro-	small, short	microbe, microphone, microcosm, microfilm, microscope

Prefixes that Describe When

after-	after	afterglow, afternoon, aftertaste, afterthought, afterward
ante-	before	antebellum, antecedent, antedate, antediluvian, anterior
epi-	after	epilogue, epitaph
post-	after	postdate, postdoctoral, posterior, postpone, postscript
pre-	before	preamble, precaution, prefix, prejudice
pro-	before	prognosis, progeny, program, prologue, prophet

The NEW Reading Teacher's Book of Lists, © 1985 Prentice-Hall, Inc., Englewood Cliffs, NJ 07632. By E. Fry, D. Fountoukidis, and J. Polk.

Prefixes that Describe Where

Prefix	Meaning	Examples
a-	on	aboard, afire, afoot, ashore, atop
ab-	from	abnormal, abhor, abolish, abstain, abstract
ac-	to	accent, accept, access, accident, acquire
ad-	to	adapt, add, addict, adhere, admit
af-	to	affair, affect, affiliate, affirm, afflict
ag-	to	agglomeration , aggrandize, aggravate, aggregate, aggressive
an-	to	annex, annihilate, annotate, announce, annul
as-	to	ascend, ascertain, aspect, aspire, assert
by-	near, aside	bypass, byplay, bystander, byway
circu-	around	circulate, circumference, circumspect, circumstance, circus
de-	from, down	debate, decay, deceive, decide, deform
dia-	through, across	diagnose, diagonal, dialogue, diameter
e-	out, away	effect, effort, eject, emigrate, erupt
em-	in	embalm, embed, embezzle, embrace, embroider
en-	in	enchant, enclose, encounter, encourage, envelop
enter-	among, between	enterprise, entertain
epi-	upon	epicenter, epidemic, epidermis, epithet
ex-	out	excel, exalt, exceed, exhaust, exit
extra-	outside	extracurricular, extraordinary, extrasensory, extraterrestrial
hypo-	under	hypochondria, hypodermic, hypothesis
im-	into	immediate, immerse, immigrate, implant, import
in-	into	incision, include, induce, inhale, infect
inter-	among, between	intercede, interpret, interrupt, intermission, international
intra-	within	intramural, intrastate, intravenus
intro-	inside	introduce, introspect, introject, introvert
mid-	middle	midriff, midshipman, midsummer, midway, midyear

Prefixes that Describe Where (continued)

Prefix	Meaning	Examples
off-	from	offset, offshoot, offshore, offspring, offstage
on-	on	oncoming, ongoing, onrush, onshore, onward
para-	beside	paradigm, paragraph, parallel, paraphrase
per-	throughout	perceive, percolate, perfect, perform, pervade
peri-	all around	perimeter, periscope, peripatetic, periphery
pro-	forward	proceed, produce, proficient, progress, project
pro-	in front of	proclaim, profane, profess
re-	back	recall, recede, reflect, repay, retract
retro-	back	retroactive, retrogress, retro-rocket, retrospect
sub-	under	subcontract, subject, submerge, subordinate, subterranean
super-	over	superimpose, superscript, supersede, superstructure, supervisor
tele-	distant	telegram, telekinesis, telephone, telescope, television
thorough-	through	thoroughbred, thoroughfare, thoroughgoing
trans-	across	transatlantic, transcend, transcribe, transfer, translate
under-	below	undercover, underground, underneath, understand, undertake
with-	back, away	withdraw, withhold, within, without, withstand

The NEW Reading Teacher's Book of Lists, © 1985 Prentice-Hall, Inc., Englewood Cliffs, NJ 07632. By E. Fry, D. Fountoukidis, and J. Polk.

Prefixes that Describe Amount or Extent of

Prefix	*Meaning*	*Examples*
equi-	equal	equal, equalibrium, equidistant, equator, equation
extra-	beyond	extraordinary, extravagant
hyper-	excessive	hyperactive, hyperbole, hypercritical, hyperglycemia, hypertension
hypo-	too little	hypoactive, hypoglycemic, hypothyroidism
is-	equal	isometric, isomorph, isosceles, isotope
multi-	many, much	multicolored, multifarious, multimillionaire, multiply, multitude
olig-	few	oligarchy, oligopoly, oligophagous, oligotrophic
omni-	all	omnibus, omnificent, omnipotent, omnivorous
out-	surpassing	outbid, outclass, outdo, outlive, outnumber
over-	too much	overactive, overbearing, overblown, overdo, overprice
pan-	all	panacea, Pandemonium, Pandora, panegyric, panorama
pene-	almost	peneplain, peninsula, penultimate, penumbra
poly-	many	polyandry, polyester, polygamy, polyglot, polysyllabic
super-	more than	superfine, superhuman, supernatural, supernova, superpower
ultra-	beyond	ultraconservative, ultramodern, ultranationalism
under-	less than	underage, underdone, underripe, undervalue, underweight

Prefixes that Express Togetherness and Separateness

Prefix	Meaning	Examples
ab-	away from	abdicate, abduct, aberrant, absent, absolve
co-	together	coauthor, cognate, coincide, cooperate, coordinate
col-	with	collaborate, collateral, colleague, collect
com-	with	combat, combine, comfort, commune, complain
con-	with	concede, concur, concert, confident, connect
syl-	together	syllable, syllogism
sym-	together	symbiosis, symbol, symmetry, sympathy, symphony
syn-	together	synchronize, syndrome, synergy, synonym, synthesis

Prefixes Expressing Negation

Prefix	Meaning	Examples
a-	not	apathy, atheist, atropy, atypical
an-	not	anemia, anarchy, anesthesia, anorexia, anonymous
counter-	opposite	counteract, countermand, counteroffensive, counterproposal, counterrevolution
de-	opposite	deactivate, deform, degrade, deplete, descend
dis-	opposite	disagree, disarm, discontinue, disgust, dishonest
il-	not	illegal, illegible, illegitimate, illiterate, illogical
im-	not	imbalance, immaculate, immature, immobilize, impossible
in-	not	inaccurate, inactive, inadvertent, incognito, indecisive
ir-	not	irrational, irreconcilable, irredeemable, irregular, irresponsible
for-	prohibit	forbid, forget, forgo, forsake, forswear
ne-	not	nefarious, never
neg-	not	negative, neglect, negotiate
non-	not	nonchalant, nonconformist, nondescript, nonpartisan, nonsense
un-	opposite	unable, undo, unbeaten, uncertain, uncomfortable

The NEW Reading Teacher's Book of Lists, © 1985 Prentice-Hall, Inc., Englewood Cliffs, NJ 07632. By E. Fry, D. Fountoukidis, and J. Polk.

The NEW Reading Teacher's Book of Lists, © 1985 Prentice-Hall, Inc., Englewood Cliffs, NJ 07632. By E. Fry, D. Fountoukidis, and J. Polk.

Prefixes that Make a Judgment

Prefix	Meaning	Examples
anti-	against	antinuclear, antisocial, antislavery, antiwar
bene-	good	benediction, benefactor, beneficial, benefit, benign
contra-	against	contraband, contraception, contradict, contraindicated, contrary
dys-	bad	dysentery, dysfunction, dyspepsia, dysphasia
eu-	good	Eucharist, eugenic, euphoria, eulogy
mal-	bad	maladjusted, malaise, malevolent, malfunction, malice
mis-	bad	misanthrope, misbehave, miscarriage, misconduct, misfortune
pro-	for	pro-American, pro-education

Miscellaneous Prefixes

Prefix	Meaning	Examples
ambi-	both, around	ambidextrous, ambience, ambiguous, ambivalent
amphi-	both, around	amphibian, amphitheater, amphora
auto-	self	autobiography, autocratic, autograph, automatic, automobile
be-	make	becalm, befriend, beguile, bewitch
hetero-	different	heterodox, heteronym, heterosexual
homo-	same	homogeneous, homogenize, homograph, homophone, homosexual
meta-	change	metabolism, metamorphosis, metaphor, metastasis
neo-	new	neoclassic, neologism, neon, neonatal, neophyte
para-	almost	paralegal, paramedic
pseudo-	false	pseudoclassic, pseudonym, pseudopod, pseudosalt
re-	again	reappear, reclassify, recopy, redo, repaint
self-	self	self-denial, self-respect, selfish, self-support, self-taught

See Also, List 38, -Ology Word Family; List 39, Phobia Word Family; List 40, Greek Roots; List 41, Latin Roots; and List 43, Suffixes and Meaning.

43. SUFFIXES AND MEANING

Suffixes are letter groups that are added to the end of a base word or root. Suffixes often add information to the meaning of the word. In this list, suffixes are grouped by meaning under each part of speech. For example, in the list of noun suffixes on the next page, there are twelve suffixes with the meaning "one who." Thus, "one who serves" is a *servant (serve + ant)* and "one who begs" is a *beggar (beg + ar)*.

Easy Suffixes—Begin by Teaching These

Noun Suffixes

More than one (Plural):
- **-s**   pens, typewriters, buildings, books, dogs

Female:
- **-ess**   hostess, murderess, tigress, governess, heiress

Study of:
- **-ology**   biology, psychology (see List 38, -Ology Word Family)

Adjective Suffixes

Relating to:
- **-like**   childlike, boylike, homelike, lifelike

Full of:
- **-ful**   careful, thoughtful, joyful, fearful, successful

Without:
- **-less**   thoughtless, tireless, careless, fearless, worthless

Comparative:
- **-er**   fatter, smaller, crazier, smarter, faster
- **-est**   fattest, smallest, craziest, smartest, fastest

Adverb Suffixes

In what manner:
- **-ily**   speedily, steadily, warily, happily, sloppily
- **-ly**   slowly, strangely, poorly, honestly, nicely

Verb Suffixes

Change of tense:
- **-ed**   talked, walked, learned, jumped, listened
- **-d**   baked, raised, managed, judged, piled
- **-ing**   singing, talking, stealing, writing, jumping

The NEW Reading Teacher's Book of Lists, © 1985 Prentice-Hall, Inc., Englewood Cliffs, NJ 07632. By E. Fry, D. Fountoukidis, and J. Polk.

More Suffixes—Continue with These

Noun Suffixes

One who:

    -ant   servant, immigrant, assistant, merchant

    -ar   beggar, liar

    -ard   drunkard, steward, coward, wizard

    -art   braggart

    -arian   librarian, humanitarian, libertarian

    -ee   payee, lessee

    -ent   superintendent, resident, regent

    -er   teacher, painter, seller, shipper, plumber

    -ess   waitress, actress, countess, seamstress

    -eur   masseur, raconteur, chauffeur, connoisseur

    -ier, yer   cashier, financier, gondolier, lawyer

    -or   actor, doctor, donor, auditor

One who practices:

    -ist   socialist, biologist, monopolist, communist

One who works with:

    -man   cameraman, craftsman, mailman, milkman, coachman

    -wright   playwright, wheelwright, shipwright

Art or skill of:

    -ship   horsemanship, showmanship, penmanship, swordsmanship

Trade or occupation:

    -ery   surgery, archery, robbery, sorcery

    -ry   dentistry, husbandry

Action or process:

    -ade   blockade, escapade, charade, parade, promenade

    -age   marriage, voyage, bondage, pilgrimage

    -ation   emancipation, computation, narration, visitation

    -cy   truancy, diplomacy, vagrancy, piracy

    -er   murder, thunder, plunder, waiver

    -ism   baptism, heroism, ostracism, despotism

    -ment   embezzlement, encirclement, development, government

    -ure   censure, failure, enclosure, exposure

Product or thing:

    -ade   lemonade, marmalade

    -ery, -ry   pottery, poetry

    -ment   instrument, ornament, fragment

    -mony   testimony, matrimony, ceremony, alimony

Material:

    -ing   bedding, roofing, bricking, stuffing, frosting

Noun Suffixes (continued)

Place for:

-arium	aquarium, planetarium, solarium
-ary	library, mortuary, sanctuary, infirmary
-orium	auditorium, emporium
-ory	laboratory, conservatory, purgatory

State or quality of:

-ance	repentance, annoyance, avoidance, resistance
-ancy	vagrancy, truancy, vacancy, dependancy
-ation	desperation, starvation, fascination, inspiration
-cy	accuracy, lunacy, bankruptcy, ecstacy
-dom	freedom, boredom, martyrdom, wisdom
-ence	violence, succulence, absence, repentance
-ency	frequency, clemency, expediency, consistency
-ery, ry	angry, imagery, bravery, savagery
-eur	hauteur, grandeur
-hood	childhood, adulthood, statehood, falsehood
-ion	champion, companion, ambition, suspicion
-ism	heroism, pacifism, racism, mysticism
-ity	necessity, felicity, civility
-ization	civilization, capitalization, standardization
-ment	amusement, refinement, predicament, amazement
-ness	happiness, kindness, goodness, darkness, preparedness
-or	error, pallor, stupor, candor, fervor
-ship	friendship, stewardship, hardship, ownership
-sion	tension, compulsion
-th	length, strength, warmth, depth
-tion	attention, caution, fascination, temptation
-tude	gratitude, fortitude, pulchritude, beatitude
-ty	loyalty, honesty, amnesty, unity, enmity

Small:

-cle	particle, corpuscle, icicle, cubicle
-cule	minuscule, molecule
-et	midget, sonnet, bassinet, cygnet
-ette	dinette, luncheonette, cigarette, majorette
-kin	lambkin, napkin, manikin
-let	owlet, rivulet, starlet, leaflet, islet
-ling	duckling, yearling, suckling, fledgling

More than one (Plural):

-a	data, criteria, memoranda
-ae (fem.)	alumnae, formulae, larvae, algae
-es	boxes, indices, crises, parentheses
-i	alumni, termini
-s	pens, typewriters, buildings

The NEW Reading Teacher's Book of Lists, © 1985 Prentice-Hall, Inc., Englewood Cliffs, NJ 07632. By E. Fry, D. Fountoukidis, and J. Polk.

Noun Suffixes (continued)

Female:

-a	sultana, Julia, Cornelia, Donna
-ess	hostess, murderess, governess, heiress, tigress
-enne	comedienne, equestrienne, tragedienne
-ette	usherette, majorette, Claudette, Bernadette
-ina	czarina, Wilhelmina
-ine	heroine, Josephine, Pauline
-trix	aviatrix, executrix

Study of, Science of:

-ology	biology, psychology (see List 38, -Ology Word Family)

Doctrine of:

-ism	capitalism, communism, socialism, hedonism, asceticism

Scientific or social system:

-ics	physics, economics, statistics, linguistics, politics

Surgical removal of:

-ectomy	tonsillectomy, appendectomy, laryngectomy

Inflammation of:

-itis	laryngitis, arthritis, bronchitis, tonsillitis

Fear of:

-phobia	claustrophobia, acrophobia (see List 39, Phobia Word Family)

Chemical:

-ine	iodine, chlorine, fluorine
-ide	fluoride, bromide, peroxide
-ose	glucose, sucrose, dextrose

Alcohol:

-ol	methanol, ethanol, glycol

Mineral or rock:

-ite	granite, anthracite, bauxite

Adjective Suffixes

Full of:

-ful	thoughtful, joyful, careful, fearful, successful
-ose	verbose, morose, comatose, bellicose
-ous	joyous, glorious, wondrous, nervous
-ulent	turbulent, succulent, corpulent, fraudulent

Made of:

-en	earthen, golden, ashen, wooden, flaxen

Without:

-less	thoughtless, tireless, ageless, worthless, careless

Adjective Suffixes (continued)

Relating to:

-al	natural, royal, neanderthal, maternal, suicidal
-an	urban, American, Indian, Alaskan, veteran
-ary	honorary, military, literary, ordinary
-esque	statuesque, picturesque, burlesque, Romanesque
-etic	alphabetic, dietetic, frenetic
-ial	filial, commercial, fluvial, remedial
-ian	barbarian, physician, Christian, Parisian
-ic	comic, historic, poetic, metallic, public
-ical	comical, historical, economical, rhetorical
-ine	feminine, bovine, feline, marine, equine
-ish	childish, whitish, Scottish, fiftyish
-like	childlike, boylike, homelike, lifelike
-ly	fatherly, motherly, scholarly, daily, timely
-oid	humanoid, asteroid, paranoid, planetoid
-ular	granular, cellular, circular, popular, regular

Inclined to:

-acious	loquacious, mendacious, audacious, fallacious
-ant	vigilant, pleasant, radiant, defiant, buoyant
-ative	demonstrative, perjorative, talkative, exploitative
-ble	gullible, perishable, voluble, durable
-ent	competent, different, ambivalent, excellent
-ive	active, passive, negative, affirmative, conclusive
-some	meddlesome, quarrelsome, tiresome, awesome

State or quality of:

-ate	fortunate, desperate, passionate, desolate
-id	candid, solid, lucid, acid, splendid, rigid
-ile	virile, agile, volatile, docile, fragile
-ious	gracious, ambitious, religious, delicious
-und	rotund, fecund, moribund, jocund
-uous	contemptuous, tempestuous, sensuous, impetuous
-y	silly, fruity, sunny, rainy, funny, gooey

Nationality, language:

-ese	Japanese, Portugese, Siamese, Chinese

Direction:

-ern	eastern, western, northern, postern
-ward	forward, backward, eastward, upward

Numbers:

-eth	twentieth, fiftieth, eightieth
-th	fifth, twelfth, hundredth, thousandth

The NEW Reading Teacher's Book of Lists, © 1985 Prentice-Hall, Inc., Englewood Cliffs, NJ 07632. By E. Fry, J. Polk, and D. Fountoukidis.

Adjective Suffixes (continued)

Comparative:
-er	fatter, smaller, crazier, smarter
-est	fattest, smallest, craziest, smartest
-most	utmost, westernmost, outermost, innermost

Verbs as adjectives:
-ed	baked, dirtied, repaired, glorified
-en	stolen, chosen, forgotten, written

Adverb Suffixes

In what manner:
-ily	speedily, steadily, warily, happily, sloppily
-ly	slowly, strangely, poorly, candidly, nicely
-ways	sideways, crossways, always, longways
-ise	clockwise, counterclockwise, lengthwise, schoolwise

To what extent:
-ly	extremely, scarcely, constantly, frequently

Verb Suffixes

To make:
-ate	activate, fascinate, annihilate, liberate
-en	strengthen, fasten, lengthen, frighten, weaken
-fy	satisfy, terrify, falsify, beautify, amplify
-ize	popularize, standardize, cauterize, computerize

Action or process:
-ade	blockade, promenade, masquarade, parade
-age	ravage, pillage
-er	discover, murder, conquer, deliver, holler
-ish	finish, flourish, nourish, punish
-ure	censure, procure, endure, inure

Repeated action:
-ble	stumble, squabble, mumble, tumble, fumble

Change tense:
-ed	talked, walked, learned, jumped
-en	taken, eaten, stolen, proven
-d	baked, tamed, managed, raised
-ing	singing, talking, stealing, jumping
-t	slept, wept, kept, swept

See Also List 40, Greek Roots; List 41, Latin Roots; List 42, Prefixes; List 44, Suffixes and Grammar; and List 68, Parts of Speech.

The NEW Reading Teacher's Book of Lists, © 1985 Prentice-Hall, Inc., Englewood Cliffs, NJ 07632. By E. Fry, J. Polk, and D. Fountoukidis.

44. SUFFIXES AND GRAMMAR

Some suffixes are best understood, not as having a particular meaning as the previous section indicates, but as expressing grammar or syntax. These suffixes enable you to express an idea in many different ways by using the variation of the key word that best fits the sentence structure.

For example, in the sentences:

1. The boy is *quiet.*
2. The boy played *quietly.*
3. The boy's *quietness* was undisturbed.

the word *quiet* was altered to fit the sentence structure. In (1) it is used as an adjective; in (2) the suffix *-ly* was added so that it could be used as an adverb; in (3) the suffix *-ness* was added so that it could be used as a noun.

Suffixes that express grammar and syntax fall into three main categories: those that show number, those that show tense or time, and those that show part of speech.

Suffixes that Show Number

-s   1. added to most nouns to show plural; for example: *cat–cats*
       2. used to show third person singular for regular verbs; for example: *he runs, she runs, it runs*

-es   1. added to nouns ending in -ch, -sh, -s, -x, or -z to show plural; for example: *churches, flashes, bosses, boxes, buzzes*
       2. used to show third person singular for regular verbs ending in -ch, -sh, -s, -x, or -z; for example: *it matches, she washes, he passes, he boxes, it buzzes*

-a   used to show the plural of certain nouns; for example: *datum–data, erratum–errata*

-i   used to show the plural of certain nouns; for example: *focus–foci, fungus–fungi*

Suffixes that Change Tense or Time

-ing   added to show continuous action; for example: *he is singing, he was singing, he will be singing, he has been singing, he had been singing, he will have been singing.*

-ed   added to show past time; for example: *she talked to him, she had talked, she has talked, she will have talked.*

-d   added to verbs ending in -e to show past time; for example: *he baked the pie, he has baked the pie, he had baked the pie, he will have baked the pie.*

-t   added to some verbs to show past time; for example: *Tom slept all day.*

-en   added to some verbs to show past completed action; for example: *he has taken that route before we have, he had taken that route before we had, he will have taken that route before we will have.*

The NEW Reading Teacher's Book of Lists, © 1985 Prentice-Hall, Inc., Englewood Cliffs, NJ 07632. By E. Fry, D. Fountoukidis, and J. Polk.

Suffixes that Change Parts of Speech

for adverbs

-ly quickly

for adjectives (See adjective suffixes on pages 115–117 for a more complete list)

-ic	tragic
-ed	baked
-ous	famous
-al	comical
-ive	responsive
-ative	talkative
-y	wordy
-an	urban

for nouns (See noun suffixes on pages 113–115 for a more complete list)

-ness	happiness
-ity	brevity
-y	bigamy
-ism	capitalism
-ion	champion
-ation	explanation
-er	worker
-eer	profiteer

for verbs

-ate	stimulate
-en	tighten
-fy	identify
-ize	characterize

See Also List 40, Greek Roots;
List 41, Latin Roots; List 42,
Prefixes; and List 43, Suffixes and Meaning.

SECTION IV
Phonics

45. INITIAL CONSONANT SOUNDS

The NEW Reading Teacher's Book of Lists, © 1985 Prentice-Hall, Inc., Englewood Cliffs, NJ 07632. By E. Fry, D. Fountoukidis, and J. Polk.

This is a list of all the initial consonant sounds. It can be used in teaching phonics, but the real reason we have included it here is to facilitate the use of the phonograms that follow.

b	p	cr	pl	sh
c	qu	dr	sl	th
d	r	fr	sc	wh
f	s	gr	sk	scr
g	t	pr	sm	spr
h	v	tr	sn	squ
j	w	wr	sp	str
k	x	bl	st	thr
l	y	cl	sw	
m	z	fl	ch	
n	br	gl	ph	

See Also List 46, Major Phonograms,
and List 47, Minor Phonograms.

46. MAJOR PHONOGRAMS

As teachers, we found it hard to get a good list of phonograms so we decided to build our own using many teacher lists and a rhyming dictionary. We think this is the most complete one in existence. A phonogram is a vowel sound plus a consonant sound, but it is often less than a syllable, hence less than a word—it needs an initial consonant or blend to make it a word. These are useful for all kinds of games and drills in reading and spelling. Major phonograms make ten or more common words.

-ab (ă)	-ace (ā)	-ack (ă)		-ad (ă)	-ade (ā)		-ag (ă)	
cab	face	back	black	bad	bade	bag	brag
gab	lace	hack	clack	dad	fade	gag	crag
jab	mace	Jack	crack	fad	jade	hag	drag
tab	pace	lack	knack	had	made	lag	flag
crab	race	Mack	shack	lad	wade	nag	shag
drab	brace	pack	smack	mad	blade	rag	slag
grab	grace	quack	snack	pad	glade	sag	snag
scab	place	rack	stack	sad	grade	tag	stag
slab	space	sack	track	tad	shade	wag	swag
stab	trace	tack	whack	Brad	spade
				Chad	trade
				clad
				glad
				shad

-ail (ā)	-ain (ā)	-ake (ā)	-all (ô)	-am (ă)	-ame (ā)	-amp (ă)	-an (ă)
bail	gain	bake	ball	dam	came	camp	ban
fail	lain	cake	call	ham	dame	damp	can
Gail	main	fake	fall	jam	fame	lamp	Dan
hail	pain	Jake	gall	Pam	game	ramp	fan
jail	rain	lake	hall	ram	lame	tamp	man
mail	vain	make	mall	Sam	name	vamp	pan
nail	brain	quake	tall	yam	same	champ	ran
pail	chain	rake	wall	clam	tame	clamp	tan
quail	drain	sake	small	cram	blame	cramp	van
rail	grain	take	squall	dram	flame	gramp	bran
sail	plain	wake	stall	gram	frame	scamp	clan
tail	slain	brake		sham	shame	stamp	flan
wail	Spain	drake		slam		tramp	plan
frail	sprain	flake		tram			scan
snail	stain	shake					span
trail	strain	snake					than
	train	stake					

124

The NEW Reading Teacher's Book of Lists, © 1985 Prentice-Hall, Inc., Englewood Cliffs, NJ 07632. By E. Fry, D. Fountoukidis, and J. Polk.

-and (ă)	-ane (ā)	-ang (ă)	-ank (ă)		-ap (ă)	-ar (ä)	-are (ā)
band	cane	bang	bank	crank	cap	bar	bare
hand	Jane	fang	dank	drank	gap	car	care
land	lane	gang	hank	flank	lap	far	dare
sand	mane	hang	lank	Frank	map	jar	fare
bland	pane	pang	rank	plank	nap	mar	mare
brand	sane	rang	sank	prank	rap	tar	rare
gland	vane	sang	tank	shank	sap	char	blare
grand	wane	tang	yank	spank	tap	scar	flare
stand	crane	clang	blank	stank	chap	spar	glare
strand	plane	slang	clank	thank	clap	star	scare
		sprang			flap		share
					scrap		snare
					slap		spare
					snap		square
					strap		stare
					trap		
					wrap		

-ark (ä)	-ash (ă)	-at (ă)	-ate (ā)	-ave (ā)	-aw (ô)		-ay (ā)	
bark	bash	bat	date	cave	caw	bay	clay
dark	cash	cat	fate	Dave	gnaw	day	cray
hark	dash	fat	gate	gave	jaw	gay	fray
lark	gash	gnat	hate	pave	law	hay	gray
mark	hash	hat	Kate	rave	paw	jay	play
park	lash	mat	late	save	raw	lay	pray
Clark	mash	pat	mate	wave	saw	may	slay
shark	rash	rat	rate	brave	claw	pay	spray
spark	sash	sat	crate	crave	craw	ray	stay
stark	brash	tat	grate	grave	draw	say	stray
	clash	vat	plate	shave	flaw	way	tray
	crash	brat	skate	slave	slaw	bray	
	flash	chat	state		squaw		
	slash	drat			straw		
	smash	flat					
	stash	scat					
	thrash	slat					
	trash	spat					
		that					

-eak (ē)	-eal (ē)	-eam (ē)	-ear (ē)	-eat (ē)	-ed (ĕ)	-eed (ē)	-eep (ē)
beak	deal	beam	dear	beat	bed	deed	deep
leak	heal	ream	fear	feat	fed	feed	jeep
peak	meal	seam	gear	heat	led	heed	keep
teak	peal	team	hear	meat	Ned	need	peep
weak	real	cream	near	neat	red	reed	seep
bleak	seal	dream	rear	peat	Ted	seed	weep
creak	veal	gleam	sear	seat	wed	weed	cheep
sneak	zeal	scream	tear	bleat	bled	bleed	creep
speak	squeal	steam	year	cheat	bred	breed	sheep
squeak	steal	stream	clear	cleat	fled	creed	sleep
streak			shear	pleat	Fred	freed	steep
			smear	treat	shed	greed	sweep
			spear	wheat	shred	speed	
					sled	steed	
					sped	treed	

-eet (ē)	-ell (ĕ)	-en (ĕ)	end (ĕ)	-ent (ĕ)	-est (ĕ)	-et (ĕ)	-ew (ü)
beet	bell	Ben	bend	bent	best	bet	dew
feet	cell	den	end	cent	guest	get	few
meet	dell	hen	fend	dent	jest	jet	hew
fleet	fell	Ken	lend	gent	lest	let	Jew
greet	hell	men	mend	Kent	nest	met	knew
sheet	jell	pen	rend	lent	pest	net	pew
sleet	Nell	wren	send	rent	rest	pet	blew
street	sell	ten	tend	sent	test	set	brew
sweet	tell	yen	vend	tent	vest	wet	chew
tweet	well	then	blend	vent	west	yet	crew
	yell	when	spend	went	zest	Chet	drew
	dwell		trend	scent	blest	fret	flew
	quell			spent	chest	whet	screw
	shell				crest		skew
	smell				quest		slew
	spell						stew
	swell						strew
							threw

-ice (ī)	-ick (ĭ)	-id (ĭ)	-ide (ī)	-ig (ĭ)	-ight (ī)	-ill (ĭ)	
dice	Dick	bid	bide	big	fight	bill	till
lice	kick	did	hide	dig	knight	dill	will
mice	lick	hid	ride	fig	light	fill	chill
nice	Nick	kid	side	gig	might	gill	drill
rice	pick	lid	tide	jig	night	hill	frill
vice	quick	quid	wide	pig	right	ill	grill
price	Rick	rid	bride	rig	sight	Jill	skill
slice	sick	grid	chide	wig	tight	kill	spill
spice	tick	skid	glide	brig	blight	mill	still
splice	wick	slid	pride	sprig	bright	pill	thrill
thrice	brick		slide	swig	flight	quill	trill
twice	chick		snide	twig	fright	rill	twill
	click		stride		plight	sill	
	flick				slight		
	slick						
	stick						
	thick						
	trick						

-im (ĭ)	-ime (ī)	-in (ĭ)	-ind (ī)	-ine (ī)	-ing (ĭ)	-ink (ĭ)	-int (ĭ)
dim	dime	bin	bind	dine	bing	kink	hint
him	lime	din	find	fine	ding	link	lint
Jim	mime	fin	hind	line	king	mink	mint
Kim	time	gin	kind	mine	ping	pink	tint
rim	chime	kin	mind	nine	ring	rink	flint
Tim	clime	pin	rind	pine	sing	sink	glint
vim	crime	sin	wind	tine	wing	wink	print
brim	grime	tin	blind	vine	zing	blink	splint
grim	prime	win	grind	wine	bring	brink	sprint
prim	slime	chin		brine	cling	chink	squint
slim		grin		shine	fling	clink	stint
swim		shin		shrine	sling	drink	
trim		skin		spine	spring	shrink	
whim		spin		swine	sting	stink	
		thin		whine	string	think	
		twin			swing		
					thing		
					wring		

-ip (ĭ)		-it (ĭ)	-ive (ī)	-ob (ŏ)	-ock (ŏ)	-od (ŏ)	-og (ŏ or ô)
dip	clip	bit	dive	Bob	dock	cod	
hip	drip	fit	five	cob	hock	God	bog
lip	flip	hit	hive	fob	knock	mod	cog
nip	grip	kit	jive	gob	lock	nod	fog
quip	ship	knit	live	job	mock	pod	hog
rip	skip	lit	chive	knob	rock	rod	jog
sip	slip	pit	drive	lob	sock	sod	log
tip	snip	quit	strive	mob	tock	Tod	tog
zip	strip	sit	thrive	rob	block	clod	clog
blip	trip	wit		sob	clock	plod	flog
chip	whip	flit		blob	crock	prod	frog
		grit		slob	flock	shod	grog
		skit		snob	frock	trod	slog
		slit			shock		smog
		spit			smock		
		split			stock		
		twit					

-oke (ō)	-old (ō)	-one (ō)	-ong (ŏ)	op (ŏ)	-ope (ō)	-ore (ô)	-orn (ô)
coke	bold	bone	bong	bop	cope	bore	born
joke	cold	cone	dong	cop	dope	core	corn
poke	fold	hone	gong	hop	hope	fore	horn
woke	gold	lone	long	mop	lope	gore	morn
broke	hold	tone	song	pop	mope	more	torn
choke	mold	zone	tong	sop	nope	pore	worn
smoke	old	clone	prong	top	pope	sore	scorn
spoke	sold	crone	strong	chop	rope	tore	shorn
stoke	told	drone	thong	crop	grope	wore	sworn
stroke	scold	phone	wrong	drop	scope	chore	thorn
		prone		flop	slope	score	
		stone		plop		shore	
				prop		spore	
				shop		store	
				slop		swore	
				stop			

The NEW Reading Teacher's Book of Lists, © 1985 Prentice-Hall, Inc., Englewood Cliffs, NJ 07632. By E. Fry, D. Fountoukidis, and J. Polk.

-ot (ŏ)	-ow (ō)	-ow (ou)	-ub (ŭ)	-uck (ŭ)	-uff (ŭ)	-ug (ŭ)	-um (ŭ)
cot	know	bow	bub	buck	buff	bug	bum
got	low	cow	cub	duck	cuff	dug	gum
hot	row	how	dub	huck	muff	hug	hum
jot	tow	now	hub	luck	puff	jug	mum
knot	blow	row	nub	muck	bluff	lug	rum
lot	flow	sow	pub	puck	fluff	mug	sum
not	glow	vow	rub	suck	gruff	pug	yum
pot	show	brow	sub	tuck	scuff	rug	chum
rot	slow	chow	tub	Chuck	snuff	tug	drum
tot	snow	plow	club	cluck	stuff	chug	glum
blot	stow	prow	flub	pluck		drug	plum
clot		scow	grub	shuck		plug	scum
plot			scrub	stuck		shrug	slum
shot			shrub	struck		slug	strum
slot			snub	truck		smug	swum
spot			stub			snug	
trot						thug	

-ump (ŭ)	-un (ŭ)	-ung (ŭ)	-unk (ŭ)	-ush (ŭ)	-ut (ŭ)	-y (ī)
bump	bun	hung	bunk	gush	but	by
dump	fun	lung	dunk	hush	cut	my
hump	gun	rung	funk	lush	gut	cry
jump	nun	sung	hunk	mush	hut	dry
lump	pun	clung	junk	rush	jut	fly
pump	run	flung	punk	blush	nut	fry
rump	sun	slung	sunk	brush	rut	ply
sump	shun	sprung	chunk	crush	Tut	pry
chump	spun	stung	drunk	flush	glut	shy
clump	stun	strung	flunk	plush	shut	sky
frump		swung	plunk	slush	slut	sly
grump		wrung	shrunk	thrush	smut	spy
plump			skunk		strut	try
slump			slunk			
stump			spunk			
trump			stunk			
			thunk			
			trunk			

See Also List 45, Initial
Consonant Sounds; and List 47, Minor Phonograms.

47. MINOR PHONOGRAMS

Minor phonograms are the same as major phonograms except that they cannot be used to make as many common words. They make at least three, but less than ten common words.

-act (ă)	-aft (ă)	-age (ā)	-aid (ā)	-air (ā)	-aise (ā)	-ait (ā)	-alk (ô)
fact	raft	cage	laid	fair	raise	bait	balk
pact	craft	page	maid	hair	praise	gait	talk
tact	draft	rage	paid	lair		trait	walk
tract	graft	sage	raid	pair			chalk
	shaft	wage	braid	chair			stalk
		stage	staid	flair			
				stair			

-ance (ă)	-ant (ă)	-ape (ā)	-ard (ä)	-arm (ä)	-arn (ä)	-arp (ä)	art (ä)
dance	can't	cape	bard	farm	barn	carp	cart
lance	pant	gape	card	harm	darn	harp	dart
chance	rant	nape	guard	charm	yarn	tarp	mart
France	grant	rape	hard			sharp	part
glance	plant	tape	lard				tart
prance	scant	grape	yard				chart
stance	slant	scrape					smart
trance		shape					start

-ase (ā)	-ask (ă)	-ast (ă)	-ass (ă)	-atch (ă)	-aught (ô)	-awn (ô)	-ax (ă)
base	ask	cast	bass	batch	caught	dawn	lax
case	cask	fast	lass	catch	naught	fawn	Max
vase	mask	last	mass	hatch	taught	lawn	tax
chase	task	mast	pass	match	fraught	pawn	wax
	flask	past	brass	scratch		yawn	flax
		vast	class	thatch		drawn	
		blast	glass			prawn	
			grass			spawn	

-aze (ā)	-ead (ĕ)	-ean (ē)	-eap (ē)	-ee (ē)	-eek (ē)	-eel (ē)	-eem (ē)
faze	dead	bean	heap	bee	leek	feel	deem
haze	head	dean	leap	fee	meek	heel	seem
blaze	lead	Jean	reap	knee	peek	keel	teem
craze	read	lean	cheap	see	seek	kneel	
	bread	mean		tee	week	peel	
	dread	wean		wee	cheek	reel	
	spread	clean		flee	creek	creel	
	thread	glean		glee	Greek	steel	
	tread				sleek	wheel	

130

The NEW Reading Teacher's Book of Lists, © 1985 Prentice-Hall, Inc., Englewood Cliffs, NJ 07632. By E. Fry, D. Fountoukidis, and J. Polk.

-een (ē)	-eer (ē)	-eigh (ā)	-eight (ā)	-ess (ĕ)	-ib (ĭ)	-ibe (ī)	-ie (ī)
queen	beer	neigh	eight	Bess	bib	jibe	die
seen	deer	weigh	weight	guess	fib	bribe	fie
teen	jeer	sleigh	freight	less	rib	scribe	lie
green	peer			mess	crib	tribe	pie
screen	queer			bless			tie
sheen	sneer			chess			vie
	steer			dress			
				press			
				stress			

-ief (ē)	-ife (ī)	-iff (ĭ)	-ift (ĭ)	-ike (ī)	-ile (ī)	-ilt (ĭ)	-ince (ĭ)
brief	fife	cliff	gift	bike	bile	jilt	mince
chief	knife	skiff	lift	dike	mile	kilt	since
grief	life	sniff	rift	hike	Nile	nilt	wince
thief	wife	stiff	drift	like	pile	quilt	prince
	strife		shift	Mike	tile	tilt	
			swift	pike	vile	wilt	
			thrift	spike	smile		
				strike	while		

-ipe (ī)	-ire (ī)	-irt (ŭ)	-ise (ī)	-ish (ĭ)	-isk (ĭ)	-iss (ĭ)	-ist (ĭ)
pipe	fire	dirt	guise	dish	disk	hiss	list
ripe	hire	flirt	rise	fish	risk	kiss	mist
wipe	tire	shirt	wise	wish	brisk	miss	wrist
gripe	wire	skirt		swish	frisk	bliss	grist
snipe	spire	squirt			whisk	Swiss	twist
stripe							
tripe							

-itch (ĭ)	-ite (ī)	-ix (ĭ)	-o (ü)	-o (ō)	-oach (ō)	-oad (ō)	-oak (ō)
bitch	bite	fix	do	go	coach	load	soak
ditch	kite	mix	to	no	poach	road	cloak
pitch	mite	six	who	so	roach	toad	croak
witch	quite			pro			
switch	rite						
	site						
	white						
	write						
	spite						

The NEW Reading Teacher's Book of Lists, © 1985 Prentice-Hall, Inc., Englewood Cliffs, NJ 07632. By E. Fry, D. Fountoukidis, and J. Polk.

oal (ō)	-oam (ō)	oan (ō)	-oar (ô)	-oast (ō)	-oat (ō)	-obe (ō)	-ode (ō)
coal	foam	Joan	boar	boast	boat	lobe	code
foal	loam	loan	roar	coast	coat	robe	lode
goal	roam	moan	soar	roast	goat	globe	mode
shoal		groan		toast	moat	probe	node
					bloat		rode
					float		strode
					throat		

-oil (oy)	-oin (oy)	-ole (ō)	-oll (ō)	-olt (ō)	-ome (ō)	-ome (ŏ)	-oo (ü)
boil	coin	dole	poll	bolt	dome	come	coo
coil	join	hole	roll	colt	home	some	goo
foil	loin	mole	toll	jolt	Nome		moo
soil	groin	pole	scroll	molt	Rome		poo
toil		role	stroll	volt	tome		too
spoil		stole	troll		chrome		woo
		whole					zoo
							shoo

-ood (ü)	-ood (ü)	-ook (ü)	-ool (ü)	-oom (ü)	-oon (ü)	-oop (ü)	-oot (ü)
good	food	book	cool	boom	coon	hoop	boot
hood	mood	cook	fool	doom	loon	loop	loot
wood	brood	hook	pool	loom	moon	droop	moot
stood		look	drool	room	noon	scoop	root
		took	school	bloom	soon	sloop	toot
		brook	spool	broom	croon	snoop	shoot
		crook	stool	gloom	spoon	swoop	
		shook		groom	swoon	troop	

-orch (ô)	-ork (ô)	-ort (ô)	-ose (ō)	-oss (ŏ)	-ost (ŏ or ô)	-ost (ō)	-otch (ŏ)
porch	cork	fort	hose	boss	host	host	notch
torch	fork	Mort	nose	loss	cost	most	blotch
scorch	York	port	pose	moss	lost	post	crotch
	stork	short	rose	toss	frost		Scotch
		snort	chose	cross			
		sport	close	gloss			
			prose				
			those				

-ote (ō)	-ough (ŭ)	-ought (ô)	-ould (ŭ)	-ounce (ou)	-ound (ou)	-ouse (ou)
note	rough	bought	could	bounce	bound	douse
quote	tough	fought	would	pounce	found	house
rote	enough	ought	should	flounce	hound	mouse
vote	slough	sought		trounce	mound	souse
wrote		brought			pound	grouse
		thought			round	
					sound	
					ground	

-out (ou)	-outh (ou)	-ove (ō)	-ove (ŭ)	-owl (ou)	-own (ou)	-own (ō)	-oy (oi)
bout	mouth	cove	dove	fowl	down	known	boy
pout	south	clove	love	howl	gown	blown	coy
scout	drouth	drove	glove	jowl	town	flown	joy
shout		grove	shove	growl	brown	grown	Roy
spout				prowl	clown		soy
sprout				scowl	crown		toy
stout					drown		
trout					frown		

-ud (ŭ)	-ude (ü)	-udge (ŭ)	-ue (ü)	-ull (ŭ)	-umb (ŭ)	-unch (ŭ)	-une (ü)
bud	dude	fudge	due	dull	dumb	bunch	June
dud	nude	judge	Sue	gull	numb	hunch	tune
mud	rude	nudge	blue	hull	crumb	lunch	prune
spud	crude	grudge	clue	lull	plumb	munch	
stud	prude	sludge	flue	mull	thumb	punch	
thud			glue			crunch	

-unt (ŭ)	-ur (ėr)	urn (ėr)	-urse (ėr)	-us (ŭ)	-ust (ŭ)	-ute (ü)
bunt	cur	burn	curse	bus	bust	jute
hunt	fur	turn	nurse	pus	dust	lute
punt	blur	churn	purse	plus	just	flute
runt	slur	spurn		thus	lust	
blunt	spur				rust	
grunt					thrust	
stunt					trust	

See Also List 45, Initial Consonant Sounds
and List 46, Major Phonograms.

48. PHONICS EXAMPLE WORDS

This is an important list at the very heart of phonics instruction. It alphabetically lists 99 single phonemes (speech sounds) and consonant blends (usually two phonemes), and it gives example words for each of these, often for their use in the beginning, middle, and end of words. These example words are also common English words, many taken from the list of Instant Words. This list solves the problem of coming up with a good common word to illustrate a phonics principle for lessons and worksheets.

A Vowel Sound: Short A

apple

(initial)			*(medial)*		
and	add	am	that	has	began
at	act	animal	can	than	stand
as	adjective	ant	had	man	black
after	answer	ax	back	hand	happen
an	ask	Africa	last	plant	fast

A Vowel Sound: Long A—Open Syllable Rule

table

(initial)	*(medial)*				
able	paper	lazy	label	vibration
acre	lady	flavor	equator	basis
agent	baby	tomato	relation	hazy
apron	radio	navy	vapor	potato
Asia	crazy	station	enable	ladle
apex	labor	basic	volcano	vacation
April				

A–E Vowel Sound: Long A—Final E Rule

cake

(initial)		*(medial)*			
ate	ape	make	late	table	baseball
able	ace	made	tale	gave	spaceship
acre		face	place	base	tablecloth
age		same	name	plane	racetrack
ache		came	wave	game	shapeless
ale		state	space	shape	

134

The NEW Reading Teacher's Book of Lists, © 1985 Prentice-Hall, Inc., Englewood Cliffs, NJ 07632. By E. Fry, D. Fountoukidis, and J. Polk.

The NEW Reading Teacher's Book of Lists, © 1985 Prentice-Hall, Inc., Englewood Cliffs, NJ 07632. By E. Fry, D. Fountoukidis, and J. Polk.

AI Vowel Sound: Long A

 nail

(initial) *(medial)*

aim	rain	mail	claim	obtain	faint
aid	train	pain	detail	paid	grain
ailment	wait	sail	explain	remain	rail
ail	tail	strait	fail	wait	
	chain	afraid	gain	plain	
	jail	brain	main	laid	

AY Vowel Sound: Long A

 hay

(medial)

			(final)		
always	gayly	jaywalk	day	pay	repay
mayor	haystack	player	say	gray	anyway
layer	wayside	daylight	away	bay	way
crayon	payment		play	stay	pray
maybe	rayon		may	birthday	lay
			today	highway	gay

A Vowel Sound: Schwa

 announce

(initial) *(medial)*

				(final)	
about	appear	several	canvass	antenna	china
above	away	national	familiar	algebra	comma
ago	again	senator	career	alfalfa	idea
alone	ahead	thousand	purchase	banana	
America	another	magazine	compass		
alike	agree	breakfast	diagram		

AL Vowel Sound: Broad O

 ball

(initial) *(medial)*

				(final)	
all	altogether	talk	scald	call	baseball
always	alternate	walk	walnut	tall	wall
also	altar	chalk	fallen	fall	stall
already	albeit	salt		overall	recall
almost	almanac	false		hall	
although	almighty	falter		small	

AU Vowel Sound: Broad O

 auto

(initial)   *(medial)*

August	Australia	audible	because	cause	launch
author	autoharp	authentic	caught	dinosaur	faucet
autumn	auction	auditor	laundry	sauce	sausage
auditorium	auburn		haul	caution	overhaul
autograph	auxilliary		daughter	exhaust	
audience	automatic		fault	fraud	

AW Vowel Sound: Broad O

saw

(initial)   *(medial)*   *(final)*

awful	lawn	yawn	crawl	law	paw
awkward	drawn	tawny	squawk	jaw	claw
awning	lawyer	drawer	scrawl	draw	flaw
awe	hawk	shawl		straw	gnaw
awl	lawful	bawl		thaw	caw
awfully				taw	

AR Vowel Sound: AIR Sound

library

(initial)   *(medial)*   *(final)*

area	January	February	declare	care	fare
	dictionary	tiara	beware	rare	stare
	vary	parent	flare	aware	glare
	primary	wary		share	welfare
	secretary	careful		spare	hare
	canary	scare		bare	square
	daring	scarcely		dare	

AR Vowel Sound: AR Sound

star

(initial)   *(medial)*   *(final)*

are	argument	card	garden	car	mar
arm	article	March	start	far	par
army	arch	farm	dark	bar	scar
art	armor	hard	yard	jar	
artist	ark	part	party	tar	
arctic	arbor	large			

The NEW Reading Teacher's Book of Lists, © 1985 Prentice-Hall, Inc., Englewood Cliffs, NJ 07632. By E. Fry, D. Fountoukidis, and J. Polk.

The *NEW Reading Teacher's Book of Lists*, © 1985 Prentice-Hall, Inc., Englewood Cliffs, NJ 07632. By E. Fry, D. Fountoukidis, and J. Polk.

B Consonant Sound: Regular

book

(initial)		*(medial)*		*(final)*	
be	back	number	subject	tub	job
by	but	problem	baby	cab	club
boy	because	remember		rob	rub
been	below	object		cub	grab
box	before	probably		rib	adverb
big	better			verb	bulb

BL Consonant Sound: BL Blend

block

(initial)				*(medial)*	
black	blame	blank	blink	oblige	obliterate
blue	bloom	blast	blur	emblem	grumbling
bleed	blossom	blend	blow	tumbler	oblivious
blood	blond	blew	blanket	nosebleed	gambler
blind	blade	blot	bleach	ablaze	rambling
				nimbly	

BR Consonant Sound: Blend

broom

(initial)			*(medial)*		
bread	bring	brush	library	daybreak	algebra
break	breath	breeze	umbrella	cobra	embrace
brick	branch	bridge	celebrate	membrane	lubricate
broad	bright	brain	vibrate	outbreak	
brother	broken	brass	abroad	zebra	
brown	brave	breakfast			

C Consonant Sound: Regular (K Sound)

cat

(initial)		*(medial)*		*(final)*	
can	call	because	across	back	check
come	country	picture	become	rock	stick
came	cut	American	quickly	sick	black
camp	car	second		lock	pick
color	cold			kick	thick
could	carry			music	electric

C Consonant Sound: S Sound

 city

(initial)			(medial)		
cent	certain	cigar	face	decide	acid
circle	civil	cyclone	since	Pacific	dancing
cycle	ceiling	cellar	pencil	percent	peaceful
circus	celebrate	cease	fancy	precise	
center	cereal		ice	process	
cell	cinder		concert	sincere	

CH Consonant Sound: Digraph

chair

(initial)		(medial)		(final)	
children	chief	pitcher	searching	which	catch
church	chart	attached	stretched	each	branch
change	chin	purchase	exchange	much	touch
chance	chest	merchant		such	inch
cheer	chain			teach	reach
check	chase			rich	watch

CL Consonant Sound: CL Blend

clock

(initial)				(medial)		
clean	clear	clever	climb	enclose	eclipse	disclose
cloth	class	cliff	click	include	acclaim	decline
clay	clap	close		cyclone	conclude	proclaim
claim	claws	cloud		exclaim	reclaim	incline
club	clerk	clues		exclude	declare	

CR Consonant Sound: CR Blend

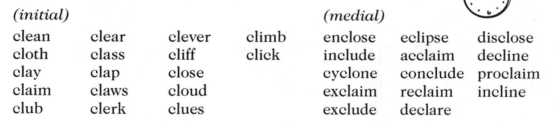 crab

(initial)				(medial)		
cry	crew	cried	cruel	across	aircraft	recruit
crack	crazy	crops	credit	secret	sacred	scarecrow
crowd	cross	crayon		increase	concrete	screen
crash	crow	creek		microscope	disease	
cream	create	crown		democrat	decree	

The NEW Reading Teacher's Book of Lists, © 1985 Prentice-Hall, Inc., Englewood Cliffs, NJ 07632. By E. Fry, D. Fountoukidis, and J. Polk.

The NEW Reading Teacher's Book of Lists, © 1985 Prentice-Hall, Inc., Englewood Cliffs, NJ 07632. By E. Fry, D. Fountoukidis, and J. Polk.

D Consonant Sound: Regular

dog

(initial)		*(medial)*		*(final)*	
do	does	study	order	and	find
day	door	under	Indians	good	need
did	done	idea	didn't	had	did
dear	different	body		said	old
down	during			red	around
deep	don't			would	end

DR Consonant Sound: DR Blend

drum

(initial)			*(medial)*		
dry	dream	drift	address	undress	hydrogen
draw	dragon	drama	hundred	withdraw	laundress
drug	drill	drain	children	daydream	redress
drove	drink	drip	dandruff	eardrum	dewdrop
drop	drive	drench	cathedral	laundry	
dress	drew	droop			

E Vowel Sound: Short E

elephant

(initial)			*(medial)*			
end	empty	ever	when	let	set	men
egg	energy	edge	then	them	went	spell
every	explain	enter	get	very	help	next
extra	enjoy	elf	left	tell	well	red
enemy	engine	else				

E Vowel Sound: Long E—Open Syllable Rule

Egypt

(initial)	*(medial)*			*(final)*	
even	cedar	meter	being	me	we
equal	demon	prefix	recent	he	be
ether	secret	react	legal	she	maybe
evil	Negro	area	really		
ecology	zebra	female	depot		

deer

EE Vowel Sound: Long E

(initial)   *(medial)*   *(final)*

eel	sleep	seem	see	bee	fee
eerie	green	teeth	three	degree	spree
	keep	sweet	tree	flee	referee
	street	week	free	knee	
	feet	screen	agree	glee	
	wheel	fifteen			
	feel				

 peach

EA Vowel Sound: Long E

(initial)   *(medial)*   *(final)*

eat	eager	ease	neat	leaf	sea
each	easel	eaves	read	feast	tea
east	Easter	easily	least	peach	flea
easy	eaten		beat	meat	plea
eagle	eastern		clean	weak	pea
			deal	peanut	

 bread

EA Vowel Sound: Short E Sound

(medial)

head	breath	feather	meadow	threaten	heaven
heavy	deaf	death	pleasant	treasure	dread
ready	ahead	measure	spread	weapon	pleasure
thread	breakfast	instead	heading	weather	widespread
steady	already	leather	sweat	overhead	gingerbread
dead					

11 eleven

E Vowel Sound: Schwa

(initial)   *(medial)*

efface	effective	happen	scientist	fuel	label
effect	efficient	problem	item	given	absent
efficiency		hundred	united	level	agent
erratic		arithmetic	quiet	heaven	hundred
essential		children	diet	even	often
erroneous		calendar	different	happen	

The NEW Reading Teacher's Book of Lists, © 1985 Prentice-Hall, Inc., Englewood Cliffs, NJ 07632. By E. Fry, D. Fountoukidis, and J. Polk.

E Vowel Sound: Silent

 **whale**

(medial)		(final)			
sometimes	homework	are	were	make	because
careful	lifetime	one	before	time	write
statement	something	there	here	more	home
safety	evening	come	came	people	
movement		little	these	place	
moreover		like	some	sentence	

ER Vowel Sound: R Sound

 letter

(medial)		(final)			
camera	afternoon	her	better	another	river
allergy	liberty	mother	sister	baker	winter
bakery	operate	over	under	wonder	liver
wonderful	federal	other	after	ever	shower
dangerous	battery	were	water	offer	lower

F Consonant Sound: Regular

 fish

(initial)		(medial)		(final)	
for	father	after	different	if	chief
first	face	before	Africa	half	stuff
find	family	often	beautiful	myself	brief
four	follow	careful		off	cliff
funny	far			leaf	itself
food	few			himself	wolf

FL Consonant Sound: FL Blend

flag

(initial)				(medial)	
flower	floor	fleet	flea	afflict	inflame
flat	flavor	flow	fluffy	inflict	afloat
flight	flood	flap		conflict	reflect
flew	flute	flock		influence	inflate
fly	flame	fling		aflame	inflexible
float	flash	flip		snowflake	

FR Consonant Sound: FR Blend

frog

(initial)

				(medial)	
free	frost	fruit	frisky	afraid	defraud
from	frank	freedom		affront	infringe
front	freshman	frozen		befriend	leapfrog
friend	frame	France		bullfrog	refrain
Friday	fresh	freighter		carefree	refresh
fry	fraction	fragile		confront	infrequent

G Consonant Sound: Regular

gate

(initial)		*(medial)*		*(final)*	
go	gun	again	segment	dog	frog
good	game	ago	regular	big	pig
got	gas	began	figure	egg	log
gave	gift	sugar		leg	bag
girl	gone	wagon		fig	
get	garden	signal		flag	

G Consonant Sound: J Sound

giant

(initial)			*(medial)*	*(final)*	
gem	gym	gesture	danger	change	page
giraffe	gypsy	genius	energy	large	village
gentlemen	ginger	genuine	region	bridge	huge
geography	gelatin	generate	engine	age	strange
generous	germ		original		
gently	general		vegetable		
			oxygen		

GL Consonant Sound: GL Blend

glass

(initial)				*(medial)*	
glad	glisten	glare	glider	eyeglass	hourglass
globe	gloom	glass	glimpse	jingling	bugler
glow	glue	glade	glitter	spyglass	angler
glory	glum	gleam	glance	smuggling	mangling
glove	glamour	glee	glaze	wiggling	singly

The NEW Reading Teacher's Book of Lists, © 1985 Prentice-Hall, Inc., Englewood Cliffs, NJ 07632. By E. Fry, D. Fountoukidis, and J. Polk.

GR Consonant Sound: Blend

grapes

(initial)   *(medial)*

grade	grand	grant	hungry	Negro	disgrace
great	green	grin	angry	program	fragrant
grow	ground	gradual	congress	regret	outgrow
grew	group	grandfather	agree	degrade	engross
grass	grab	gravity	degree	engrave	
gray	grain				

GH: Silent

eight

(medial)   *(final)*

daughter	eighth	delight	thought	high	sleigh
might	night	light	fought	sigh	although
brighter	neighbors	right	bought	bough	plough
throughout	fight	sight	caught	through	dough
highway	thoroughly	tight	taught	weigh	neigh
				though	

H Consonant Sound: Regular

hand

(initial)   *(medial)*

he	help	half	high	behind	rehearse
had	here	his	hit	ahead	behold
have	happy	hen	house	unhappy	unhook
her	home	hero		behave	ahoy
him	hard	hide		overhead	
how	has	hill		autoharp	

I Vowel Sound: Short I

Indian

(initial)   *(medial)*

in	it	ill	with	will	different
is	invent	include	did	big	until
if	important	India	this	still	miss
into	insect	isn't	little	give	begin
inch	instead	inside	which	his	city
			him		

I Vowel Sound: Long I—Open Syllable Rule

  iron

(initial)   *(medial)*

I	icy	bicycle	pilot	variety	title
idea	Irish	tiny	quiet	dinosaur	spider
I'll	iodine	silent	triangle	giant	diagram
iris	Iowa	rifle	climate	lion	China
I'm	ivory				
item					

I–E Vowel Sound: Long I—Final E Rule

  ice

(initial)   *(medial)*

idle	five	fire	nine	mile	drive
ire	white	write	bite	size	wire
isle	ride	life	like	wide	mine
I've	time	side	line	describe	wife

IR Vowel Sound: R Sound

girl

(medial)   *(final)*

girl	skirt	thirteen	shirk	circuit	fir
first	birthday	girth	mirth	girdle	sir
third	thirsty	birth	confirm	stirrup	stir
shirt	affirm	circus	Virginia	dirty	tapir
dirt	circle	thirty	firm		whir
					astir

J Consonant Sound: Regular

jar

(initial)   *(medial)*

just	jet	June	object	project	unjust
jump	job	jungle	enjoy	adjust	majesty
January	joke	junior	subject	dejected	majority
jaw	joy	jacket	major	overjoyed	rejoice
July	juice	join	banjo	adjoin	
			adjective	reject	

K Consonant Sound: Regular

kite

(initial)		(medial)		(final)	
kind	kiss	monkey	market	like	work
key	kitten	broken	packing	make	mark
kill	kid	turkey	stroking	book	speak
king	kettle	worker		look	milk
keep	kick			cake	bank
kin	keen			cook	break

KN Consonant Sound: N

knife

(initial)					(medial)
knee	knelt	knack	knockout	knell	unknown
knew	knit	kneel	knickers	kneecap	doorknob
know	knock	knapsack	knothole	knives	penknife
knowledge	knight	knob	knoll	knotty	acknowledge
knot	knuckle	knead	knave	known	knick knack
					knock-kneed

L Consonant Sound: Regular

letter

(initial)		(medial)		(final)	
little	large	only	really	will	oil
like	last	below	follow	all	tell
long	line	along	family	girl	until
look	learn	children		school	spell
live	left			shall	well
land	light			small	vowel

M Consonant Sound: Regular

man

(initial)		(medial)		(final)	
me	more	number	important	from	farm
my	mother	American	example	them	room
make	move	something	family	am	arm
much	must	complete		seem	team
many	made			warm	form
may	men			him	bottom

N Consonant Sound: Regular

 nut

(initial)		(medial)		(final)	
not	name	many	until	in	man
no	number	under	any	on	even
new	need	answer	animal	can	own
night	never	country		when	open
next	near			an	been
now	next			then	than

NG Consonant Sound: NG

king

(medial)		(final)			
slingshot	gangster	sing	long	bang	spring
lengthen	singer	bring	song	lung	strong
longing	hanger	thing	gang	wing	fang
kingdom	gangplank	going	hang	ring	hung
youngster	gangway	swing	young	fling	string
					wrong

O Vowel Sound: Short

box

(initial)		(medial)			
odd	opera	not	fox	follow	rock
olive	oxygen	box	drop	got	bottom
opposite	operate	hot	pop	problem	copy
oxen	on	stop	pot	top	job
October	occupy	body	clock	product	cannot
opportunity					

O Vowel Sound: Long O—Open Syllable Rule

 **radio**

(initial)		(medial)	(final)		
open	odor	October	go	zero	echo
over	omit	program	no	cargo	volcano
obey	oboe	Roman	so	piano	
ocean	okra	moment	hello	Negro	
Ohio		poem	ago	potato	
		total	also	hero	
		broken	auto		

The NEW Reading Teacher's Book of Lists, © 1985 Prentice-Hall, Inc., Englewood Cliffs, NJ 07632. By E. Fry, D. Fountoukidis, and J. Polk.

The NEW Reading Teacher's Book of Lists, © 1985 Prentice-Hall, Inc., Englewood Cliffs, NJ 07632. By E. E. Fry, D. Fountoukidis, and J. Polk.

O–E Vowel Sound: Long O—Final E Rule

 rope

(initial)	(medial)				
owe	home	rode	whole	rose	stove
	those	nose	slope	spoke	awoke
	hope	stone	bone	smoke	phone
	note	joke	tone	drove	
	alone	globe	pole	vote	

OA Vowel Sound: Long O

 boat

(initial)	(medial)				
oak	coat	toast	approach	croak	coal
oat	soap	goat	loaf	soak	toad
oath	road	goal	groan	cloak	moan
oatmeal	coast	loan	foam	roach	throat
oaf	load	float	roast	boast	coach

OW Vowel Sound: Long O

 window

(initial)	(medial)		(final)		
own	bowl	crowbar	show	follow	mow
owe	stowaway	bowling	low	tomorrow	glow
owing	snowball	mower	slow	throw	know
owner	towboat		snow	blow	crow
			row	grow	arrow
			yellow	flow	borrow

OW Vowel Sound: OU Diphthong

 owl

(medial)			(final)		
down	crown	towel	how	somehow	endow
town	cowboy	powder	now	eyebrow	vow
brown	power	tower	cow	bow	prow
flower	vowel	chowder	plow	scow	avow
crowd	downward	shower	allow	sow	snowplow

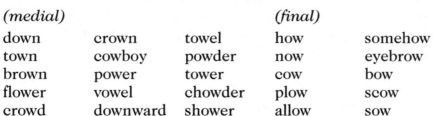

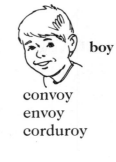
boy

OY Vowel Sound: OI Diphthong

(initial)	*(medial)*		*(final)*		
oyster	royal	joyous	toy	decoy	convoy
	voyage	disloyal	joy	newsboy	envoy
	loyal	loyalty	enjoy	annoy	corduroy
	boycott	enjoyment	employ	soy	
	annoying	joyful	destroy	viceroy	
	employer	boyish	coy	Troy	
	boyhood		cowboy	alloy	

violin

O Vowel Sound: Schwa

(initial)	*(medial)*		*(final)*
other	oblige	mother	action	kimono
original	obstruct	money	canyon
official	oppose	atom	weapon
observe	occasion	second	period
opinion	oppress	nation	mission
objection	opossum	method	riot

oil

OI Vowel Sound: OI Diphthong

(initial)	*(medial)*				
oilcloth	join	broil	coil	sirloin	joint
oilwell	point	spoil	moisture	disappoint	embroider
oily	voice	avoid	exploit	toil	typhoid
ointment	coin	poison	doily	void	
	choice	boil	soil	broiler	
	noise	turmoil	rejoice		

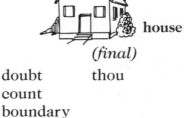
house

OU Vowel Sound: OU Diphthong

(initial)		*(medial)*		*(final)*
out	outer	hour	aloud	doubt	thou
our	outline	sound	found	count
ounce	outside	about	council	boundary
oust	outlook	around	ground
ourselves	outcry	round	loud
outdoors	outfield	scout	cloud
ouch		amount	mountain

The NEW Reading Teacher's Book of Lists, © 1985 Prentice-Hall, Inc., Englewood Cliffs, NJ 07632. By E. Fry, D. Fountoukidis, and J. Polk.

O Vowel Sound: Broad O

 dog

(initial)

			(medial)		
off	onto	offhand	soft	wrong	moth
office	offset	offshore	log	cloth	frost
officer	offspring	ostrich	long	toss	cross
often	onward		along	coffee	belong
on	onset		cost	strong	
offer	oncoming		across	song	

OR Vowel Sound: OR Sound

fork

(initial) *(medial)* *(final)*

or	Oregon	short	score	corner	for
order	organ	horn	form	store	more
ore	ordinary	fork	before	north	nor
orbit	oral	forget	horse	force	
orchestra	orchard	born	story		
ordinary	orchid	cord	important		

OO Vowel Sound: 1-Dot U, or Short OO

book

(medial)

look	took	foot	shook	brook	cook
good	wood	stood	goodbye	wool	dogwood
hook	rook	soot	lookout	notebook	rookie
afoot	hoof	cookie	football	understood	handbook
hood	crook	nook	wooden	neighborhood	overlook
motherhood					

OO Vowel Sound: 2-Dot U, or Long OO

moon

(initial) *(medial)* *(final)*

ooze	soon	tooth	mood	too	bamboo
	school	cool	roof	zoo	cuckoo
	room	goose	loose	shampoo	boo
	food	troop	balloon	woo	igloo
	shoot	fool	noon	coo	
	smooth	boot		tattoo	
	pool	tool		kangaroo	

pencil

P Consonant Sound: Regular

(initial)		(medial)		(final)	
put	point	open	perhaps	up	ship
people	piece	example	happy	sleep	top
page	pass	paper		jump	step
pair	person	important		help	map
part	paper	upon		stop	deep
picture	pull			group	drop

telephone

PH Consonant Sound: F

(initial)		(medial)		(final)	
photo	phase	alphabet	cellophane	photograph	telegraph
phonics	phantom	orphan	emphasis	phonograph	graph
phrase	phonetic	nephew	gopher	autograph	triumph
physical	pharmacy	sulphur	graphic	paragraph	
physician	phoenix	geography	trophy		
pheasant	phenomenon		sophomore		

plate

PL Consonant Sound: PL Blend

(initial)			(medial)		
play	place	player	supply	display	airplane
plant	plan	pleasant	multiply	explain	applaud
plain	plane	plot	employ	supplying	apply
please	planets	plank	reply	surplus	complain
plow	plastic	plug	perplex		
plus	platform		imply		

propeller

PR Consonant Sound: PR Blend

(initial)				(medial)	
pretty	president	present	probably	surprise	approach
price	prince	problem	prove	April	approximate
press	program	produce	pray	improve	appropriate
prize	practice	property	products	apron	impression
print	prepare	provide		express	

The NEW Reading Teacher's Book of Lists, © 1985 Prentice-Hall, Inc., Englewood Cliffs, NJ 07632. By E. Fry, D. Fountoukidis, and J. Polk.

The NEW Reading Teacher's Book of Lists, © 1985 Prentice-Hall, Inc., Englewood Cliffs, NJ 07632. By E. Fry, D. Fountoukidis, and J. Polk.

Q Consonant Sound: KW Sound

queen

(initial)   *(medial)*

quart	quiet	quote	square	liquid	squirm
quite	quack	quill	equal	equipment	sequence
question	quail	quality	squirrel	equator	squeak
quick	quake		frequent	equivalent	inquire
quit	quilt		require	squash	
queer	quiz		equation	earthquake	

R Consonant Sound: Regular

ring

(initial)   *(medial)*   *(final)*

run	rest	very	large	our	other
red	ride	part	story	their	over
right	road	word	form	for	water
ran	rock	around		year	her
read	room			dear	after
rat	rod			your	near

S Consonant Sound: Regular

saw

(initial)   *(medial)*   *(final)*

some	sound	also	question	this	less
so	say	person	inside	us	across
see	sentence	answer	system	likes	its
said	side	himself		makes	gas
soon	same			yes	bus
set	sea			miss	perhaps

S Consonant Sound: Z Sound

eyes

(medial)   *(final)*

music	observe	please	is	odds	news
easy	museum	cheese	as	says	hers
busy	present	wise	was	suds	does
those	result	these	his	yours	
because	season		has	tongs	
desert	poison		ours	days	

SC Consonant Sound: SC Blend

 **scale**

(initial)

				(medial)	
score	scatter	scream	scoop	describe	inscribe
school	scholar	scallop	scrub	telescope	unscramble
screen	scout	screw		description	microscopic
scratch	scarce	scared		microscope	unscrupulous
scarf	scramble	scab		nondescript	telescoping
scar	scrape			unscrew	descriptive

SH Consonant Sound: Digraph

 shoe

(initial)   *(medial)*   *(final)*

(initial)		*(medial)*		*(final)*	
she	shot	dashed	ashes	wish	rush
shall	shirt	splashing	friendship	wash	dish
show	shell	sunshine		fish	crash
ship	sheet	worship		push	bush
short	shop	fisherman		finish	flash
shape	shut			fresh	establish

SK Consonant Sound: SK Blend

 skate

(initial)   *(medial)*   *(final)*

(initial)			*(medial)*	*(final)*	
sky	skeleton	skillet	outskirts	desk	mask
skin	skull	skirmish	askew	task	husk
skill	skid	skinny	muskrat	ask	dusk
skunk	sketch	skylark	numskull	brisk	
skirt	ski	skeptic	rollerskate		
skip	skim		muskmelon		
			masked		

SL Consonant Sound: SL Blend

slide

(initial)   *(medial)*

(initial)				*(medial)*	
slow	sled	slope	sly	asleep	oversleep
sleep	slave	slam	slash	landslide	snowslide
slept	sleeve	slate	slab	onslaught	grandslam
slip	slant	slipper	sleek	enslave	nonslip
slid	slice	sleet	slimy	bobsled	
slap	slight	slim		manslaughter	

The NEW Reading Teacher's Book of Lists, © 1985 Prentice-Hall, Inc., Englewood Cliffs, NJ 07632. By E. Fry, D. Fountoukidis, and J. Polk.

SM Consonant Sound: SM Blend

smoke

(initial)   *(medial)*

smile	smash	smock	smote	smuggler	blacksmith
smooth	smear	smoky	smokestack	smattering	gunsmith
smell	smith	smudge	smelt	smorgasbord	silversmith
small	smolder	smuggle	smite		locksmith
smart	smack	smug	smithy		
smother	smog	smitten	smoker		

SN Consonant Sound: SN Blend

snake

(initial)

snow	snuggle	snapshot	sniff	snooze	snuff
snowball	snip	sneak	sniffle	snorkel	snowman
snare	snarl	snatch	snipe	snort	sniper
sneeze	snap	sneakers	snob	snout	snowy
snore	snack	sneer	snoop	snub	
snug	snail				

SP Consonant Sound: SP Blend

spoon

(initial)   *(medial)*   *(final)*

sports	speed	spider	inspect	despair	clasp
space	spell	spend	respect	inspire	crisp
speak	spot	spark	respond	despite	gasp
spring	spin		despise		grasp
spread	spoke		unspeakable		wasp
special	spare		respectful		lisp
					wisp

stamp

ST Consonant Sound: ST Blend

(initial)   *(medial)*   *(final)*

stop	story	stick	instead	restless	best
step	street	stone	destroy	poster	cast
stay	stand	stood	restore	tasty	dust
state	star		westward		fast
still	study		haystack		least
store	strong		destruction		past
					west

SW Consonant Sound: SW Blend

swing

(initial)

swim	switch	sweet	swollen	swampy	swarthy
swell	swallow	swift	sway	swirl	swat
swept	swung	swan	swine	swarm	swerve
sweat	swam	swagger	swoop	swear	sworn
sweater	swamp	swap	swindle	swelter	swish
sweep					

T Consonant Sound: Regular

top

(initial)		*(medial)*		*(final)*	
to	took	city	later	not	what
two	table	into	sentence	at	set
take	ten	water	until	it	part
tell	talk	after		out	got
too	today			get	put
time	told			but	want

TH Consonant Sound: Digraph Voiceless

three

(initial)		*(medial)*		*(final)*	
thank	thought	something	toothbrush	with	truth
think	thread	author	python	both	death
thing	threw	nothing		ninth	south
third	thumb	athlete		worth	fifth
thirty	thunder	faithful		cloth	bath
thick	threat	bathtub		teeth	

TH Consonant Sound: Digraph Voiced

feather

(initial)		*(medial)*		*(final)*
the	though	mother	weather	smooth
that	thus	other	gather	
them	thy	brother	breathing	
they	thence	father	rhythm	
this	their	although	farther	
there	then	bother	leather	
than	thou	clothing	northern	
these		either		

The NEW Reading Teacher's Book of Lists, © 1985 Prentice-Hall, Inc., Englewood Cliffs, NJ 07632. By E. Fry, D. Fountoukidis, and J. Polk.

TR Consonant Sound: Blend

truck

(initial)			*(medial)*		
track	trick	trouble	extra	control	country
tractor	travel	trap	electric	sentry	patrol
train	tree	trail	central	waitress	
trade	trim	triangle	attract	contract	
truly	trip	traffic	entry	patron	
try	true		subtract	contrast	

TW Consonant Sound: TW Blend

twins

(initial)					*(medial)*
twelve	twirl	twinkle	twinge	twelfth	between
twenty	twine	twist	twang	twill	entwine
twice	tweed	twitter	twentieth	twiddle	untwist
twig	twilight	twitch	tweet		intertwine

U Vowel Sound: Short U

umbrella

(initial)			*(medial)*		
up	unhappy	unless	but	number	such
us	upon	umpire	run	must	hunt
under	usher		much	study	summer
until	unusual		just	hundred	jump
ugly	uproar		cut	sudden	gun
uncle	upset		funny	sun	

U Vowel Sound: Long U—Open Syllable Rule

music

(initial)	*(medial)*			*(final)*	
unit	unify	future	humid	fugitive	menu
united	unique	human	museum	funeral	
Utah	utilize	valuable	continuous	beautiful	
uniform		humor	fuel	unusual	
universe		January	bugle	musician	
usual		pupil	cubic	puny	
university		community	communicate		

U Vowel Sound: 1-Dot U

bull

(medial)

bullet	bush	cushion	bull's-eye	pulpit	bulldog
full	bushel	ambush	bushy	fully	armful
pull	sugar	bulletin	pullet	bullfrog	bully
push	pudding	handful	pushcart	fulfill	bullfight
put	butcher	pulley	bulldozer	bulwark	output

U Vowel Sound: 2-Dot U

ruler

(medial)

June	flute	tune	punctuation	revolution	tuna
July	prune	conclusion	constitution	ruby	influence
truth	parachute	tube	duty	prudent	solution
junior	cruel	February	nutrition	situation	rhubarb
rule	numeral	aluminum	reduce	ruin	truly
crude					

UR Vowel Sound: R Sound

church

(initial)	*(medial)*			*(final)*	
urn	turn	purple	further	fur	spur
urban	burn	hurt	purpose	sulfur	cur
urchin	hurry	turkey	burst	murmur	bur
urge	curl	curb	surf	concur	
urgent	Thursday	nurse	turtle	occur	
	purse	surface		slur	

V Consonant Sound: Regular

Valentine

(initial)		*(medial)*		*(final)*	
very	vowel	over	however	give	live
visit	van	even	cover	five	move
voice	verb	never	several	love	above
vote	vase	river		gave	leave
view	violin			twelve	wave
vest	valley			have	believe

The NEW Reading Teacher's Book of Lists, © 1985 Prentice-Hall, Inc., Englewood Cliffs, NJ 07632. By E. Fry, D. Fountoukidis, and J. Polk.

The NEW Reading Teacher's Book of Lists, © 1985 Prentice-Hall, Inc., Englewood Cliffs, NJ 07632. By E. Fry, D. Fountoukidis, and J. Polk.

W Consonant Sound: Regular

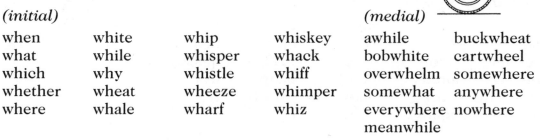 **window**

(initial)   *(medial)*

we	water	would	away	awake	halfway
with	way	wave	reward	aware	sidewalk
will	were	win	forward	unwind	upward
was	word	woman	want	highway	midway
work	week	wait	sandwich	backyard	tapeworm

WH Consonant Sound: Digraph (HW Blend)

wheel

(initial)   *(medial)*

when	white	whip	whiskey	awhile	buckwheat
what	while	whisper	whack	bobwhite	cartwheel
which	why	whistle	whiff	overwhelm	somewhere
whether	wheat	wheeze	whimper	somewhat	anywhere
where	whale	wharf	whiz	everywhere	nowhere
				meanwhile	

WR Consonant Sound: R

wrench

(initial)   *(medial)*

write	wrestle	wretch	wrung	awry	typewriter
writing	wrist	wrinkle	wry	rewrite	monkeywrench
written	wreath	wrapper	wrangle	handwriting	typewritten
wrote	wring	wrathful		unwrap	
wrong	wreck	wreckage		playwright	
wrap	wren	wriggle		shipwreck	

X Consonant Sound: KS Sound

box

(medial)   *(final)*

Mexico	explain	fox	fix	complex	vex
Texas	axis	ax	relax	index	wax
mixture	oxen	six	next	lax	sex
extremely	extra	tax	mix	hex	perplex
sixty	excuse	ox	prefix	lox	
expert	exclaim				

Y Consonant Sound: Consonant

 yarn

(initial)   *(medial)*

you	youth	yam	yew	lawyer	vineyard
year	yawn	yank	yeast	canyon	papaya
yellow	yard	yak	yen	beyond	dooryard
yes	yet	yodel	yolk	courtyard	stockyard
yell	your	yacht	yonder	barnyard	backyard
young					

Y Vowel Sound: Long E

 baby

(medial)   *(final)*

anything	very	happy	country	early
babysit	any	lady	city	money
everyone	many	story	really	quickly
ladybug	pretty	family	body	heavy
bodyguard	only	study	usually	ready
copying	funny	every	easy	energy
everything				

Y Vowel Sound: Long I Sound

 fly

(medial)   *(final)*

myself	type	my	sky	shy	reply
nylon	lying	by	July	defy	sly
cycle	ryhme	why	fry	dry	deny
dying	python	buy	apply	ally	
style	hyena	cry	pry	spy	

Z Consonant Sound: Regular

zebra

(initial)   *(medial)*   *(final)*

zero	zipper	lazy	citizen	size	quiz
zoo	zoom	crazy	frozen	freeze	whiz
zone		puzzle	breeze	prize	buzz
zest		dozen	grazing		fizz
zenith		magazine	organize		fuzz
zigzag		realize	seize		jazz
zinc					adz

See Also List 46, Major Phonograms,
and List 49, Phonetically Irregular Words.

The NEW Reading Teacher's Book of Lists, © 1985 Prentice-Hall, Inc., Englewood Cliffs, NJ 07632. By E. Fry, D. Fountoukidis, and J. Polk.

49. PHONICALLY IRREGULAR WORDS

The NEW Reading Teacher's Book of Lists, © 1985 Prentice-Hall, Inc., Englewood Cliffs, NJ 07632. By E. Fry, D. Fountoukidis, and J. Polk.

As every reading teacher knows, there are many words that do not follow regular phonics rules. Here are two such groups of common words. The first group contains common words with silent consonants. The second group contains common words with other types of phonic irregularities. Clearly, these are words that students need to be taught to recognize as sight words.

Words with Silent Consonants

The following words with silent consonants were taken from List 4, Instant Words. The words are listed in order of frequency, with those that are most frequent listed first. Two types of consonants that could be considered silent were *not* included in this list: (1) double consonants, where the second consonant adds nothing to the sound of the first (example, *all*); and (2) consonant digraphs (example, *ch, th, ph,* and *gh* pronounced as *"f"*).

would	light	black	window	design
write	thought	listen	edge	straight
could	might	quickly	sign	stick
know	often	scientists	snow	caught
back	night	known	bright	thick
through	walk	island	although	sight
right	enough	brought	couldn't	eight
answer	watch	though	catch	science
should	talk	check	climbed	adjective
high	knew	picked	wrote	stretched
				bought
				track

Words with Other Phonic Irregularities

a	earth	have	off	something	water
again	enough	heard	old	sure	were
any	example	kind	on	the	what
are	eyes	learn	once	their	where
become	father	live	one	there	who
been	few	many	only	they	women
both	find	measure	other	to	words
color	four	most	people	today	work
come	friends	mother	picture	two	world
country	from	mountain	piece	usually	you
do	give	move	said	want	young
does	great	of	some	was	your
door	group				

See Also List 19, Spelling Demons—Elementary.

SECTION V
Comprehension

50. SIGNAL WORDS

These are words that the author uses to tell us how to read. Signal words help us to understand how information is organized and provide clues about what is important. Teach signal words one group at a time. Give your students a few examples from a category and have them add others as they run across them in their reading.

1. Continuation signals (*Warning—there are more ideas to come*):

and	also	another
again	and finally	first of all
a final reason	furthermore	in addition
last of all	likewise	more
moreover	next	one reason
other	secondly	similarly
too	with	

2. Change-of-direction signals (*Watch out—we're doubling back*):

although	but	conversely
despite	different from	even though
however	in contrast	instead of
in spite of	nevertheless	otherwise
the opposite	on the contrary	on the other hand
rather	still	yet
while	though	

3. Sequence signals (*There is an order to these ideas*):

first, second, third	A, B, C
in the first place	for one thing
then	next
before	now
after	while
into (*far into the night*)	until
last	during
since	always
o'clock	on time
later	earlier

4. Illustration signals (*Here's what that principle means in reality*):

for example	specifically
for instance	to illustrate
such as	much like
in the same way as	similar to

5. Emphasis signals (*This is important*):

a major development	it all boils down to
a significant factor	most of all
a primary concern	most noteworthy
a key feature	more than anything else
a major event	pay particular attention to
a vital force	remember that
a central issue	should be noted
a distinctive quality	the most substantial issue
above all	the main value
especially important	the basic concept
especially relevant	the crux of the matter
especially valuable	the chief outcome
important to note	the principal item

6. Cause, condition, or result signals (*Condition or modification coming up*):

because	if	of
for	from	so
while	then	but
that	until	since
as	whether	in order that
so that	therefore	unless
yet	thus	due to
resulting from	consequently	

7. Spatial signals (*Answers the "where" question*):

between	on	by
here	there	left
right	these	close to
near	this	side
middle	west	beside
east	about	north
south	around	over
under	away	in front of
across	into	behind
toward	beyond	above
below	opposite	upon
outside	inside	alongside
over	out	far
in	adjacent	near
next to		

The NEW Reading Teacher's Book of Lists, © 1985 Prentice-Hall, Inc., Englewood Cliffs, NJ 07632. By E. Fry, D. Fountoukidis, and J. Polk.

The NEW Reading Teacher's Book of Lists, © 1985 Prentice-Hall, Inc., Englewood Cliffs, NJ 07632. By E. Fry, D. Fountoukidis, and J. Polk.

8. Comparison-contrast signals (*We will now compare idea A with idea B*):

and	or	also
too	best	most
either	less	less than
more than	same	better
even	then	half
much as	like	analogous to
but	different from	still
yet	however	although
opposite	rather	while
though		

9. Conclusion signals (*This ends the discussion and may have special importance*):

as a result	consequently	finally
from this we see	in conclusion	in summary
hence	last of all	therefore

10. Fuzz signals (*Idea not exact, or author not positive and wishes to qualify a statement*):

almost	if	looks like
maybe	could	some
except	should	alleged
nearly	might	reputed
seems like	was reported	purported
sort of	probably	

11. Nonword emphasis signals
> exclamation point (!)
> underline
> *italics*
> **bold type**
> subheads, like The Conclusion
> > indention of paragraph
> graphic illustrations
> numbered points (1,2,3)
> very short sentence: *Stop war.*
> "quotation marks"

See Also List 63, Test and Workbook Words;
and List 65, Important Modifiers.

51. PROPAGANDA TECHNIQUES

These are persuasion devices that are frequently found in advertising and political campaigning. Teach them to your students and then have them bring in examples.

Name calling. Using a derogatory term to create a negative emotional attitude for an individual or thing. (*You don't want a polluting, gas-guzzling automobile! Buy a milliped cycle instead!*)

Glittering generality. Using a shred of truth as a base for a sweeping generalization. (*His past experience as Mar County chairman makes him the best qualified of the three candidates.*)

Card stacking. Telling the facts for one side only. (*This method of staff reduction cuts operating costs; reduces insurance, pension, and other long-range costs; and provides for easier staff training and supervision.* The firing of 60 teachers and doubling of classes is not mentioned.)

Testimonials. Using the testimony of someone to persuade you to think as they do. (*I would never have believed that there was such a difference in hair color products. Then I tried Sizzlelights. My hair never looked so shimmery. For shimmery hair I will always use Sizzlelights.*)

Prestige identification. Using a well-known figure to lend importance or prestige to a product. (The TV personality who explains the simple aim-and-shoot procedure for cameras, the benefits of decaffeinated coffee, or the superior quality of a cooking oil.)

Bandwagon. Using the argument that everyone's doing it, so you should, too. (*Thirty million Americans can't be wrong. They buy B-stone tires at their local B-stone store. Join those who know a value. Buy B-stone!*)

Plain folks. Someone just like you, who has your problems and understands your life, uses X product. Therefore, you should, too. (An older, not very attractive woman demonstrates that holding a frypan is painful for her because of arthritis. She then uses X product, there is a time lapse, and she states that the pain is gone, and now she can lift the pan effortlessly. Therefore, if you suffer from painful arthritis as she does, you also will be relieved of the pain by using X.)

Red herring. Highlighting a minor detail as a way to draw attention from the important issue. (*Never-ware cookware will look beautiful on your shelf for generations!* No mention of its cooking value is made.)

Exigency. Creating the impression that your action is required immediately, or the opportunity will be lost forever. (*For a short time only, the limited, signed edition of* Gladstoned *is being offered. Don't wait another minute. Order yours, now, before supplies are depleted.*)

Transfer. Attempting to have you transfer your feelings about one thing to another thing. (*Make your home a showplace. Get NU-Color shutters today and be proud of your home.*)

Innuendo. Hinting that there may be something being kept hidden. (*Only John T. Belt did not voluntarily disclose his financial position before the primary.*)

Snob appeal. Trying to persuade by making you feel you're one of the elite if you use brand X or think Y. (*Live a legend of elegance with Lennet china and crystal. Limited edition available to club members only.*)

Flag waving. Connecting the use of a product with patriotism. (*Switch to American coal. Let's end our dependency on foreign oil.* or *Let's make our town [school, company, team, etc.] the best.*)

The NEW Reading Teacher's Book of Lists, © 1985 Prentice-Hall, Inc., Englewood Cliffs, NJ 07632. By E. Fry, D. Fountoukidis, and J. Polk.

See Also List 54, Comprehension Skills.

52. COMPREHENSION QUESTIONS

Here are some question types to help you add variety to your questioning. These questions can be adapted for use with any prose. Examples of each question type are based on the story of Cinderella.

Vocabulary

1. Questions to help students understand the meaning of a particular word. For example: What does the word *jealous* mean? What did the stepsisters do that shows that they were jealous?

2. Questions to help students understand words used in the text in terms of their own lives. For example: Have you ever known someone who was jealous? Have you ever been jealous? Why?

3. Questions to help students understand multiple meanings of words. For example: What does *ball* mean in this story? Can you think of any other meaning of the word *ball*?

Pronoun Referents

4. Questions to help students understand what or who some pronouns refer to and how to figure them out. For example: In the second sentence of the third paragraph, who does "she" refer to? How do you know?

Causal Relations

5. Questions to help students recognize causal relations stated directly in the text. For example: Why were Cinderella's stepsisters jealous of Cinderella?

6. Questions to help students recognize causal relations not directly stated in the text. For example: Why did the stepmother give Cinderella extra work to do on the day of the ball?

Sequence

7. Questions to help students understand that the sequence of some things is unchangeable. For example: What steps did the Fairy Godmother follow in order to make a coach for Cinderella? Could the order of these steps be changed? Why or why not?

8. Questions to help students understand that the sequence of some things is changeable. For example: What chores did Cinderella do on the day of the ball? Could she have done some of them in a different order? Why or why not?

Comparison

9. Questions to encourage the students to compare things within the text. For example: How did the behavior of the stepsisters differ from the behavior of Cinderella?

10. Questions to encourage students to compare elements of the story with elements of other stories. For example: In what ways are the stories of Cinderella and Snow White similar? In what ways are they different?

11. Questions to encourage students to compare elements of the story with their own experiences. For example: If you were in Cinderella's place how would you have acted toward your stepsisters? Is this similar or different from the way Cinderella acted?

Generalizing

12. Questions to encourage students to generalize from one story to another. For example: Are most heroines of fairy tales as kind as Cinderella? Give some examples to support your answer.

13. Questions to encourage students to generalize from what they read to their own experiences. For example: Can we say that most stepmothers are mean to their stepchildren? Why or why not?

Predicting Outcomes

14. Questions to encourage students to think ahead to what may happen in the future. For example: After Cinderella's beautiful dress changes back to rags what do you think happens?

Detecting Author's Point of View

15. Questions to help students detect the author's point of view. For example: What is the author's opinion of the stepsisters and what makes you think this? Support your answer with examples from the story.

See Also List 54, Comprehension Skills;
List 55, Comprehension Thesaurus; and
Section VII, Testing.

The NEW Reading Teacher's Book of Lists, © 1985 Prentice-Hall, Inc., Englewood Cliffs, NJ 07632. By E. Fry, D. Fountoukidis, and J. Polk.

53. SENTENCE TUNES

If you have any doubt that changing the way you say something can change the meaning, this example should convince you. Your students will enjoy playing with this sentence and should be able to create their own multi-tuned sentences.

Directions: Emphasize italicized word to change meaning.

I did not say you stole my red bandana.

(*Someone else said it*)

I *did* not say you stole my red bandana.

(*Disputatious denial*)

I did *not* say you stole my red bandana.

(*Disputatious denial*)

I did not *say* you stole my red bandana.

(*I implied or suspected*)

I did not say *you* stole my red bandana.

(*Someone else stole it*)

I did not say you *stole* my red bandana.

(*You did something else with it*)

I did not say you stole *my* red bandana.

(*You stole someone else's*)

I did not say you stole my *red* bandana.

(*You stole one of another color*)

I did not say you stole my red *bandana*.

(*You stole something else red*)

The NEW Reading Teacher's Book of Lists, © 1985 Prentice-Hall, Inc., Englewood Cliffs, NJ 07632. By E. Fry, D. Fountoukidis, and J. Polk.

54. COMPREHENSION SKILLS

This is a traditional list of comprehension skills such as might be found in any textbook about reading or on the scope and sequence chart of a basal reader.

VERY TRADITIONAL COMPREHENSION SKILLS

Author's intent, purpose, and bias
Cause and effect
Classification, categories
Comparison
Conclusion
Detail recognition
Empathy and emotional reaction
Evaluation, subjective and by external
    criteria, judgment
Exaggeration and hyperbole recognition
Extending interpretation, extrapolation
Factual recall
Following directions
Generalization

Inference
Literary style
Main idea
Mental imagery
Mood
Organization
Plot, story problem
Propaganda detection
Restatement
Sequence, time relationships
Separation of fact from opinion
    (figurative from literal)
Summarizing
Whole-part recognition

The NEW Reading Teacher's Book of Lists, © 1985 Prentice-Hall, Inc., Englewood Cliffs, NJ 07632. By E. Fry, D. Fountoukidis, and J. Polk.

MORE MODERN APPROACH TO COMPREHENSION SKILLS

Student Observable Action	**Cognitive Action**
Output	*Thinking*

RECOGNIZING

Examples: Multiple-choice item, Underlining, Matching
True-false
Selecting correct answer in context, or from choices given

RECALLING

Examples: Write short answer,
Completion (cloze),
Remembering, not selecting

PARAPHRASING

Examples: Summarizing,
Restating in own words

CLASSIFYING

Examples: Clustering ideas in article,
Putting facts or ideas into some class (columns), Outline, make table

FOLLOWING DIRECTIONS

Examples: Assemble toy,
Pencil activities,
Point to area on screen

GRAPHING

Examples: Draw a map, picture,
time line, curve, graph, flow chart

ORAL READING

Intonation, Phrasing

DIRECTLY STATED FACTS

Little or no interpretation,
Most common items,
Literal comprehension

MAIN IDEA

Very common but complicated and subjective concept; involves conclusion, purpose, and/or summary

FACTS TO SUPPORT MAIN IDEA

Common and sometimes useful concepts, similar to relationship

SEQUENCE

Time order, Flashbacks,
May be partly inferred

EXTRAPOLATION

Going beyond stated facts, Predicting,
Inference, Trends, Traits, Unstated conclusions, Use of previous learning

APPRECIATION

Value, Judgments, Worth
Pleasing to reader, Is it good?
Would others think it good?
Emotional response

EVALUATION

Validity, Truthfulness
Usefulness, Reality, Opinion, Fact

AUTHOR'S INTENT

Persuasion, Goals, Propaganda, Mood, Style

SCHEMA

Plot, Script, Plan, Proposition,
Organization, Units, Networks

VOCABULARY

Word or phrase meaning in context, Figurative language, Other meanings of word

RELATIONSHIPS

Cause and effect, comparisons, Relate one part or character to another,
Anaphora referents

OTHER COMPREHENSION FACTORS

The Reader

Age, IQ,
Education,
Background, SES,
Out of school experiences
Fatigue, Health

READERS PURPOSE

Find out content, Learn,
Study for test,
Get general idea quickly,
Recreation,
Goals, Rewards

TIME

Delay, Need to remember,
Immediate post test, Action

ENVIRONMENT

Classroom, Home,
Distractions,
Light, Noise, Chair

Type of Material

Fiction, Stories,
Expository articles, Textbooks,
Advertisements,
Forms, Poetry
Different subjects (for example, history,
science)

READABILITY

Difficulty level,
Clear writing,
Personal words,
Legibility, Imagery

LENGTH

Sentence, Paragraph,
Chapter, Book

GRAPHS

Comprehend illustrations,
bar charts, maps, tables

The NEW Reading Teacher's Book of Lists, © 1985 Prentice-Hall, Inc., Englewood Cliffs, NJ 07632. By E. Fry, D. Fountoukidis, and J. Polk.

See Also List 52, Comprehension Questions;
List 55, Comprehension Thesaurus; and
List 57, Study Skills List.

55. COMPREHENSION THESAURUS

Here is a Comprehension Thesaurus with which you can generate an impressive ten thousand and eighty-seven (that's 10,087) different comprehension terms. Impress your principal by using a new one every day for the next 56 years.

Directions: Select any term from Part A and link it with any term in Part B to form a Reading Comprehension Skill. (For those who don't recognize it, this list is largely "tongue in cheek," but it does make a point about the confusing multiplicity of comprehension terminology.)

PART A: The Action

Getting	Organizing	Providing
Identifying	Outlining	Reading (for)
Understanding	Using	Following
Classifying	Locating	Previewing
Recalling	Retelling	Apprehending
Selecting	Reasoning (about)	Determining
Finding	Interpreting	Working (with)
Recognizing	Comprehending	Visualizing
Summarizing	Demonstrating	Thinking (about)
Grasping	Applying	Thinking Critically
Drawing	Obtaining	Getting Excited (about)
Evaluating	Predicting	Dealing (with)
Relating	Contrasting	Judging
Paraphrasing	Proving	Translating
Comparing	Anticipating	Synthesizing
Transforming	Internalizing	Checking
Clarifying	Sifting	Deriving
Specifying	Inferring	Integrating
Matching	Referring (to)	Actively Responding (to)
Criticizing	Drawing	Describing
Analyzing	Making	Questioning
Noting	Concluding	Verbalizing
Perceiving	Forecasting	Processing
Extending	Extrapolating	Encoding
Restating	Foreshadowing	Learning
Reacting (to)	Producing (from memory)	

PART B: The Concept

Main ideas	Ambiguous statements	Climax
Central thoughts	Mood	Outcome
Author's purpose	Tone	Objective ideas
Author's intent	Inference	Subjective ideas
Point of view	Inference about author	Events
Thought units	Conjecture	Interactions
Story content	Information	Relevancies
Details	Text information	Semantic constraints
Supporting details	Important things	Linguistic constraints
Essential details	Humor	Convictions
Specifics	Directions	Inclinations
Specific facts	Trends	Characterization
Inferences	Goals	Personal reaction
Wholes and parts	Aims	Effects
Conclusions	Principles	Comparisons
Propositions	Generalizations	Time
Propositional relationships	Universals	Event to time relationship
Schema	Abstractions	Tense
Schemata	Abstract ideas	Propaganda
Constructs	Structures	Flashbacks
Meanings	Judgments	Repetitive refrain
Scenarios	Literary style	Personification
Scripts	Elements of style	Answers to questions
Sense	Elements	Directly stated answers
Classifications	Imagery	Indirectly stated answers
Categories	Mental imagery	Extended answers
Multiple meanings	Cause and effect	Various purposes
Connotations	Organization	Validity
Denotations	Story line	Antecedents
Causal relations	Story problem	References
Sequence	Plot	Experiences
Sequence of events	Plot structure	Vicarious experiences
Sequence of ideas	Time of action	Concrete experiences
Chronological sequence	Types of literature	Concepts
Trends	Context	Familiar concepts
Seriation	Affective content	Unfamiliar concepts
Anaphora	Answers	Vocabulary
Associations	General idea	Vocabulary in context
Facts	Facts	Word Meaning
Deep structure	Concepts	Terminology
Analogies	Relationships	Descriptions
Figurative language	Lexical relationships	Criteria
Metaphors	Textual relationships	Attributes
Similes	Written works	Content

See Also List 54, Comprehension Skills.

The NEW Reading Teacher's Book of Lists, © 1985 Prentice-Hall, Inc., Englewood Cliffs, NJ 07632. By E. Fry, D. Fountoukidis, and J. Polk.

SECTION VI
Study Skills

56. TAXONOMY OF GRAPHS

This is a simplified version of a more complete Taxonomy of Graphs. Its purpose is to show some of the varieties of graphical expression used by writers and read by readers. Teachers should encourage students to use graphs to express ideas and to supplement writing. Graph comprehension can be taught using many of the same questions used to teach paragraph comprehension (main idea, inference, sequence, etc.).

An Illustrated Version of a Taxonomy of Graphs

by Edward Fry

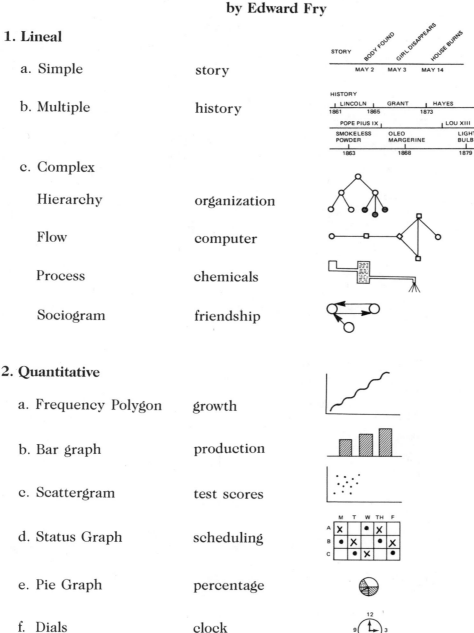

1. Lineal

  a. Simple   story

  b. Multiple   history

  c. Complex

      Hierarchy   organization

      Flow   computer

      Process   chemicals

      Sociogram   friendship

2. Quantitative

  a. Frequency Polygon   growth

  b. Bar graph   production

  c. Scattergram   test scores

  d. Status Graph   scheduling

  e. Pie Graph   percentage

  f. Dials   clock

3. Spatial

a. Two Dimensions
   (single plane)   map   floor plan

b. Three Dimensions
   (multiplane)   relief map   math shapes

4. Pictorial

a. Realistic

b. Semipictorial

c. Abstract

5. Hypothetical

a. Conceptual

b. Verbal

6. Near Graphs

a. High Verbal Outline   Main Idea
                                 a. Detail
                                 b. Another detail

b. High Numerical

Table	
25	4.2
37	6.1
71	7.3

c. Symbols

d. Decorative Design

The NEW Reading Teacher's Book of Lists, © 1985 Prentice-Hall, Inc., Englewood Cliffs, NJ 07632. By E. Fry, D. Fountoukidis, and J. Polk.

57. STUDY SKILLS LIST

These study skills should be taught throughout elementary school and into high school. Be sure to integrate them into your lessons regularly and encourage students to use them on an ongoing basis.

I. Organizing for Study
  Time planning[1]
  Place
  Tools
  Reference works

II. Reading[2]
  Using signal words[3]
  Using text aids
    —Table of Contents
    —Introductions
    —Headings
    —Summaries
    —Glossaries
    —Appendices
    —Index

  Surveying the text
  Reading to answer questions[4]
  Determining organizational patterns
    —Chronological order
    —Cause and effect
    —Comparison and contrast
    —Functional
    —Simple/Complex

  Pencil activities
    —Underlining
    —Notetaking
    —Outlining
    —Summarizing
    —Graphing[5]

  Reading for different purposes
    —Skimming[6]
    —Scanning
    —Reading to learn
    —Reading for pleasure[7]
  Increasing reading speed

---

[1]See also List 58, Time Planning.
[2]See also List 54, Comprehension Skills.
[3]See also List 50, Signal Words.
[4]See also List 52, Comprehension Questions.
[5]See also List 56, Taxonomy of Graphs.
[6]See also List 59, Skimming Illustration.
[7]See also Section IX, Books.

The NEW Reading Teacher's Book of Lists, © 1985 Prentice-Hall, Inc., Englewood Cliffs, NJ 07632. By E. Fry, D. Fountoukidis, and J. Polk.

III. Learning New Vocabulary
    Using context
    Roots, prefixes and suffixes[1]
    Using the dictionary

IV. Using Visual Aids
    Maps (reading and symbols)
    Pictures
    Graphs[2]
    Tables
    Signs and Symbols[3]

V. Listening to Lectures
    Taking notes
    Listening skills

VI. Preparing for Tests
    Making study sheets
    Making up test questions
    Recitation or self-testing
    Mnemonic devices[4]

VII. Taking Tests[5]
    Essay Exams
    Objective exams
    —Multiple choice
    —Matching
    —True-False
    Quantitative exams

VIII. Writing Research Papers
    Using the library[6]
    Using reference books
    Narrowing a topic
    Making a bibliography
    Using note cards
    Making an outline
    Writing the rough draft
    Using footnotes

---

[1]See also List 40, Greek Roots; List 41, Latin Roots; List 42, Prefixes;
    List 43, Suffixes and Meaning; and List 44 Suffixes and Grammar.
[2]See also List 56, Taxonomy of Graphs.
[3]See also List 98, General Signs and Symbols.
[4]See also List 60, Memory Aids; and List 61, Mnemonic Device.
[5]See also List 62, Test-Taking Strategies; List 63, Test and Workbook Words;
    List 64, Essay Test Words; and List 65, Important Modifiers.
[6]See also List 102, Library Classifications.

The NEW Reading Teacher's Book of Lists, © 1985 Prentice-Hall, Inc., Englewood Cliffs, NJ 07632. By E. Fry, D. Fountoukidis, and J. Polk.

58. TIME PLANNING CHART

A time planning chart is a standard study skills tool. This is a practical one, just in case you don't have one readily available for your students. Use it to encourage leisure reading and studying.

STUDY, READING, WORK, RECREATION SCHEDULE

	Mon.	Tues.	Wed.	Thurs.	Fri.	Sat.	Sun.
Study Period During School Day						a.m.	
After School After-noon						p.m.	
Early Evening							
Late Evening							

Directions: Fill in every square with one or two of the following activities:

1. STUDY: Homework assignments, activity related to courses you are taking.
2. READING: Reading primarily books for your pleasure, or, at most, supplemental or extra-interest material for course you are taking.
3. WORK: Work that you do outside of school for pay, or at home.
4. RECREATION: Talking to friends, watching TV, sports, goofing around.

See Also List 56, Taxonomy of Graphs; and List 57, Study Skills List.

59. SKIMMING ILLUSTRATION

This illustration gives a good picture of skimming. In order for students to become proficient at skimming, they need lots of practice. Twice a week for half a year isn't too much.

Usually the first paragraph will be read at average speed all the way through. It often contains an introduction or overview of what will be talked about.

Sometimes, however, the second paragraph contains the introduction or overview. In the first paragraph, the author might just be "warming up" or saying something clever to attract attention.

Reading a third paragraph completely might be unnecessary but ...   ...
...   .
...   .
...   .
...   .
...   .
...   .
the main idea is usually contained in the opening sentence

...   .
...   . topic sentence   ...   .
...   .
...   .
...   .
...   .
...   .

Besides the first sentence, the reader should get some but not all the detail from the rest of the paragraph... ...
...   .
...   .
...   .
...   .

...   .
...   .
...   .
...   .
...   .   names   ...
...   .
...   ...   date   ...   .
...   .
...   .
This tells you nothing   ...   ...
...   .
...   .
...   .

hence, sometimes the main idea is in the middle or at the end of the paragraph.

Some paragraphs merely repeat ideas ...   .   names   ...   ...
...   .
...   .
...   .

Occasionally the main idea can't be found in the opening sentence. The whole paragraph must then be read.

Then leave out a lot of the next paragraph ...   .
...   .
...   .
...   .
...   . to make up time
...   .
...   .

The NEW Reading Teacher's Book of Lists, © 1985 Prentice-Hall, Inc., Englewood Cliffs, NJ 07632. By E. Fry, D. Fountoukidis, and J. Polk.

Remember to keep up a very fast rate

... ...
... ...
... ...
... ... 800 w.p.m.
... ...
... ...
... ...

Don't be afraid to leave out half or more of each paragraph... ... ...

... ...
... ...
... ...
... ...
... ...

Don't get interested and start to read everything ... ...

... ...
... ...
... ...
... ...
... ...

skimming is work ... ...

... ...
... ...
... ...
... ...

Lowered comprehension is expected

... ...
... ... 50% ... ...
... ...
... ...
... ... not too low
... ...
... ...

Skimming practice makes it easier

... ...
... ...
... ...
... ...
... ...
... ... gain confidence ... ...
... ...
... ...
... ...

Pehaps you won't get anything at all from a few paragraphs ... ...

... ...
... ...
... ...
... ...
... ... don't worry
... ...
... ...

Skimming has many uses ... ...

... ...
... ... reports ...
... ...
... ... newspapers ... ...
... ...
... ... supplementary
... ... text ... ...

The ending paragraphs might be read more fully as often they contain a summary.

Remember that the importance of skimming is to get only the author's main ideas at a very fast speed.

See Also List 54, Comprehension Skills; and List 57, Study Skills List.

60. MEMORY AIDS

Here are some techniques that are useful in memorizing. Show your students how to use these techniques when they study for your tests.

1. **Study actively.** You are more likely to remember material if you write it down or say it out loud than if you merely read it or hear it.
2. **Make sure you understand.** If you understand what you're trying to learn, you'll find that you can remember it better and for a longer period of time.
3. **Associate new information with old.** When learning something new, try to compare it with something similar that you are already familiar with.
4. **Make up examples.** When learning general principles, try to make up examples of your own. In addition to helping you remember the principle better, this will also help you check your understanding. If you're not sure that your example is correct, check it with your teacher.
5. **Visualize what you're trying to learn.** This can involve creating a mental image or drawing a graph (a time line to help with time sequences, a hierarchical chart for organizations or family trees, etc.). (See List 56, Taxonomy of Graphs, for other ideas.)
6. **Group items into categories.** If you have to learn a long list of things, try to group simiar items together. For example, to memorize a shopping list you would want to group vegetables together, meats together, dairy products, and so on.
7. **Be selective.** Most of the time you will not be able to memorize every detail, and if you try you may end up learning almost nothing. Concentrate on general concepts and a few examples to go with each. Pay particular attention to information the teacher indicates is important. Teachers frequently send signals to help you identify what is most important (information written on the chalk board, or repeated several times orally, or prefaced by statements such as "You should know this."). (See List 50, Signal Words.)
8. **Space your study sessions.** You are more apt to remember material if you study over several days rather than in one crash session.
9. **Use key words.** For example, to learn this list of suggestions for improving your memory, pick out a key word for each suggestion and then learn just the key words. To learn items 1 through 9, you might choose the following key words: active, understand, associate, examples, visualize, group, selective, space, key words.
10. **Learn how many items are on the list.** When learning lists, make sure you learn the number of items on the list. For example, in item 9, it is not enough to learn the key words. You also should learn that there are nine items. This will aid you in recalling all of the items.

The NEW Reading Teacher's Book of Lists, © 1985 Prentice-Hall, Inc., Englewood Cliffs, NJ 07632. By E. Fry, D. Fountoukidis, and J. Polk.

The NEW Reading Teacher's Book of Lists, © 1985 Prentice-Hall, Inc., Englewood Cliffs, NJ 07632. By E. Fry, D. Fountoukidis, and J. Polk.

11. **Rhymes and sayings can be helpful.** For example, how many of us can remember the number of days in the months without:

> Thirty days has September,
> April, June, and November;
> All the rest have thirty-one,
> Excepting February alone,
> Which has just four and twenty-four,
> And every leap year one day more.

12. **Use alliteration.** Repeating initial sounds can be helpful in remembering information. For example, to remind sailors entering a harbor to keep the red harbor light on their right, they learn:

> Red to right returning.

13. **Try acrostics.** Sometimes you can use the first letter of a list of words to form another word or sentence. These are referred to as acrostics and are similar to acronyms (see List 34, Acronyms and Initializations). For example, "ROY G. BIV" can help us remember the colors of the spectrum: Red, Orange, Yellow, Green, Blue, Indigo, and Violet.

14. **Exaggerate.** This is especially helpful when you are using visualization. Try to make your images big, colorful, and with lots of details. This will make them interesting and easier to remember.

15. **Have confidence.** Don't go around saying, "I can't remember names." You can if you try.

See Also List 57, Study Skills,
and List 61, Mnemonics Device.

61. MNEMONIC DEVICE

This mnemonic device has actually been known for centuries. It is still impressive as a study technique. Done with a bit of showmanship, it will provide great entertainment also. Your students can impress their parents by memorizing a list of twenty objects in just a few minutes (after they study and learn the mnemonic device).

The following is (1) an interesting trick with which the students can interest and amuse their friends, (2) a serious experiment in psychology clearly demonstrates the power of associative learning, and (3) a useful skill that can sometimes help the student to remember a long and not necessarily related list of facts (useful in passing some examinations and in going to the grocery shop).

First, let us give an example of how the trick might be done in school. The student asks his or her friends to call out slowly a list of objects—any objects. The friends call out "clock-chair-hammer," and so on. Often a friend will write them down on the blackboard so that the others will not forget them: "1. clock; 2. chair; 3. hammer." The student does not look at the blackboard. After twenty objects, or however many the students decide, someone calls a halt and immediately announces that he or she has memorized all the objects and can call them out in any order—forwards, backwards, every other way—in fact, he or she can tell them the number of any object (without looking at the board). The friends say that they do not believe the student; one of them asks, "What is number 3?" The student immediately replies, "Hammer." Then after a few such questions, the student demonstrates complete mastery by calling off the whole list either forwards or backwards.

Now almost anyone can do this trick, once he or she knows how. The secret lies in memorizing a set of "key objects." You must first take a little time to memorize (make mental associations between) a "key object" and the number. For example, the key object for number one is "sun" and the key object for number two is "shoe," and so on. (see the list on the following page). You must learn the association between the key object and the number so well that whenever you say "one" to yourself you visualize "sun." You should easily be able to learn the first ten key objects and their numbers in a short learning session on the first day, ten more the next day, and so on. After you have learned the key objects well, you are ready to do the trick. When the first friend calls out the word "clock" as the first item for you to memorize, you must mentally picture a "clock" next to a "sun," which is your key object for number 1. After you have made a clear mental picture of a clock next to a sun, you then allow the next friend to call out a second item to be memorized, such as "chair"; you then mentally picture a chair with your key object, a shoe, sitting on it. You control the rate at which your friends can call out names of objects; at first, you will go rather slowly, but after you have done the trick a few times you can go more rapidly.

The NEW Reading Teacher's Book of Lists, © 1985 Prentice-Hall, Inc., Englewood Cliffs, NJ 07632. By E. Fry, D. Fountoukidis, and J. Polk.

Key Objects

1 Sun	11 Elephant
2 Shoe	12 Twig
3 Tree	13 Throne
4 Door	14 Fort
5 Hive	15 Fire
6 Sticks	16 Silver coin
7 Heaven (an angel)	17 Sea
8 Gate	18 Apron
9 Sign	19 Knife
10 Pen	20 Baby

There are several important learning principles involved in this trick that also apply to other learning. One is the "mental visualization"—it is a powerful factor in memory, and can be developed with relatively little practice. Another important factor is self-confidence; if you say beforehand "I can't do it" you probably won't be able to. Self-confidence is also important during the trick, for you must concentrate only on the object to be remembered, you cannot worry about "Did I learn the first three things?" Exaggeration of mental pictures, making them large, brightly colored, or even purposefully distorted, will often aid memory.

This type of memorizing is not a new discovery. It was well known by the ancient people of both Greece and India.

The key objects have been chosen to take advantage of another learning principle—that of rhyming. The first ten objects all have an end-rhyme with the name of the number. The second ten objects all begin with the same sound as the name of the number, except for 20, where a rough rhyme is used to avoid confusion with 12. If you wish to extend the list of objects to 50 or 100, or to change any of the suggested list, you can choose any key objects that you wish. The important thing is that they be easily visualized and never change.

See Also List 56, Taxonomy of Graphs; List 60, Memory Aids; and List 62, Test-Taking Strategies.

SECTION VII
Testing

62. TEST-TAKING STRATEGIES

Teaching these strategies should help make your students "test wise" and improve their performance on essay and objective tests. Although a few students may use these strategies on their own, most will need instruction and encouragement.

General

- If you have a choice of seats, try to sit in a place where you will be least disturbed (e.g., not by a door).
- When you first receive the test, glance over it, noting the types of questions and the numbers of points to be awarded for them.
- Budget your time, making sure you allow sufficient time for the questions that are worth the most points.
- Read directions carefully. Underline important direction words, such as *choose one, briefly,* and so on.
- Start with the questions that are easiest.
- Be alert for information in some questions that may provide help with other more difficult questions. If you find such information, be sure to note it before you forget.

Objective Tests

- Before you start, find out if there is a penalty for guessing and if you can choose more than one answer.
- Read the questions and all possible answers carefully.
- Be especially careful about questions with the choices *all of the above* and *none of the above.*
- Underline key words and qualifiers such as *never, always,* and so on.
- Answer all of the questions you know first.
- Make a mark next to those you can't answer so you can go back to them later.
- After you complete the questions you know, go back and reread the ones you didn't answer the first time.
- If you still can't answer a question the second time through, here are some strategies to try:
  1. For a multiple choice item, read the question; then stop and try to think of an answer. Look to see if one of the choices is similar to your answer.
  2. Start by eliminating those answers that you know are not correct and then choose among the remaining alternatives.
  3. Read through all of the answers very carefully, and then go back to the question. Sometimes you can pick up clues just by thinking about the different answers you have been given to choose from.

4. Try paraphrasing the question and then recalling some examples.

5. For a multiple choice item, try reading the question separately with each alternative answer.

- If there is no penalty for guessing, make sure you answer all questions, even if you have to guess blindly.
- If there is a penalty for guessing, you usually should guess if you can eliminate one of the choices.
- If you have time, check over the exam. Change an answer only if you can think of a good reason to do so. Generally you're better off if you stick with your first choice.

Essay Tests

- Read through all of the questions carefully.
- Mark the important direction words that tell you what you're to do: *compare, trace, list,* and so on.
- Number the parts of the question so you don't forget to answer all of them.
- Take time to try to understand what the question is asking. Don't jump to conclusions on the basis of a familiar word or two.
- As you read through the questions, briefly jot down ideas that come into your mind.
- Briefly outline your answers before you begin to write. Refer back to the question to be sure your answer is focused on the question.
- As you write, be careful to stick to your outline.
- If possible, allow generous margins so you can add information later if you need to.
- Don't spend so much time on one question that you don't have time for other questions.
- If you have time, proofread what you have written. This is a good time to double-check to make sure you have answered all of the parts of the questions.
- If you run short of time, quickly outline answers to the questions that remain. List the information without worrying about complete sentences.

The NEW Reading Teacher's Book of Lists, © 1985 Prentice-Hall, Inc., Englewood Cliffs, NJ 07632. By E. Fry, D. Fountoukidis, and J. Polk.

Quantitative Tests

- Read the questions carefully to make sure you understand what is being asked.
- Do the questions you are sure of first.
- Budget your time to allow for questions worth the most points.
- Don't just write answers. Make sure to show your work.
- As you work out answers try to do it neatly and to write down each step. This helps you avoid careless mistakes and makes it possible for the tester to follow your work. It may make the difference between partial credit and no credit for a wrong answer.
- Check your answer when you finish to make sure it makes sense. If it doesn't seem logical, check again.
- If you are missing information needed to calculate an answer, check to see if it was given in a previous problem or if you can compute it in some way.
- Check to see if you have used all of the information provided. You may not always need to, but you should double-check to be sure.
- If you have time, go back and check your calculations.

See Also List 50, Signal Words;
List 52, Comprehension Questions;
List 58, Time Planning Chart;
List 60, Memory Aids;
List 61, Mnemonic Device;
List 64, Essay Test Words;
List 65, Important Modifiers; and
List 66, Cloze Variations.

63. TEST AND WORKBOOK WORDS

These words are found in directions in workbook exercises and in tests. It is absolutely essential that students understand and pay close attention to them. These key words are perhaps most effectively taught in context. Each time you give students a test or a written exercise, point them out and review their meaning.

answer sheet	definition	name	reason
best	directions	next	rhyming
blank	does not belong	none of these	right
booklet	end	not true	row
check your work	error	opposite	same as
choose	example	pairs	sample
circle	finish	paragraph	section
column	following	passage	second
compare	go on to next page	print	stop
complete	item	probably	true
contrast	mark	put an X	underline
correct	match	question	wait for directions
crossout	missing	read	

64. ESSAY TEST WORDS

These words occur in essay test questions. In order for students to perform well on essay tests, they must understand the types of answers that these words require. When you give essay tests, try to use a variety of these words and take the opportunity to instruct the students on their meaning.

analyze	define	formulate	point out	show how
apply	demonstrate	general	predict	significance
argue	describe	generalize	propose	solve
assess	develop	give an example of	prove	specify
categorize	diagram	identify	provide	state
cause	differentiate	illustrate	rank	suggest
cite evidence	discuss	interpret	react	summarize
classify	distinguish	justify	reason	support
compare	draw conclusions	list	recall	survey
construct	effect	mention	recommend	tell
contrast	enumerate	organize	relate	trace
convince	estimate	outline	relationship	utilize
create	evaluate	paraphrase	select	why
criticize	explain			

65. IMPORTANT MODIFIERS

These are easy words, but ones sometimes skipped over by careless readers. Failure to pay attention to these modifiers can result in a wrong answer, even though the student actually knows the right answer. One way to help avoid this is to teach your students to underline these words as they take tests.

all	best	few	less	most	often	sometimes
always	every	good	many	never	seldom	usually
bad	equal	invariably	more	none	some	worst

The NEW Reading Teacher's Book of Lists, © 1985 Prentice-Hall, Inc., Englewood Cliffs, NJ 07632. By E. Fry, D. Fountoukidis, and J. Polk.

66. CLOZE VARIATIONS

The NEW Reading Teacher's Book of Lists, © 1985 Prentice-Hall, Inc., Englewood Cliffs, NJ 07632. By E. Fry, D. Fountoukidis, and J. Polk.

Cloze is a sentence completion technique in which a word (or part of a word or several words) is omitted and the student fills in the missing part. Cloze can be used as a test or drill of reading comprehension or language ability, as a research tool, or as a measure to estimate readability or passage difficulty.

To estimate the readability or difficulty level appropriate for instruction, one suggested criterion is that a student be able to fill in 35 to 44 percent of the exact missing words when every fifth word is deleted from a 250-word passage.

Cloze passages can be made easily by the teacher on any subject or any type of material. All you need to do is omit parts of the passage and ask the students to fill in the missing parts. Here is a list of some possible variations:

1. Passage Variations—different kinds of passage to start with

    a. Content of Passage
        (1) Science
        (2) History
        (3) Literature, etc.

    b. Difficulty of Passage
        (1) Readability level
        (2) Imageability
        (3) Legibility

    c. Length of Passage
        (1) Sentence
        (2) Paragraph
        (3) 500 words, etc.

2. Deletion Variations—different kinds of deletions or blanks

    a. Mechanical—automatic or no judgment used in deletions
        (1) Delete every nth word (5th, 10th, etc.).
        (2) Randomized deletion but average every nth word.

    b. Selective—judgment used in selecting deletions
        (1) Delete structure words or content words only.
        (2) Delete only one part of speech. (For example, nouns omitted.)
        (3) Delete particular letters (blends, bound morphemes, prefixes, vowels, consonants, etc.).
        (4) Delete only words or letters that best fit a particular skill objective.

    c. Size of Deletion
        (1) One word, two words, etc.
        (2) One letter, two letters, etc.

The NEW Reading Teacher's Book of Lists, © 1985 Prentice-Hall, Inc., Englewood Cliffs, NJ 07632. By E. Fry, D. Fountoukidis, and J. Polk.

3. Cueing Variations—different prompts or hints

  a. No cues.

  b. Multiple choice (referred to as "Maze"). If this is used, distractor words (wrong choices) can be varied as follows:
    (1) Similar to correct answer in length or different.
    (2) Similar or different in phonemes.
    (3) Similar or different in meaning.

  c. One or more letters, depending on how many letters have been deleted.

4. Administration Variations

  a. Preparation
    (1) Student reads complete passage (no blanks) before answering.
    (2) Student listens to complete passage before answering.
    (3) Student is given a brief introduction to passage.
    (4) No preparation.

  b. Answering
    (1) Student reads passage and writes answers.
    (2) Teacher reads passage orally and student writes answers.
    (3) Teacher reads passage orally and student gives answers orally.
    (4) Student told to guess or not to guess.

5. Scoring Variations

  a. Score as correct only exact word, or score synonym as correct.

  b. Correct spelling required or not required.

  c. Self-correction, teacher correction, other-student correction.

  d. Discuss answers or no discussion.

See Also List 52, Comprehension Questions;
and List 70, Basic Sentence Patterns.

67. TESTING TERMS

The NEW Reading Teacher's Book of Lists, © 1985 Prentice-Hall, Inc., Englewood Cliffs, NJ 07632. By E. Fry, D. Fountoukidis, and J. Polk.

Most school districts give tests. Most teachers get the results of those tests. What do those test scores mean? How do you interpret them? One place to start is with an understanding of the terminology that test makers use. Familiarity with these terms will help you to explain test results to interested and sometimes anxious students and parents.

Achievement tests. Tests that measure how much students have learned in a particular subject area.

Aptitude tests. Tests that attempt to predict how well students will do in learning new subject matter in the future.

CEEB test scores. College Entrance Examination Board test scores. This type of score is used by exams such as the Scholastic Aptitude Test. It has a mean of 500 and a standard deviation of 100.

Correlation coefficient. A measure of the strength and direction (positive or negative) of the relationship between two things.

Criterion-referenced tests. Tests for which the performance of the test taker is compared with a fixed standard or criterion. The primary purpose is to determine if the test taker has mastered a particular unit sufficiently to proceed to the next unit.

Diagnostic tests. Tests that are used to identify individual students' strengths and weaknesses in a particular subject area.

Grade equivalent scores. The grade level for which a score is the real or estimated average. For example, a grade equivalent score of 3.5 is the average score of students halfway through the third grade.

Mean. The arithmetic average of a group of scores.

Median. The middle score in a group of scores.

Mode. The score that was obtained by the largest number of test takers.

Normal distribution. A bell-shaped distribution of test scores in which scores are distributed symmetrically around the mean and where the mean, median, and mode are the same.

Norming population. The group of people to whom the test was administered in order to establish performance standards for various age or grade levels. When the norming population is composed of students from various sections of the country, the resulting standards are called *national norms*. When the norming population is drawn from a local school or school district, the standards are referred to as *local norms*.

Norm-referenced tests. Tests for which the results of the test taker are compared with the performance of others (the norming population) who have taken the test.

Percentile rank. A comparison of an individual's raw score with the raw score of others who took the test (usually this is a comparison with the norming population). This comparison tells the test taker the percentage of other test takers whose scores fall below his or her own score.

Raw score. The initial score assigned to test performance. This score usually is the number correct; however, sometimes it may include a correction for guessing.

Reliability. A measure of the extent to which a test is consistent in measuring whatever it purports to measure. Reliability coefficients range from 0 to 1. In order to be considered highly reliable a test should have a reliability coefficient of 0.90 or above. There are several types of reliability coefficients: *parallel-form* reliability (the correlation of performance on two different forms of a test), *test-retest* reliability (the correlation of test scores from two different administrations of the same test to the same population), *split-half* reliability (the correlation between two halves of the same test), and *internal consistency* reliability (a reliability coefficient computed using a Kuder-Richardson formula).

Standard deviation. A measure of the variability of test scores. If most scores are close to the mean, the standard deviation will be small. If the scores have a wide range, then the standard deviation will be large.

Standard error of measurement (SEM). An estimate of the amount of measurement error in a test. This provides an estimate of how much a person's actual test score may vary from his or her hypothetical true score. The larger the SEM, the less confidence can be placed in the score as a reflection of an individual's true ability.

Standardized tests. Tests that have been given to groups of students under standardized conditions and for which norms have been established.

Stanine scores. Whole number scores between 1 and 9 which have a mean of 5 and a standard deviation of 2.

True score. The score that would be obtained on a given test if that test were perfectly reliable. This is a hypothetical score.

Validity. The extent to which a test measures what it is supposed to measure. Two common types of validity are *content validity* (the extent to which the content of the test covers situations and subject matter about which conclusions will be drawn) and *predictive validity* (the extent to which predictions made from the test are confirmed by evidence gathered at some later time).

See Also List 63, Test and Workbook Words;
List 64, Essay Test Words; and List 65,
Important Modifiers.

The NEW Reading Teacher's Book of Lists, © 1985 Prentice-Hall, Inc., Englewood Cliffs, NJ 07632. By E. Fry, D. Fountoukidis, and J. Polk.

SECTION VIII
Language Arts

68. PARTS OF SPEECH

Over the centuries that English has been spoken and written, patterns of word usage have developed. These patterns form the grammar or syntax for the language and govern the use of the eight parts of speech.

NOUN. A word that names a person, place, thing, or idea. It can act or be acted upon. *Examples:*

> Roger, Father McGovern, the Yankees, bowlers, cousins, neighborhood, Baltimore, attic, Asia, Newark Airport, Golden Gate Bridge, glove, class, triangle, goodness, strength, stupidity, joy, perfection.

PRONOUN. A word that is used in place of a noun. *Examples:*

> he, you, they, them, it, her, our, your, its, their, anybody, both, nobody, someone, several, himself, ourselves, themselves, yourself, itself, who, whom, which, what, whose.

ADJECTIVE. A word that is used to describe a noun or pronoun, telling what kind, how many or which one. *Examples:*

> green, enormous, slinky, original, Italian, some, few, eleven, all, none, that, this, these, those, third.

VERB. A word that shows physical or mental action, being, or state of being. *Examples:*

> swayed, cowered, dance, study, hold, think, imagine, love, approve, considered, am, is, was, were, has been, seems, appears, looks, feels, remains.

ADVERB. A word that is used to describe a verb, telling where, how, or when. *Examples:*

> quietly, lovingly, skillfully, slyly, honestly, very, quite, extremely, too, moderately, seldom, never, often, periodically, forever.

CONJUNCTION. A word that is used to join words or groups of words. *Examples:*

> and, or, either, neither, but, because, while, however, since, for.

PREPOSITION. A word used to show the relationship of a noun or pronoun to another word. *Examples:*

> across, below, toward, within, over, above, before, until, of, beyond, from, during, after, at, against.

INTERJECTION. A word that is used alone to express strong emotion. *Examples:*

> Heavens! Cheers! Oh! Aha! Darn!

See Also List 43, Suffixes and Meaning;
List 68, Parts of Speech; and List 69, Irregular Verb Forms.

The NEW Reading Teacher's Book of Lists, © 1985 Prentice-Hall, Inc., Englewood Cliffs, NJ 07632. By E. Fry, D. Fountoukidis, and J. Polk.

69. IRREGULAR VERB FORMS

Most rules have exceptions, and exceptions can cause problems. Here is an extensive list of verbs and their principal parts that do not follow the usual pattern.

Present	Past	Past Participle
am	was	been
are (pl.)	were	been
beat	beat	beaten
begin	began	begun
bend	bent or bended	bent or bended
bet	bet	bet
bite	bit	bitten
bleed	bled	bled
blow	blew	blown
break	broke	broken
bring	brought	brought
build	built	built
burst	burst	burst
catch	caught	caught
choose	chose	chosen
come	came	come
cost	cost	cost
creep	crept	crept
cut	cut	cut
dig	dug	dug
dive	dived or dove	dived
do	did	done
draw	drew	drawn
dream	dreamed or dreamt	dreamed or dreamt
drink	drank	drunk
drive	drove	driven
eat	ate	eaten
fall	fell	fallen
feed	fed	fed
feel	felt	felt
fight	fought	fought
fly	flew	flown
forbid	forbade	forbidden
forget	forgot	forgotten
forgive	forgave	forgiven
freeze	froze	frozen
get	got	got or gotten
give	gave	given
go	went	gone
grow	grew	grown
grind	ground	ground
hang	hung or hanged	hung
has	had	had
hear	heard	heard

The NEW Reading Teacher's Book of Lists, © 1985 Prentice-Hall, Inc., Englewood Cliffs, NJ 07632. By E. Fry, D. Fountoukidis, and J. Polk.

Present	Past	Past Participle
hide	hid	hidden
hold	held	held
hurt	hurt	hurt
is	was	has been
keep	kept	kept
kneel	kneeled or knelt	kneeled or knelt
know	knew	known
lay	laid	laid
leap	leaped or leapt	leaped or leapt
leave	left	left
lend	lent	lent
let	let	let
lie	lay	lain
light	lit	lit
lose	lost	lost
make	made	made
mean	meant	meant
mow	mowed	mowed or mown
put	put	put
read	read	read
ride	rode	ridden
ring	rang	rung
rise	rose	risen
run	ran	run
say	said	said
saw	sawed	sawed or sawn
see	saw	seen
sell	sold	sold
sew	sewed	sewed or sewn
set	set	set
shake	shook	shaken
shed	shed	shed
shine	shined or shone	shined or shone
shoot	shot	shot
show	showed	shown or showed
shrink	shrank or shrunk	shrunk
shut	shut	shut
sing	sang	sung
sink	sank	sunk
sit	sat	sat
sleep	slept	slept
slide	slid	slid
sow	sowed	sowed or sown
speak	spoke	spoken
spend	spent	spent
spin	spun	spun
split	split	split
spread	spread	spread
spring	sprang or sprung	sprung

Present	Past	Past Participle
stand	stood	stood
steal	stole	stolen
stick	stuck	stuck
sting	stung	stung
strike	struck	struck
string	strung	strung
spit	spit	spit
sweat	sweat or sweated	sweat or sweated
sweep	swept	swept
swear	swore	sworn
swim	swam or swum	swum
swing	swung or swang	swung
take	took	taken
teach	taught	taught
tear	tore	torn
tell	told	told
think	thought	thought
throw	threw	thrown
understand	understood	understood
wake	woke or waked	woken or waked
wear	wore	worn
weave	wove	woven
weep	wept	wept
wet	wet	wet
win	won	won
wind	wound	wound
write	wrote	written

See Also List 43, Suffixes and Meaning;
and List 68, Parts of Speech.

The NEW Reading Teacher's Book of Lists, © 1985 Prentice-Hall, Inc., Englewood Cliffs, NJ 07632. By E. Fry, D. Fountoukidis, and J. Polk.

70. BASIC SENTENCE PATTERNS

Parts of speech are put together to form sentences. The list of basic sentence patterns and variations show the most common arrangements of words.

N/V	noun/verb	*Children sang.*
N/V/N	noun/verb/noun	*Bill paid the worker.*
N/V/ADV	noun/verb/adverb	*Ann sewed quickly.*
N/LV/N	noun/linking verb/noun	*Arthur is President.*
N/LV/ADJ	noun/linking verb/adjective	*Chris looks sleepy.*
N/V/N/N	noun/verb/noun/noun	*Chuck gave Marie flowers.*

VARIATIONS OF BASIC SENTENCE PATTERNS

NEGATIVE—*It is raining./It is not raining.*

QUESTION—*The bottle is empty./Is the bottle empty?*

USE OF THERE—*A man is at the door./There is a man at the door.*

REQUEST—*You mow the grass./Mow the grass.*

PASSIVE—*The dog chased the fox./The fox was chased by the dog.*

POSSESSIVE—*Robert owns this car./This is Robert's car.*

See Also List 71, Punctuation Guidelines, and List 72, Capitalization Guidelines.

The NEW Reading Teacher's Book of Lists, © 1985 Prentice-Hall, Inc., Englewood Cliffs, NJ 07632. By E. Fry, D. Fountoukidis, and J. Polk.

71. PUNCTUATION GUIDELINES

Review these guidelines with your students regularly. Have students refer to them when proofreading their writing.

Use a PERIOD (.)

—At the end of a statement or command
The rain suddenly stopped.

—After abbreviations or initials
Ave., A.M., B.T. Hayes, Thurs.

—In decimals
$2.75

Use a COMMA (,)

—In dates
February 1, 1950

—To separate city and state
Elizabeth, New Jersey

—To set off direct quotations
Carol said, "Let's go."
"If we leave now," she said, "we'll be on time."

—After addressing a person directly
Alicia, would you like an apple?

—After "yes" or "no" at the beginning of a sentence
No, I would like an orange.

—To separate words, phrases, or clauses in a series
Jen, Chris, Dave, and Ryan raced.
I looked in the cellar, behind the garage, and in the attic.

—After the greeting and closing in letters
Dear Anthony, Sincerely,

—To set off interrupting elements
Alice, the daughter, answered.
Reading, I believe, is a worthy pastime.
Memorial Day, May 30, is the day of the picnic.

The NEW Reading Teacher's Book of Lists, © 1985 Prentice-Hall, Inc., Englewood Cliffs, NJ 07632. By E. Fry, D. Fountoukidis, and J. Polk.

The NEW Reading Teacher's Book of Lists, © 1985 Prentice-Hall, Inc., Englewood Cliffs, NJ 07632. By E. Fry, D. Fountoukidis, and J. Polk.

Use a QUESTION MARK (?)

—At the end of an inquiry or question
Where did she go?
She did?
It's impossible, isn't it?

—To express doubt
He weighs 250 (?) pounds.

Use the EXCLAMATION MARK (!)

—After a word or words that show strong feeling or surprise
It's a miracle! Fire!

Use an APOSTROPHE (')

—In contractions—to show a letter is missing
won't, couldn't, we'll, can't

—With possessive forms to show ownership
reporter's notes, teachers' voices

Use QUOTATION MARKS (" ")

—Around a title of a story, poem or song
I heard "Jingle Bells" played by the school band.

—Around direct quotations
Jennifer reported, "The horse's saddle is missing."

—When using slang or special meaning
It is "bunk."

Use PARENTHESES ( )

—To set off or supplement any information
He was two meters (over six feet) tall.

—To set off numbers or letters in a sentence
You have two choices: a) dinner at the Plaza, or b) lunch at the cafeteria.

Use a COLON (:)

—In a business letter or memo
Dear Sir:

To: From:

—In expressions of time
7:15 A.M.   11:59 P.M.

—Before a list or series
There are only three candidates: Mark, Sara, and Arnold.

—Before a strong assertion
We have one goal: to elect Marsha Steward mayor.

—To show the speaker in a dialogue
Mary: I'll ask her opinion.
Al: No, I'd rather ask myself.

—In ratios
The proportion of oil to gas is 1:3.

Use a SEMICOLON (;)

—To join independent clauses
Elise read the book; Alaine saw the movie; Liz did both.

Note: A comma may also separate independent clauses.

See Also List 70, Basic Sentence Patterns;
and List 72, Capitalization Guidelines.

The NEW Reading Teacher's Book of Lists, © 1985 Prentice-Hall, Inc., Englewood Cliffs, NJ 07632. By E. Fry, D. Fountoukidis, and J. Polk.

72. CAPITALIZATION GUIDELINES

The NEW Reading Teacher's Book of Lists, © 1985 Prentice-Hall, Inc., Englewood Cliffs, NJ 07632. By E. Fry, D. Fountoukidis, and J. Polk.

Review these guidelines with your students and provide practice exercises for problem areas. Give "proofreading" assignments to help students become sensitive to the proper use of upper case letters.

Capitalize the pronoun I.

I often sleep late on weekends.

Capitalize the first word of any sentence.

Kittens are playful.

Capitalize the first word and all important words in titles of books, magazines, newspapers, stories, etc.

The Lion, the Witch, and the Wardrobe

Capitalize names of specific people, places, events, date, and documents.

Eunice Jones, Toronto, Fourth of July, Thanksgiving, September, the Constitution

Capitalize the names of organizations and trade names.

Ford Motor Company, Tide detergent

Capitalize titles of respect.

Mr. Cox, Ms. Blake, Judge Rand

Capitalize names of races, languages, religions, and deity.

Negro, German, Catholic, the Almighty, Jehovah

Capitalize the first word in a direct quotation.

Ann inquired, "Where is the suntan lotion?"

See Also List 70, Basic Sentence Patterns; and List 71, Punctuation Guidelines.

73. SYLLABLES

The teaching of syllabication rules is somewhat controversial. Some say you should, and some say it is not worth the effort. Syllables sometimes are part of phonics lessons because syllabication affects vowel sounds (for example, an open vowel rule), and sometimes they are part of spelling or English lessons. There is no close agreement on various lists of syllabication rules, and some of the rules have plenty of exceptions. We are not urging you to teach them, but neither are we urging you to refrain from doing so.

Syllabication Rules*

Rule 1. VCV†	A consonant between two vowels tends to go with the second vowel unless the first vowel is accented and short.
	Example: *bro-ken, wag-on*
Rule 2. VCCV	Divide two consonants between vowels unless they are a blend or digraph.
	Example: *pic-ture, ush-er*
Rule 3. VCCCV	When there are three consonants between two vowels, divide between the blend or the digraph and the other consonant.
	Example: *an-gler*
Rule 4. Affixes	Prefixes always form separate syllables (*un-hap-py*), and suffixes form separate syllables only in the following cases:

a. The suffix -*y* tends to pick up the preceding consonant.

Example: *fligh-ty*

b. The suffix -*ed* tends to form a separate syllable only when it follows a root that ends in *d* or *t*.

Example: *plant-ed.*

c. The suffix -*s* never forms a syllable except when it follows an *e*.

Example: *at-oms, cours-es*

Rule 5. Compounds	Always divide compound words.
	Example: *black-bird*
Rule 6. Final *le*	Final *le* picks up the preceding consonant to form a syllable.
	Example: *ta-ble*

*Source: P. Costigan, *A Validation of the Fry Syllabification Generalization*. Unpublished master's thesis. Rutgers University, New Brunswick, NJ, 1977. Available from ERIC.

*†V = vowel; C = consonant.

The NEW Reading Teacher's Book of Lists, © 1985 Prentice-Hall, Inc., Englewood Cliffs, NJ 07632. By E. Fry, D. Fountoukidis, and J. Polk.

Rule 7. Vowel
Clusters

Do not split common vowel clusters, such as:

a. *R*-controlled vowels (*ar, er, ir, or,* and *ur*).

Example: *ar-ti-cle*

b. Long vowel digraphs (*ea, ee, ai, oa,* and *ow*).

Example: *fea-ture*

c. Broad *o* clusters (*au, aw,* and *al*).

Example: *au-di-ence*

d. Diphthongs (*oi, oy, ou,* and *ow*).

Example: *thou-sand*

e. Double *o* like *oo*.

Example: *moon*

Rule 8. Vowel
Problems

Every syllable must have one and only one vowel sound.

a. The letter *e* at the end of a word is silent.

Example: *come*

b. The letter *y* at the end or in the middle of a word operates
as a vowel.

Example: *ver-y, cy-cle*

c. Two vowels together with separate sounds form separate
syllables.

Example: *po-li-o*

Common Syllables

These are the 150 most common unweighted nonword graphemic syllables in the English language, ranked in order of frequency.*

McGuffey and the New England Primer both made extensive use of syllables in teaching beginning reading. Modern teachers and teaching methods do not.

Syllables may or may not come back into favor as a teaching unit. In the meantime, dictionaries use them, and a few, mostly remedial, teaching methods use them.

1	ing	35	ers	70	ful	105	land	140	ward
	er		ment		ger		light		age
	a		or		low		ob		ba
	ly		tions		ni		of		but
5	ed		ble		par		pos		cit
	i	40	der	75	son	110	tain	145	cle
	es		ma		tle		den		co
	re		na		day		ings		cov
	tion		si		ny		mag		da
10	in		un		pen		ments		dif
	e	45	at	80	pre	115	set	150	ence
	con		dis		tive		some		ern
	y		ca		car		sub		eve
	ter		cal		ci		sur		hap
15	ex		man		mo		ters		ies
	al	50	ap	85	on	120	tu		
	de		po		ous		af		
	com		sion		pi		au		
	o		vi		se		cy		
20	di		el		ten		fa		
	en	55	est	90	tor	125	im		
	an		la		ver		li		
	ty		lar		ber		lo		
	ry		pa		can		men		
25	u		ture		dy		min		
	ti	60	for	95	et	130	mon		
	ri		is		it		op		
	be		mer		mu		out		
	per		pe		no		rec		
30	to		ra		ple		ro		
	pro	65	so	100	cu	135	sen		
	ac		ta		fac		side		
	ad		as		fer		tal		
	ar		col		gen		tic		
			fi		ic		ties		

*Sakiey, Fry, Goss & Loldman (1980). Syllable Frequency Count. *Visible Language XIV,* 2.

See Also List 32, Compound Words; List 42, Prefixes;
List 43, Suffixes; List 48, Phonics Example Words.

The NEW Reading Teacher's Book of Lists, © 1985 Prentice-Hall, Inc., Englewood Cliffs, NJ 07632. By E. Fry, D. Fountoukidis, and J. Polk.

74. DESCRIPTIVE WORDS

What do telling tales, and writing poetry or reports have in common? They depend on descriptive words to create vivid and accurate images in the reader's mind. A good stock of descriptive words will bolster the quality of your students' writing exercises. Use these lists of adjectives and adverbs to nudge reluctant writers into developing characters and setting, or to help students "retire" overused words.

Ability—Condition

able	confident	gentle	lucky	smooth
adequate	courageous	hardy	manly	spirited
alive	curious	healthy	mighty	stable
assured	daring	heavy	modern	steady
authoritative	determined	heroic	open	stouthearted
bold	durable	important	outstanding	strong
brainy	dynamic	influential	powerful	super
brave	eager	innocent	real	sure
busy	easy	intense	relaxed	tame
careful	effective	inquisitive	rich	tough
capable	energetic	jerky	robust	victorious
cautious	fearless	knotted	secure	virile
clever	firm	light	sharp	zealous
competent	forceful	lively	shy	
concerned	gallant	loose	skillful	

Anger—Hostility

agitated	combative	evil	irritated	rude
aggravated	contrary	fierce	mad	savage
aggressive	cool	furious	mean	severe
angry	cranky	hard	nasty	spiteful
annoyed	creepy	harsh	obnoxious	tense
arrogant	cross	hateful	obstinate	terse
belligerent	cruel	hostile	outraged	vicious
biting	defiant	impatient	perturbed	vindictive
blunt	disagreeable	inconsiderate	repulsive	violent
bullying	enraged	insensitive	resentful	wicked
callous	envious	intolerant	rough	wrathful

Depression—Sadness—Gloom

abandoned	depressed	forsaken	low	ruined
alien	desolate	gloomy	miserable	rundown
alienated	despairing	glum	mishandled	sad
alone	despised	grim	mistreated	scornful
awful	despondent	hated	moody	sore
battered	destroyed	homeless	mournful	stranded
blue	discarded	hopeless	obsolete	tearful
bored	discouraged	horrible	ostracized	terrible
burned	dismal	humiliated	overlooked	tired
cheapened	downcast	hurt	pathetic	unhappy
crushed	downhearted	jilted	pitiful	unloved
debased	downtrodden	kaput	rebuked	whipped
defeated	dreadful	loathed	regretful	worthless
degraded	estranged	lonely	rejected	wrecked
dejected	excluded	lonesome	reprimanded	
demolished	forlorn	lousy	rotten	

Distress

afficted	displeased	hindered	puzzled	tormented
anguished	dissatisfied	impaired	ridiculous	touchy
awkward	distrustful	impatient	sickened	troubled
baffled	disturbed	imprisoned	silly	ungainly
bewildered	doubtful	lost	skeptical	unlucky
clumsy	foolish	nauseated	speechless	unpopular
confused	futile	offended	strained	unsatisfied
constrained	grief	pained	suspicious	unsure
disgusted	helpless	perplexed	swamped	weary
disliked				

Fear—Anxiety

afraid	dreading	insecure	overwhelmed	tense
agitated	eerie	intimidated	panicky	terrified
alarmed	embarrassed	jealous	restless	timid
anxious	fearful	jittery	scared	uncomfortable
apprehensive	frantic	jumpy	shaky	uneasy
bashful	frightened	nervous	shy	upset
dangerous	hesitant	on edge	strained	worrying
desperate	horrified			

The NEW Reading Teacher's Book of Lists, © 1985 Prentice-Hall, Inc., Englewood Cliffs, NJ 07632. By E. Fry, D. Fountoukidis, and J. Polk.

The *NEW Reading Teacher's Book of Lists*, © 1985 Prentice-Hall, Inc., Englewood Cliffs, NJ 07632. By E. Fry, D. Fountoukidis, and J. Polk.

Inability—Inadequacy

anemic	disabled	incapable	powerless	unable
ashamed	exhausted	incompetent	puny	uncertain
broken	exposed	ineffective	shaken	unfit
catatonic	fragile	inept	shaky	unimportant
cowardly	frail	inferior	shivering	unqualified
crippled	harmless	insecure	sickly	unsound
defeated	helpless	meek	small	useless
defective	impotent	mummified	strengthless	vulnerable
deficient	inadequate	naughty	trivial	weak
demoralized				

Joy—Elation

amused	enchanted	glorious	joyful	smiling
blissful	enthusiastic	good	jubilant	splendid
brilliant	exalted	grand	magnificent	superb
calm	excellent	gratified	majestic	terrific
cheerful	excited	great	marvelous	thrilled
comical	exuberant	happy	overjoyed	tremendous
contented	fantastic	hilarious	pleasant	triumphant
delighted	fit	humorous	pleased	vivacious
ecstatic	funny	inspired	proud	witty
elated	gay	jolly	relieved	wonderful
elevated	glad	jovial	satisfied	

Love—Affection—Concern

admired	conscientious	giving	mellow	reliable
adorable	considerate	good	mild	respectful
affectionate	cooperative	helpful	moral	sensitive
agreeable	cordial	honest	neighborly	sweet
altruistic	courteous	honorable	nice	sympathetic
amiable	dedicated	hospitable	obliging	tender
benevolent	devoted	humane	open	thoughtful
benign	empathetic	interested	optimistic	tolerant
brotherly	fair	just	patient	trustworthy
caring	faithful	kind	peaceful	truthful
charming	forgiving	kindly	pleasant	understanding
charitable	friendly	lenient	polite	unselfish
comforting	generous	lovable	reasonable	warm
congenial	genuine	loving	receptive	worthy

Quantity

ample	few	lots	paucity	scarcity
abundant	heavy	many	plentiful	skimpy
chock-full	lavish	meager	plenty	sparing
copious	liberal	much	profuse	sparse
dearth	light	numerous	scads	sufficient
empty	loads	oodles	scant	well-stocked

Sight—Appearance

adorable	crinkled	foggy	motionless	skinny
alert	crooked	fuzzy	muddy	smoggy
beautiful	crowded	glamorous	murky	sparkling
blinding	crystalline	gleaming	nappy	spotless
bright	curved	glistening	narrow	square
brilliant	cute	glowing	obtuse	steep
broad	dark	graceful	round	stormy
blonde	deep	grotesque	rotund	straight
bloody	dim	hazy	pale	strange
blushing	distinct	high	poised	ugly
chubby	dull	hollow	quaint	unsightly
clean	elegant	homely	shadowy	unusual
clear	fancy	light	shady	weird
cloudy	filthy	lithe	sheer	wide
colorful	flat	low	shiny	wizened
contoured	fluffy	misty	shallow	

Size

ample	elfin	immense	miniature	stupendous
average	enormous	large	minute	tall
behemoth	fat	little	petite	tiny
big	giant	long	portly	towering
bulky	gigantic	mammoth	prodigious	vast
colossal	great	massive	puny	voluminous
diminutive	huge	microscopic	short	wee
dwarfed	hulking	middle-sized	small	

Smell—Taste

acrid	fragrant	putrid	sour	sweet
antiseptic	fresh	ripe	spicy	tangy
bitter	juicy	rotten	stale	tart
choking	medicinal	salty	sticky	tasty
clean	nutty	savory	strong	tasteless
delicious	peppery	smoky	stuffy	

The NEW Reading Teacher's Book of Lists, © 1985 Prentice-Hall, Inc., Englewood Cliffs, NJ 07632. By E. Fry, D. Fountoukidis, and J. Polk.

The NEW Reading Teacher's Book of Lists, © 1985 Prentice-Hall, Inc., Englewood Cliffs, NJ 07632. By E. Fry, D. Fountoukidis, and J. Polk.

Sound

bang	groan	melodic	screech	thud
booming	growl	moan	shrill	thump
buzz	harsh	mute	silent	thunderous
clatter	high-pitched	noisy	snarl	tinkle
cooing	hiss	purring	snort	voiceless
crash	hoarse	quiet	soft	wail
crying	hushed	raspy	splash	whine
deafening	husky	resonant	squeak	whispered
faint	loud	screaming	squeal	

Time

ancient	daylight	late	outdated	sunrise
annual	decade	lengthy	periodic	sunset
brief	dusk	long	punctual	swift
brisk	early	modern	quick	tardy
centuries	eons	moments	rapid	twilight
continual	evening	noon	short	whirlwind
crawling	fast	noonday	slowly	years
dawn	flash	old	speedy	yearly
daybreak	intermittent	old-fashioned	sporadic	young

Touch

boiling	dirty	grubby	shaggy	stinging
breezy	dry	hard	sharp	tender
bumpy	dusty	hot	silky	tight
chilly	filthy	icy	slick	uneven
cold	fluffy	loose	slimy	waxen
cool	flaky	melted	slippery	wet
creepy	fluttering	plastic	slushy	wooden
crisp	frosty	prickly	smooth	yielding
cuddly	fuzzy	rainy	soft	
curly	gooey	rough	solid	
damp	greasy	sandpapery	sticky	

See Also List 25, Similes; List 26, Metaphors;
List 27, Idiomatic Expressions; and
List 28, Common Word Idioms.

75. LITERARY TERMS

Every area of knowledge has its own specialized vocabulary—literature included. Knowing literary terms and their meanings will help students recognize the use of these elements of literature. Recognizing and discussing them in class is a sure beginning to a deeper understanding of the author's skill, and an appreciation of literature. It also will enable students to understand articles of literary criticism.

Accent. When a part of a word, phrase or sentence is spoken with greater force or stronger tone it is accented.

Allegory. Objects and characters in a story are equated with meanings outside the literal meaning of the story.

Alliteration. When two or more words have the same beginning sound. Example: *Mary made mittens.*

Anadiplosis. Repeating the ending word of a clause as the beginning of the next one. Example: *Pleasure might cause her to read, reading might cause her to know, knowledge might piety win, and piety grace obtain.*

Assonance. Repetition of an internal vowel sound in two or more words. Example: *He feeds the deer.*

Ballad. A long narrative poem that tells a story. It usually has strong rhythm and rhyme.

Chiasmus. The reversal of syntax or word order for effect. Example: *Empty his bottle, and his girlfriend gone.*

Epic. A long narrative poem that centers on the deeds of a great hero.

Form. The structure of a literary piece. For example, traditional poetry has lines and stanzas.

Hyperbole. An exaggeration. Example: *The waves during the storm were one hundred feet high.*

Imagery. Choosing words to create strong pictures or images in the reader's mind. Example: *A blanket of soft snow covered the sleeping tractor.*

Kenning. A short simile or metaphor for a thing not actually named. Example: *sky candle* for the sun.

Metaphor. The comparison of two things without using the words "like" or "as." For example: *Habits are first cobwebs, then cables.*

Metonymy. Naming something associated with what is really being talked about rather than naming the subject directly. Example: *pen* in place of *writing*.

Ode. A poem written in praise of someone or something.

Onomatopoeia. A word in which the sound of the words gives the meaning of the word. For example: *Ouch!*

Oxymoron. The joining of two contradictory terms. Example: *glorious pain.*

Personification. Giving nonhuman things human characteristics. Example: *The wind whispered throughout the night.*

The NEW Reading Teacher's Book of Lists, © 1985 Prentice-Hall, Inc., Englewood Cliffs, NJ 07632. By E. Fry, D. Fountoukidis, and J. Polk.

Poetry. An expression of feeling in words, usually having form, rhythm, and rhyme.

Rhyme. When two or more words have the same ending sound.

Rhythm. The repetition of a pattern of accented and unaccented syllables.

Simile. The comparison of two things using the words "like" or "as." Example: *He runs like a gazelle.*

Stanza. A group of related lines in a poem, similar to a paragraph in prose.

See Also List 68, Parts of Speech;
and List 86, Caldecott and Newbery Awards.

76. INTEREST INVENTORY—PRIMARY

Use the interest inventory to get to know your students. You will find special talents, hobbies, and needs that will help you help your students.

1. In school the thing I like to do best is _____.

2. Outside of school the thing I like to do best is _____.

3. If I had a million dollars I would _____.

4. When I grow up I will _____.

5. I hate _____.

6. My favorite animal is _____.

7. The best sport is _____.

8. When nobody is around I like to _____.

9. The person I like best is _____.

10. Next summer I hope to _____.

11. I like to collect _____.

12. My favorite place to be is _____.

13. The things I like to make are _____.

14. The best book I ever read was _____.

15. The best TV show is _____.

16. What I think is funny is _____.

See Also List 77, Interest Inventory—Intermediate.

The NEW Reading Teacher's Book of Lists, © 1985 Prentice-Hall, Inc., Englewood Cliffs, NJ 07632. By E. Fry, D. Fountoukidis, and J. Polk.

77. INTEREST INVENTORY—INTERMEDIATE

Assigning a topic for a report, suggesting a good book, selecting meaningful examples all can be helped by knowing students' preferences and interests. Use the interest inventory during the first week of school.

1. Outside of school my favorite activity is _____.

2. I work at _____. My job is _____.

3. The sport(s) I like to watch best is (are) _____.

4. The sport(s) I like to play best is (are) _____.

5. After high school I plan to _____.

6. The job I want to be doing as an adult is _____.

7. In school my favorite subject(s) is (are) _____.

8. The subject(s) in which I get the best grade is (are) _____.

9. I would like to learn more about _____.

10. My main hobbies or leisure time activity is (are) _____.

11. For pleasure I read _____.

12. I spend about _____ hours or _____ minutes a week reading for fun.

13. The best book I have ever read was (Title) _____.

14. The book I am reading now is (Title) _____.

15. My favorite magazine(s) is (are) _____.

16. The part of the world that interests me the most is _____.

17. When I am finished with school, I hope to live in _____.

18. The kinds of books or stories I like to read are _____.

19. My favorite TV show is _____.

20. What makes me mad is _____.

21. What makes me laugh is _____.

22. My favorite person is _____.

23. Next summer I plan to _____.

See Also List 76, Interest Inventory—Primary.

The NEW Reading Teacher's Book of Lists, © 1985 Prentice-Hall, Inc., Englewood Cliffs, NJ 07632. By E. Fry, D. Fountoukidis, and J. Polk.

78. BOOK REPORT ALTERNATIVES

Once you have enticed your students to read, consult this list of alternatives for forty exciting things to do in place of writing a book report.

1. Draw a time line to illustrate the events in the story.
2. Construct a story map to show the plot and setting.
3. Create a jacket for the book, complete with illustrations and blurbs.
4. Prepare a chart showing the characters, their relationships, and a few biographical facts about each.
5. Create a poster-sized ad for the book.
6. Have a panel discussion if several students read the same book.
7. Dramatize an incident or an important character alone or with others.
8. Do a radio announcement to publicize the book.
9. Have individual conferences with students to get their personal reactions.
10. Appoint a committee to conduct peer discussion and seminars on books.
11. Illustrate the story, take slides, coordinate music and narration, and give a multimedia presentation.
12. Write a play based on the continuation of the story or a new adventure for the characters.
13. Give a demonstration of what was learned from a how-to book.
14. Compose a telegram about the book, limited to twenty words.
15. Dramatically read a part of the book to the class to get them hooked.
16. Keep a diary of one of the characters in the story, using first person.
17. Write a letter to the author telling why you liked the book, your favorite parts, what you would have done with the plot.
18. Be a newspaper columnist, write a review for the book section.
19. Explain how the story might have ended if a key character or incident was changed.
20. Write a letter to the key character to tell him or her how to solve the problem.
21. Write a newspaper article based on an incident from the book.
22. Write a biography of the leading character, using information from the book.
23. Write an obituary article about a key character, giving an account of what he or she was best known for.
24. Give a testimonial speech citing the character for special distinctions noted in the book.
25. Compare the movie and book versions of the same story.
26. Make a diorama to show the time and setting of the story.

The NEW Reading Teacher's Book of Lists, © 1985 Prentice-Hall, Inc., Englewood Cliffs, NJ 07632. By E. Fry, D. Fountoukidis, and J. Polk.

The NEW Reading Teacher's Book of Lists, © 1985 Prentice-Hall, Inc., Englewood Cliffs, NJ 07632. By E. Fry, D. Fountoukidis, and J. Polk.

27. Have a character day. Dress up as your favorite character in the story and relive some of the story.

28. Rewrite the story as a TV movie, including staging directions.

29. Examine the story for the author's craft and try to write a story of your own, imitating the use of tone, setting, style, and so on.

30. Memorize your favorite lines, or write them down for future quoting.

31. Make sketches of some of the action sequences.

32. Read the story into a tape recorder so that others may listen to it.

33. Research the period of history in which the story is set.

34. Make a list of similes, metaphors, or succinct descriptions used in the book.

35. Make puppets and present a show based on the book.

36. Build a clay or papier-mâché bust of a key character.

37. Give a "chalk talk" about the book.

38. Paint a mural that shows the key incidents in the story.

39. Rewrite the story for students in a lower grade. Keep it interesting.

40. File information about the book in a classroom cross-reference. Include author, story type, list of books it is similar to, and so on.

See Also List 79, Book Report Form.

79. BOOK REPORT FORM

This form can be duplicated and distributed for reports on short stories, plays, and books.

TITLE _____

AUTHOR _____

PUBLISHER _____

COPYRIGHT DATE _____

ILLUSTRATOR _____

THEME OR MAIN IDEA:

MAIN CHARACTERS:

SETTING:

SUMMARY:

OPINION/RECOMMENDATIONS:

See Also List 78, Book Report Alternatives.

The NEW Reading Teacher's Book of Lists, © 1985 Prentice-Hall, Inc., Englewood Cliffs, NJ 07632. By E. Fry, D. Fountoukidis, and J. Polk.

SECTION IX
Books

80. BASAL READERS

The NEW Reading Teacher's Book of Lists, © 1985 Prentice-Hall, Inc., Englewood Cliffs, NJ 07632. By E. Fry, D. Fountoukidis, and J. Polk.

Basal readers are used in an estimated 95 percent of the elementary classrooms in the United States. The core of a basal reading series consists of students' texts, workbooks, teachers' guides, and supplementary materials. Many offer computerized management programs to help plan lessons and track progress for individual students.

Aaron, Ira E., et al. *Scott Foresman Reading Program.* Glenview, Ill.: Scott Foresman, 1983.

Allington, Richard L. *Reading for Success.* Glenview, Ill.: Scott Foresman, 1985.

The American Readers. Lexington, Mass.: D. C. Heath, 1980.

Clymer, Theodore, et al. *Ginn Reading Program.* Lexington, Mass.: Ginn & Co. 1985.

Durr, William K., *Houghton Mifflin Reading Program.* Boston: Houghton, Mifflin, 1983.

Early, Margaret. *The Bookmark Reading Program.* New York: Harcourt Brace Jovanovich, 1983.

Fay, Leo C. and Anderson, Paul S. *Rand McNally Reading Program: The Young America Basic Series.* Chicago: Riverside, 1981.

Harris, Theodore L., et al. *Keys to Reading.* Oklahoma City: Economy, 1980.

Headway. LaSalle, Illinois: Open Court, 1980.

McCracken, Glenn and Walcott, Charles C . *Lippincott Basic Reading.* New York: Harper & Row, 1981.

Otto, Wayne, et al. *The Merrill Linguistic Reading Program.* Columbus, Ohio: Charles E. Merrill, 1983.

Ruddell, Robert B., et al. *Pathfinder—Allyn and Bacon Reading Program.* Boston: Allyn & Bacon, 1980.

Smith, Carl B. and Wardhaugh, Ronald. *Macmillan Reading Series R.* New York: Macmillan, 1983.

Weiss, Bernard, et al. *The Holt Basic Reading System.* New York: Holt, Rinehart & Winston, 1980.

See Also List 81, Basal Readers—Braille and Large Print
and List 82, Old-Time Readers.

81. BASAL READERS—BRAILLE AND LARGE PRINT

Many of the major basal reading programs are available in Braille or large-print editions. If you have students in your class with visual problems, contact the American Printing House for the Blind, 1839 Frankfort Avenue, Louisville, KY 40206, for catalogs of reading and other educational materials that are available in special editions.

Aaron, Ira E., et al. *Scott Foresman Reading Systems.* Glenview, Ill.: Scott Foresman, 1971-1972. Grades 2-6.

Aaron, Ira E., et al. *Scott Foresman Reading Unlimited.* Glenview, Ill.: Scott Foresman, 1976. Grades 1-6 (Levels 2-31).

Amato, Dolores, et al., *Harper & Row Reading Basics Plus.* New York: Harper & Row, 1976. Grades 1-6.

Clymer, Theodore, et al. *Ginn 360: Reading Program.* Lexington, Mass.: Ginn & Co., 1969-1970. Grades 1-6 (Levels 3-13).

Clymer, Theodore, et al. *Ginn 720: Rainbow Edition.* Lexington, Mass.: Ginn & Co., 1976, 1979. Grades 1-6 (Levels 3-13).

Early, Margaret. *Bookmark Reading Program.* New York: Harcourt Brace Jovanovich, 1970. Grades 1-6.

Eller, William and Hester, Kathleen B. *Laidlaw Reading Program.* River Forest, Ill.: Laidlaw Brothers, Grades 1-6 (Levels 3-13).

Harris, Theodore. *Keys to Reading.* Oklahoma City: Economy. Grades 1-6.

Johnson, Marjorie S. *American Book Reading Program.* New York: American Book Co. Grades 1-6 (Levels C-N).

McCracken, Glenn and Walcutt, Charles C. *Lippincott Basic Reading Series.* New York: Harper & Row, 1969-1971.

Ruddell, Robert B., et al. *Pathfinder-Allyn and Bacon Reading Program.* Boston: Allyn & Bacon, 1978. Grades 1-6 (Levels 8-20).

Scott Foresman Basics in Reading. Glenview, Ill.: Scott Foresman, 1978. Grades 1-6. Available in Braille only.

Smith, Carl B. and Wardhaugh, Ronald. *Macmillan Reading Series R.* New York: Macmillan, 1980. Grades 1-6 (Levels 7-36).

Van Roekel, Byron H. and Kluwe, Mary Jean. *Design for Reading.* New York: Harper & Row, 1972. Grades 1-6 (Levels 4-17).

Weiss, Bernad, *Holt Basic Reading Program.* New York: Holt, Rinehart, & Winston, 1973. Grades 1-6 (Levels 7-15).

The NEW Reading Teacher's Book of Lists, © 1985 Prentice-Hall, Inc., Englewood Cliffs, NJ 07632. By E. Fry, D. Fountoukidis, and J. Polk.

82. OLD-TIME READERS

History buffs will especially appreciate this list of books that were used long ago to teach reading. These are the ancestors to the modern basal reading programs we use today.

Hornbook. Used in colonial times, it was not really a book but a paddle that had a printed page attached to one side. The page was covered with "horn," a cellophane-like layer of cow's horn, to protect the paper from grubby little fingers. The page contained the alphabet, the Lord's Prayer, and sometimes some syllables or short phrases.

Battledore. Also used in colonial times, this was a folded piece of paper with contents similar to the hornbook.

New England Primer. This was a tiny book (only three or four inches tall) containing the alphabet, lists of syllables, aphorisms like, "In Adams Fall We sinneth all," and "He that ne'er learns his ABC, for ever will a blockhead be," and prayers and "catechism" questions and answers. The first copies were printed in England in 1683, and later American versions were known as the *American Primer* and the *New York Primer*.

He that ne er learns his A, B, C,
For ever will a Blockhead be ;

But he that learns thefeLetters fair
Shall have aCoach to take the Air.

The NEW Reading Teacher's Book of Lists, © 1985 Prentice-Hall, Inc., Englewood Cliffs, NJ 07632. By E. Fry, D. Fountoukidis, and J. Polk.

The Holy Bible. A standard "reader" that followed the New England Primer.

Grammatical Institute Part Three. Despite its name, this reader was written by none other than famous dictionary author Noah Webster in about 1782. Part One was spelling, which later had its title changed to *The American Spelling Book* (also known as the "Blue Black Speller") and became an all-time phenomenon. It sold over 12,700,000 copies before Webster died in 1843. In 1866 alone, it sold an amazing 1,596,000 copies. The speller has some of the aspects of a primer with short stories, and it is still in print. You can buy one from the trade book department of American Book Company.

American Preceptor. Written by Celeb Bingham in 1794, this reader went through 68 editions and sold over 640,000 copies.

English Readers. This reader became the most popular book of the early 1800s. It was written in 1799 by Lindley Murray and lasted until the famous McGuffey Reader was published.

McGuffey Readers. First published in 1836, over 122,000,000 copies had been sold making them among the greatest selling books of all time before they finally met their major decline in 1920. They were successful because they were among the earliest graded or leveled readers of increasing difficulty; because they appealed to the strong moral values of the time, without the doctrinaire religion of the earlier texts; and because of the more modern advertising and selling techniques of the publishers. William Holmes McGuffey was a successful Ohio elementary school teacher who later became a college professor and president of Miami University in Ohio. You can still buy them, too, from American Book Company's Trade Book Department.

Sanders, Hillard, and **Swinton** were different authors of various reading series that competed with McGuffey because, despite the *McGuffey Readers'* enormous popularity, it did not have a monopoly, especially along the East Coast.

The NEW Reading Teacher's Book of Lists, © 1985 Prentice-Hall, Inc., Englewood Cliffs, NJ 07632. By E. Fry, D. Fountoukidis, and J. Polk.

83. ELEMENTARY HI/LO BOOKS

The best way to become a proficient, lifelong reader is to read. Hi/Lo books generate a high level of interest, yet have a low level of difficulty. These may be just the thing to give extra practice to struggling students.

Allen, Marjorie. *One, Two, Three—Ah-Choo!* New York: Coward, McCann & Geoghegan, 1980.

Charming story about a young boy with allergies who wants a pet that won't make him sneeze. Hermit crab solution is satisfactory and funny.

Benchley, Nathaniel. *Sam the Minuteman.* New York: Harper & Row, 1969.

Young Sam joins his father and friends for a taste of the battle during the American Revolution. Pictures by illustrator Arnold Lobel capture the drama and exhaustion of the struggle.

Boegehold, Betty. *Three to Get Ready.* New York: Harper & Row, 1965.

Three delicately illustrated kittens tell their own stories. All about the dangers and delights of living out in the world.

Hoff, Syd. *Danny and the Dinosaur.* New York: Harper & Row, 1958.

Danny befriends a dinosaur at the museum and together they meet friends, have adventures, and part sadly.

Lobel, Arnold. *Frog and Toad Together.* New York: Harper & Row, 1971.

Frog and Toad are two appealing characters. In this book, Toad plants seeds, bakes cookies, and has a nightmare; as always, his old friend Frog is there to share.

Minarik, Else Holmehund. *Little Bear.* New York: Harper & Row, 1957.

Four stories about an imaginative bear and his accepting, encouraging mother. Warm and loving relationship.

Minarik, Else Holmehund. *No Fighting, No Bighting.* New York: Harper & Row, 1958.

Told as a story-within-a-story. Two quarreling siblings spend an afternoon with their storytelling Cousin Joan in a turn-of-the-century parlor.

Sharmat, Marjorie Weinman. *Little Devil Gets Sick.* New York: Doubleday, 1980.

Little Devil has a dreadful cold and none of his home remedies work. Whimsical and entertaining.

Suess, Dr. *The Cat in the Hat.* New York: Random House, 1957.

An incredible, talented feline visitor shocks brother and sister with his antics while mother is away. Classic.

Yolen, Jane. *Spider Jane on the Move.* New York: Coward, McCann & Geoghegan, 1980.

Spider Jane is a crochety, lovable inhabitant of a scrupulously clean web who must deal with moving, vacations, and a crabby Uncle Fred who insists on becoming a "webguest."

See Also List 84, Secondary Hi/Lo Books.

84. SECONDARY HI/LO BOOKS

Exciting, well-written books on topics of interest to teens may be the key to getting your students "hooked on books." Secondary students who need additional instruction in reading skills often have difficulty finding books of interest that they can read independently and enjoy. This is just a sample of some of the books that are available. Your librarian can suggest others.

Dolan, Ed. *The Bermuda Triangle and Other Mysteries of Nature.* New York: Franklin Watts Triumph Series, 1980.

Nonfiction book about Bermuda Triangle, Abominable Snowman, and UFOs. Factual material handled in a highly interesting manner. Very well-written and fascinating.

Durham, John. *A New Life for Sarita.* New York: Scholastic Action Series, 1971.

Chicano teenager struggles with old-world father who wants to impose traditional female behavior on her. The struggle is realistic and the solution subtle. Classic.

Greenya, John. *One Punch Away.* New York: Scholastic Action Series, 1972.

Black teenager learns to box in detention center. Becomes a winner and finds himself. Realistic boxing background.

Hallman, Ruth. *Midnight Wheels.* Philadelphia: Westminister Press, 1979.

Exciting adventure story featuring a young woman who is an auto mechanic. Nontraditional roles and rousing excitement pack a wallop.

Miner, Jane. *Choices.* New York: Scholastic Action Series, 1980.

Foster child, George, makes a series of painful choices as he learns that his uncle is exploitive and his loyalty is elsewhere. Exciting adventure and good character development.

Platt, Kin. *Dracula.* New York: Franklin Watts Triumph Series, 1979.

Charming combination of supernatural, mystery, and comedy genres. Teenager lets his imagination run wild with wonderful results..

Purification, Les. *Karate Ace.* New York: Scholastic Sprint Series, 1976.

Apparently timid teen learns karate and turns the tables on bullies in the neighborhood. Kids will identify with the underdog. Factual material on karate very authoritative.

Sunshine, Madeline. *A Member of the Family.* New York: Scholastic Sprint Series, 1976.

Friends teach a boy a lesson about love and friendship by helping him overcome his shame about retarded sister. Realistic background on retardation. Excellent characterization.

White, Wallace. *One Dark Night.* New York: Franklin Watts Triumph Series.

Boy learns that his uncle, the sheriff, is evil. Excitement and confrontation lead to subtle solution. Prose is well-written.

Wood, Phyllis Anderson. *I Think This Is Where We Came In.* Philadelphia: Westminister Press, 1976.

Two boys and a teenage girl on a camping trip pick up an injured dog. During their adventures, they discover their own individuality, find romance, and learn much. Fine characterization.

See Also List 85, All-Time Favorites and List 88, Bibliotherapy.

The NEW Reading Teacher's Book of Lists, © 1985 Prentice-Hall, Inc., Englewood Cliffs, NJ 07632. By E. Fry, D. Fountoukidis, and J. Polk.

85. ALL-TIME FAVORITES

Any list of chidren's books is necessarily subjective. Different authorities would select different books. This list of all-time favorites is selected from a much longer list of Books to Read in the *World Book Encyclopedia*, 1983. B = beginning readers (preschool and kindergarten); Y = young readers (grades 1–3); I = intermediate readers (grades 4–6); and O = older readers (grades 7 and up).

Aesop's Fables. Watts, 1967, **Y.**

Alcott, Louisa May. *Little Women.* Boston: Little Brown, 1968, **I.**

Andersen, Hans Christian. *The Complete Fairy Tales and Stories.* New York: Doubleday, 1974, **all ages.**

Barrie, Sir James. *Peter Pan.* New York: Random House, 1957, **I.**

Baum, L. Frank. *The Wizard of Oz.* Reilly and Lee, 1956, **I.**

Bemelmans, Ludwig. *Madeline.* New York: Viking, 1962, **B.**

Brunhoff, Jean de. *The Story of Babar.* New York: Random House, 1960, **B.**

Carroll, Lewis. *Alice in Wonderland and Through the Looking Glass.* New York: Grosset & Dunlap, 1963, **I.**

Chaucer, Geoffrey. *Chanticleer and the Fox.* New York: Thomas Y. Crowell, 1958, **B.**

Collodi, Carlo. *The Adventures of Pinocchio.* Macmillan, 1963, **I.**

Dickens, Charles. *A Christmas Carol.* Philadelphia: Lippincott, 1966, **I.**

Frank, Anne. *The Diary of a Young Girl.* New York: Doubleday, 1967, **O.**

Goble, Paul. *The Girl Who Loved Wild Horses.* Scarsdale, NY: Bradbury, 1978, **B.**

Grahame, Kenneth. *The Wind in the Willows.* New York: Scribner's, 1961, **O.**

Grimm, Jakob and Wihelm. *The Complete Fairy Tales.* New York: Pantheon, 1974, **Y** and **I.**

Keats, Ezra Jack. *The Snowy Day.* New York: Viking, 1963, **B.**

Lang, Andrew (ed.). *The Blue Fairy Book.* New York: McKay, 1948, **I.**

McCloskey, Robert. *Make Way for Ducklings.* New York: Viking, 1963, **B.**

Milne, A. A. *Winnie-the-Pooh.* New York: Dutton, 1954, **I.**

Potter, Beatrix. *The Tale of Peter Rabbit.* New York: Frederick Warne, 1958, **B.**

Sendak, Maurice. *Where the Wild Things Are.* New York: Harper, 1963, **B.**

Seuss, Dr. *The Cat in the Hat.* New York: Random House, 1957, **B.**

Spyri, Johanna. *Heidi.* New York: Grosset, 1945, **I.**

Stevenson, Robert Louis. *A Child's Garden of Verses.* New York: Golden Press, 1951, **Y.**

Stevenson, Robert Louis. *Treasure Island.* New York: Scribner's, 1939, **O.**

Swift, Jonathan. *Gulliver's Travels.* Duell, 1961, **O.**

Tolkien, J. R. R. *The Hobbit.* New York: Houghton, 1937, **I.**

Travers, P. L. *Mary Poppins.* New York: Harcourt, 1962, **I.**

Twain, Mark. *The Adventures of Tom Sawyer.* New York: Harper, 1938, **O.**

White, E. B. *The Trumpet of the Swan.* New York: Harper, 1970, **I.**

Wilder, Laura Ingalls. *Little House in the Big Woods.* New York: Harper, 1953, **I.**

See Also List 83, Elementary Hi/Lo Books; and List 84, Secondary Hi/Lo Books.

86. CALDECOTT AND NEWBERY AWARD WINNERS

The NEW Reading Teacher's Book of Lists, © 1985 Prentice-Hall, Inc., Englewood Cliffs, NJ 07632. By E. Fry, D. Fountoukidis, and J. Polk.

Since 1938, the Caldecott Medal has been awarded annually to the artist of the most distinguished American picture book for children published during the preceding year. It was named for Randolph Caldecott, a famous English illustrator of books for children. In cases where only one name is given, the book was written and illustrated by the same person.

Caldecott Medal Winners

1938   *Animals of the Bible* by Helen Dean Fish, illustrated by Dorothy P. Lathrop. Philadelphia: Lippincott.

1939   *Mei Li* by Thomas Handforth. New York: Doubleday.

1940   *Abraham Lincoln* by Ingri and Edgar Parin d'Aulaire. New York: Doubleday.

1941   *They Were Strong and Good* by Robert Lawson. New York: Viking.

1942   *Make Way for Ducklings* by Robert McCloskey. New York: Viking.

1943   *The Little House* by Virginia Lee Burton. Boston: Houghton Mifflin.

1944   *Many Moons* by James Thurber, illustrated by Louis Slobodkin. New York: Harcourt Brace Jovanovich.

1945   *Prayer for a Child* by Rachel Field, illustrated by Elizabeth Orton Jones. New York: Macmillan.

1946   *The Rooster Crows ...* (traditional Mother Goose), illustrated by Maud and Miska Petersham. New York: Macmillan.

1947   *The Little Island* by Golden MacDonald, illustrated by Leonard Weisgard. New York: Doubleday.

1948   *White Snow, Bright Snow* by Alvin Tresselt, illustrated by Roger Duvoisin. New York: Lothrop.

1949   *The Big Snow* by Berta and Elmer Hader. New York: Macmillan.

1950   *Song of the Swallows* by Leo Politi. New York: Scribner's.

1951   *The Egg Tree* by Katherine Milhous. New York: Scribner's.

1952   *Finders Keepers* by William Lipkind, illustrated by Nicolas Mordvinoff. New York: Harcourt Brace Jovanovich.

1953   *The Biggest Bear* by Lynd Ward. Boston: Houghton Mifflin.

1954   *Madeline's Rescue* by Ludwig Bemelmans. New York: Viking.

1955   *Cinderella, or the Little Glass Slipper* by Charles Perrault, translated and illustrated by Marcia Brown. New York: Scribner's.

1956   *Frog Went A-Courtin'* edited by John Langstaff, illustrated by Feodor Rojankovsky. New York: Harcourt Brace Jovanovich.

1957   *A Tree is Nice* by Janice May Udry, illustrated by Marc Simont. New York: Harper.

1958   *Time of Wonder* by Robert McCloskey. New York: Viking.

1959   *Chanticleer and the Fox* adapted from Chaucer and illustrated by Barbara Cooney. New York: Thomas Y. Crowell.

1960   *Nine Days to Christmas* by Marie Hall Ets and Aurora Labastida, illustrated by Marie Hall Ets. New York: Viking.

1961   *Baboushka and the Three Kings* by Ruth Robbins, illustrated by Nicolas Sidjakov. New York: Parnassus.

1962   *Once a Mouse ...* by Marcia Brown. New York: Scribner's.

1963   *The Snowy Day* by Ezra Jack Keats. New York: Viking.

1964   *Where the Wild Things Are* by Maurice Sendak. New York: Harper.

The NEW Reading Teacher's Book of Lists, © 1985 Prentice-Hall, Inc., Englewood Cliffs, NJ 07632. By E. Fry, D. Fountoukidis, and J. Polk.

1965   *May I Bring a Friend?* by Beatrice Schenk de Regniers, illustrated by Beni Montresor. New York: Atheneum.

1966   *Always Room for One More* by Sorche Nic Leodhas, illustrated by Nonny Hogrogian. New York: Holt, Rinehart & Winston.

1967   *Sam, Bangs & Moonshine* by Evaline Ness. New York: Holt, Rinehart & Winston.

1968   *Drummer Hoff* by Barbara Emberley, illustrated by Ed Emberley. Englewood Cliffs, N.J.: Prentice-Hall.

1969   *The Fool of the World and the Flying Ship* by Arthur Ransome, illustrated by Uri Shulevitz. New York: Farrar, Straus & Giroux.

1970   *Sylvester and the Magic Pebble* by William Steig. New York: Windmill.

1971   *A Story—A Story* by Gail E. Haley. New York: Atheneum.

1972   *One Fine Day* by Nonny Hogrogian. New York: Macmillan.

1973   *The Funny Little Woman* retold by Arlene Mosel, illustrated by Blair Lent. New York: Dutton.

1974   *Duffy and the Devil* by Harve Zemach, illustrated by Margot Zemach. New York: Farrar, Straus & Giroux.

1975   *Arrow to the Sun* adapted and illustrated by Gerald McDermott. New York: Viking.

1976   *Why Mosquitoes Buzz in People's Ears* retold by Verna Aardema, illustrated by Leo and Diane Dillon. New York: Dial Press.

1977   *Ashanti to Zulu: African Traditions* by Margaret Musgrove, illustrated by Leo and Diane Dillon. New York: Dial Press.

1978   *Noah's Ark* by Peter Spier. New York: Doubleday.

1979   *The Girl Who Loved Wild Horses* by Paul Goble. Scarsdale, New York: Bradbury.

1980   *Ox-Cart Man* by Donald Hall. Viking.

1981   *Fables* by Arnold Lobel. New York: Harper.

1982   *Jumanji* by Chris van Allsburg. Boston: Houghton Mifflin.

1983   *Shadow* translated by Blaise Cendrars, illustrated by Marcia Brown. New York: Scribner's.

1984   *The Glorious Flight Across the Channel with Louis Bleriot* by Alice and Martin Provensen. New York: Viking.

1985   *Saint George and the Dragon* as retold by Margaret Hodges, illustrated by Trina Schart Hyman. Boston: Little, Brown.

The Newbery Medal is awarded annually to the author of the most distinguished contribution to American literature for children. The award, named after John Newbery, an 18th-century publisher of quality children's books, has been offered since 1922 as an incentive for quality in children's books.

Newbery Award Winners

1922 *The Story of Mankind* by Hendrik Willem van Loon. New York: Liveright.
1923 *The Voyages of Doctor Dolittle* by Hugh Lofting. Philadelphia: J. B. Lippincott.
1924 *The Dark Frigate* by Charles B. Hawes. Atlantic/Little.
1925 *Tales from Silver Lands* by Charles J. Finger. New York: Doubleday.
1926 *Shen of the Sea* by Arthur Bowie Chrisman. New York: Dutton.
1927 *Smoky, The Cowhorse* by Will James. New York: Scribner's.
1928 *Gay-neck: The Story of a Pigeon* by Dhan Gopal Mukerji. New York: Dutton.
1929 *The Trumpeter of Krakow* by Eric P. Kelly. New York: Macmillan.
1930 *Hitty, Her First Hundred Years* by Rachel Field. New York: Macmillan.
1931 *The Cat Who Went to Heaven* by Elizabeth Coatsworth. New York: Macmillan.
1932 *Waterless Mountain* by Laura Adams Armer. New York: Longman.
1933 *Young Fu of the Upper Yangtze* by Elizabeth Foreman Lewis. Winston.
1934 *Invincible Louisa* by Cornelia Meigs. Boston: Little Brown.
1935 *Dobry* by Monica Shannon. New York: Viking.
1936 *Caddie Woodlawn* by Carol Brink. New York: Macmillan.
1937 *Roller Skates* by Ruth Sawyer. New York: Viking.
1938 *The White Stag* by Kate Seredy. New York: Viking.
1939 *Thimble Summer* by Elizabeth Enright. New York: Rinehart.
1940 *Daniel Boone* by James Daugherty. New York: Viking..
1941 *Call It Courage* by Armstrong Sperry. New York: Macmillan.
1942 *The Matchlock Gun* by Water D. Edmonds. New York: Dodd.
1943 *Adam of the Road* by Elizabeth Janet Gray. New York: Viking.
1944 *Johnny Tremain* by Esther Forbes. Boston: Houghton Mifflin.
1945 *Rabbit Hill* by Robert Lawson. New York: Viking.
1946 *Strawberry Girl* by Lois Lenski. Philadelphia: J.B. Lippincott.
1947 *Miss Hickory* by Carolyn Sherwin Bailey. New York: Viking.
1948 *The Twenty-one Balloons* by William Pene du Bois. New York: Viking.
1949 *King of the Wind* by Marguerite Henry. Chicago: Rand McNally.
1950 *The Door in the Wall* by Marguerite de Angeli. New York: Doubleday.
1951 *Amos Fortune, Free Man* by Elizabeth Yates. Aladdin.
1952 *Ginger Pye* by Eleanor Estes. New York: Harcourt Brace Jovanovich.
1953 *Secret of the Andes* by Ann Nolan Clark. New York: Viking.
1954 *And Now Miguel* by Joseph Krumgold. New York: Thomas Y. Crowell.
1955 *The Wheel on the School* by Meindert DeJong. New York: Harper.
1956 *Carry on, Mr. Bowditch* by Jean Lee Latham. Boston: Houghton Mifflin.
1957 *Miracles on Maple Hill* by Virginia Sorensen. New York: Harcourt Brace Jovanovich.
1958 *Rifles for Watie* by Harold Keith. New York: Thomas Y. Crowell.
1959 *The Witch of Blackbird Pond* by Elizabeth George Speare. Boston: Houghton Mifflin.
1960 *Onion John* by Joseph Krumgold. New York: Thomas Y. Crowell.
1961 *Island of the Blue Dolphins* by Scott O'Dell. Boston: Houghton Mifflin.
1962 *The Bronze Bow* by Elizabeth George Speare. Boston: Houghton Mifflin.
1963 *A Wrinkle in Time* by Madeleine L'Engle. New York: Farrar, Straus & Giroux.

The NEW Reading Teacher's Book of Lists, © 1985 Prentice-Hall, Inc., Englewood Cliffs, NJ 07632. By E. Fry, D. Fountoukidis, and J. Polk.

The NEW Reading Teacher's Book of Lists, © 1985 Prentice-Hall, Inc., Englewood Cliffs, NJ 07632. By E. Fry, D. Fountoukidis, and J. Polk.

1964   *It's Like This, Cat* by Emily Cheney Neville. New York: Harper.

1965   *Shadow of a Bull* by Maia Wojciechowska. New York: Atheneum.

1966   *I, Juan de Pareja* by Elizabeth Borton de Trevino. New York: Ferrar, Straus & Giroux.

1967   *Up a Road Slowly* by Irene Hunt. Follett.

1968   *From the Mixed-Up Files of Mrs. Basil E. Frankweiler* by E. L. Konigsburg. New York: Atheneum.

1969   *The High King* by Lloyd Alexander. New York: Holt.

1970   *Sounder* by William H. Armstrong. New York: Harper.

1971   *Summer of the Swans* by Betsy Byars. New York: Viking.

1972   *Mrs. Frisby and the Rats of NIMH* by Robert C. O'Brien. New York: Atheneum.

1973   *Julie of the Wolves* by Jean C. George. New York: Harper.

1974   *The Slave Dancer* by Paula Fox. Bradbury.

1975   *M. C. Higgins, The Great* by Virginia Hamilton. New York: Macmillan.

1976   *The Grey King* by Susan Cooper. New York: Atheneum.

1977   *Roll of Thunder, Hear My Cry* by Mildred D. Taylor. New York: Dial Press.

1978   *Bridge to Terabithia* by Katherine Paterson. New York: Thomas Y. Crowell.

1979   *The Westing Game* by Ellen Raskin. New York: Dutton.

1980   *A Gathering of Days: A New England Girl's Journal, 1830–32* by Joan Blos. New York: Greenwillow.

1981   *Jacob Have I Loved* by Katherine Paterson. New York: Thomas Y. Crowell.

1982   *A Visit to William Blake's Inn: Poems for Innocent and Experienced Travelers* by Nancy Willard. New York: Harcourt Brace Jovanovich.

1983   *Dicey's Song* by Cynthia Voigt. New York: Atheneum.

1984   *Dear Mr. Henshaw* by Beverly Cleary. New York: Morrow.

1985   *The Hero and the Crown* by Robin McKinley. New York: Greenwillow.

See Also List 85, All-Time Favorites.

87. PICTURE BOOKS

For pre-readers the books on this list are just the thing. The pictures tell the story without words. Children can "read" the pictures and enjoy these first experiences with books.

Anno, Mitsumasa. *Topsy-Turvies: Pictures to Stretch the Imagination.* New York: John Weatherhill Inc., 1970.

Carle, Eric. *Do You Want to Be My Friend?* New York: Harper, 1971.

De Paola, Tomie. *Pancakes for Breakfast.* New York: Harcourt Brace Jovanovich, 1978.

Goodall, John. *The Midnight Adventures of Kelly, Dot and Esmeralda.* New York: Atheneum, 1973.

Goodall, John. *Paddy Pork's Holiday.* New York: Atheneum, 1976.

Goodall, John. *The Surprise Picnic.* New York: Atheneum, 1977.

Hoban, Tana. *Big Ones, Little Ones.* New York: Greenwillow, 1976.

Hoban, Tana. *Over, Under, Through, and Other Spatial Concepts.* New York: Macmillan, 1973.

Keats, Ezra Jack. *Skates!* Scholastic, Inc., 1981.

Krahn, Fernando. *April Fools.* New York: Dutton, 1974.

Mayer, Mercer. *Frog Goes to Dinner.* New York: Dial Press, 1974.

Mayer, Mercer. *Frog, Where Are You?* New York: Dial Press, 1980.

Mayer, Mercer. *The Great Cat Chase.* New York: Scholastic, 1975.

Mayer, Mercer. *Hiccup.* New York: Dial Press, 1976.

Sesame Street. *Can You Find What's Missing?* Illustrated by Carol Nicklaus. New York: Random House, 1974.

Ward, Lynd. *The Silver Pony.* New York: Houghton Mifflin, 1973.

See Also List 80, Basal Readers; and List 83, Elementary Hi/Lo Books.

The *NEW Reading Teacher's Book of Lists*, © 1985 Prentice-Hall, Inc., Englewood Cliffs, NJ 07632. By E. Fry, D. Fountoukidis, and J. Polk.

88. BIBLIOTHERAPY

The NEW Reading Teacher's Book of Lists, © 1985 Prentice-Hall, Inc., Englewood Cliffs, NJ 07632. By E. Fry, D. Fountoukidis, and J. Polk.

This is a very special book list for it deals with books that address children's problems. These books are used in "bibliotherapy" or in helping children better understand their own problems by reading about other children with similar problems.

General

The Bookfinder: A Guide to Children's Literature about the Needs and Problems of Youth Aged 2-15, by Sharon S. Dreyer. American Guidance Service, Inc., 1977. Volume 2, published in 1981, picks up where the first volume leaves off. It includes annotations of books published 1975–1978. Both these volumes include an index and a listing of annotations for titles dealing with different problems and needs of young people.

Children's Books for Times of Stress: An Annotated Bibliography, by Ruth J. Gillis. Bloomington, Ind.: Indiana University Press, 1978. Lists 261 books published between 1932 and 1976 under broad headings: Behavior, Family, Difficult Situations, New Situations, Self Concept, Friendship, and Emotion.

Handicapped

Books about Handicaps for Children and Young Adults, by Patricia Bisshopp. Meeting Street School, 667 Waterman Ave., East Providence, RI 02940. Bibliography for all areas of physically and emotionally handicapped.

Large Type Books in Print. New York: Bowker. Annual beginning with 1982 edition. Books for visually handicapped in 14-point type or greater. Subject, author, and title indexes.

"A Look Behind the Wall of Silence," *Ohio Library Association Bulletin* (April 1977), by Louise M. Wright. Discusses suggested readings for young deaf people and books to help others understand hearing impaired.

Notes from a Different Drummer: A Guide to Juvenile Fiction Portraying the Handicapped, by Barbara H. Baskin and Karen H. Harris. New York: Bowker, 1977. Annotated guide to books that have mentally or physically handicapped characters.

We the Handicapped: Bibliotherapy Reference Guide. Detroit: We the Handicapped. A list of 455 books with annotations on the physically disabled. Contains titles of fiction and nonfiction, listed by juvenile or adult level.

Death and Divorce

Books to Help Children Cope with Separation and Loss, by Joanne E. Berstein. New York: Bowker, 1983. Annotated book list grouped by subject.

Minorities

Americans All. Champaign, Ill.: Garrard. Series of biographies of great Americans of all races, creeds and national origins. Each emphasizes courage, character, and personal determination. Elementary grades.

Good Reading for the Disadvantaged Reader: Multi-Ethnic Resources, by George Spache. Champaign, Ill.: Garrard, 1975. Annotated list of books and AV materials for use in developing self-concept among seven minority groups, including inner city children.

Living City Adventure Series. New York: Globe Books. Series of short stories that focus on problems and hopes of multiethnic young people. Junior and senior high school students.

Open Door Books. Chicago: Children's Press. A series of thirty-six autobiographical books of minority men and women who have faced modern society and won. Intermediate through junior high.

Careers

Key Resources in Career Education: An Annotated Guide, by Daniel W. Tiedman, Washington, D.C.: National Institute of Education, USDHEW, 1976.

Values and Human Relationships

"Books to Promote Insight into Family Life Problems," *English Journal* (November 1956), by Jean DeSales Bertram. Approaches to solving family living problems explored through fourteen well-known novels.

Reading Ladders for Human Relations. Virginia M. Reid, ed. Washington, D.C.: American Council on Education, rev. ed., 1972. Annotated listing of books for children and young people around themes of individual growth, family and group relationships and searching for values.

Values Resource Guide, Annotated for the Elementary School Teacher, by Mate Hune. Washington, D.C.: American Association of Colleges for Teacher Education. An index and guide to values related books, films, poems, and so on.

See Also List 89, Book List Collection.

The NEW Reading Teacher's Book of Lists, © 1985 Prentice-Hall, Inc., Englewood Cliffs, NJ 07632. By E. Fry, D. Fountoukidis, and J. Polk.

89. BOOK LIST COLLECTION

General

These lists are sources that librarians and others use for locating and ordering books. Many of these references can be found in school or public libraries. They contain titles of thousands of books, annotations, and review or recommendations as well.

Adventuring with Books: A Book List for Elementary Schools. Shelton Root and Committee on the Elementary School Book List, ed. National Council of Teachers of English, 2nd ed., 1973. Annotated listings for preschool through grade 8, with notations on interest level and difficulty.

Aids to Choosing Books for Children. Ingeborg Boudreau. Children's Book Council, 1969. Annotated bibliography of book lists and review media to help librarians, teachers, and parents in book selection. Includes both general and specialized book lists.

Best Books for Children. Bowker, 1959 to date. An annual catalog of titles that is annotated and arranged by level of difficulty and subject matter.

The Best in Children's Books: The University of Chicago Guide to Children's Literature, 1973–1978. Zena Sutherland. University of Chicago Press, 1980. Reviews indexed by topic, type of literature, and reading level.

Bibliography of Books for Children. Bonnie Baron. Association for Childhood Education International, 1977. Annotated list of books for children from preschool through elementary grades, grouped by type and subject.

Book Bait: Detailed Notes on Adult Books Popular with Young People. Elinor Walker. American Library Association, 3rd ed., 1979. Describes adult books that young people have enjoyed.

Books for Beginning Readers. Elizabeth Guilefoile. National Council of Teachers of English, 1962. Bibliography of more than 300 easy-reading books for beginners.

Children and Books. Zena Sutherland, Dianne L. Monson, and May Hill Arbuthnot. Scott, Foresman & Co., 6th ed., 1981. This book is designed primarily as a text for library science majors; however, it contains a wealth of book lists and information about reading material for young people.

Children and Poetry: A Selective Annotated Bibliography. Virginia Haviland and William Jay Smith. Library of Congress, 2nd ed., 1979. A selective guide to both old and new poetry for children.

Children's Books Too Good to Miss. May Hill Arbuthnot, Margaret Mary Clark, Harriet Geneva Long, and Ruth M. Hadlow. University Press Books, 7th ed., 1980. List of books, grouped by age, which every child should be exposed to.

Children's Catalog. Wilson Co. Comprehensive list of reviews of books for preschool through intermediate-grade children. Five-year cumulations and yearly supplements.

Fantasy for Children: An Annotated Checklist. Ruth Nadelman Lynn. Bowker, 1979. A bibliographic guide to works of fantasy, divided by type and theme.

Gateways to Readable Books. Dorothy Withrow, Helen Carey, and Bertha Hirzel. Wilson, 1975. An annotated list of books likely to appeal to reluctant adolescent readers.

Good Reading for Poor Readers. George Spache. Garrard, rev. ed., 1978. Listing of trade books, textbooks, workbooks, games, magazines, newspapers, book lists, and book clubs that may be of use in working with reading disabled students. Readability information is included.

The NEW Reading Teacher's Book of Lists, © 1985 Prentice-Hall, Inc., Englewood Cliffs, NJ 07632. By E. Fry, D. Fountoukidis, and J. Polk.

High Interest-Easy Reading for Junior and Senior High School Students. Marian White, ed. National Council for Teachers of English, rev. ed., 1979. Annotated list of high interest, low reading level titles arranged by subject.

The Horn Book Magazine. Horn Book. Magazine about children's books, authors, and so on, with section for reviews. Published six times per year.

An Index to Young Readers' Collective Biographies. Judith Silverman. Bowker, 3rd ed., 1979. Includes listings for over seven thousand individuals.

Junior High School Library Catalog. Estelle A. Fidell and Gary L. Bogart. Wilson, 3rd ed., 1975. Reviews of nearly four thousand books for grades 7–9 listed by topic, author, and title. Yearly supplements available.

Notable Children's Books, 1940–1970. American Library Association, 1977. A reappraisal of ALA's Children's Services Division's annual Notable lists, from 1940 to 1970. Annotations given for each title.

A Parent's Guide to Children's Reading. Nancy Larrick. Bantam, 1975. A useful paperback that has been well received through four printings.

School Library Journal. Bowker. Published August through May. Reviews approximately 1,500 titles, sometimes with dissenting opinions.

Senior High School Library Catalog. Wilson, 11th ed., 1977. Review of over four thousand titles and references by title, author, and subject. Yearly supplements available.

Stories to Tell to Children. Sara C. Bryant. Carnegie Library of Pittsburgh. Frequently revised. One of the best bibliographies of folk and fairy tale literature for the storyteller.

The World of Books for Children: A Parent's Guide. Abby Campbell Hunt. Sovereign, 1979. Guide to recommended children's books arranged by subject within age level.

Your Reading: A Booklist for Junior High Schools. Charles B. Willard and Committee on the Junior High School Book List of National Council of Teachers of English. Walker, 1975. Annotated guide to almost 1,300 books for sixth through ninth graders.

Books for Particular Subject Areas

The AAAS Science Booklist. Hilary J. Deason. American Association for the Advancement of Science, 3rd. ed., 1970. Annotated list of science and mathematics books for high school and college students.

American Historical Fiction and Biography for Children and Young People. Jeanette Hotchkiss. Scarecrow, 1973. Annotated list arranged chronologically by subject. Reading level information provided.

Appraisal: Children's Science Books. Harvard Graduate School of Education. Approximately fifty books reviewed in each issue that is published three times per year.

Children's Books to Enrich the Social Studies for the Elementary Grades. Helen Huus. National Council for Social Studies, 1966. Annotated bibliography arranged by topic to cover world history and geography from early times to the present.

The NEW Reading Teacher's Book of Lists, © 1985 Prentice-Hall, Inc., Englewood Cliffs, NJ 07632. By E. Fry, D. Fountoukidis, and J. Polk.

Books for Particular Ethnic Groups

Asia: A Guide to Books for Children. The Asia Society, 1966. Annotated listings arranged by country. Approximate grade level provided.

A Bicultural Heritage: Themes for the Exploration of Mexican and Mexican-American Culture in Books for Children and Adolescents. Isabel Schon. Scarecrow Press, 1978. Annotated bibliography of English fiction and nonfiction.

The Black Experience and the School Curriculum: Teaching Materials for Grades K-12; An Annotated Bibliography. Katherine Baxter. Wellsprings Ecumenical Center, 1968. Annotated lists of books grouped by history, social studies, biography, fiction, and poetry.

The Black Experience in Children's Books. Barbara Rollock. New York Public Library, rev. ed., 1974. Annotated bibliography grouped by subject matter and age, about life in America, in the islands, in Africa, and in England.

Books for the Chinese-American Child: A Selected List. Cecilia Mei-Chi Chen. Cooperative Children's Book Center, 1969. Selective list of books.

Books in Spanish for Children and Young Adults: An Annotated Guide. Isabel Schon. Scarecrow, 1978. Annotations of Spanish language books.

Books on American Indians and Eskimos: A Selection Guide for Children and Young Adults. Mary Jo Lass-Woodfin. American Library Association, 1978. Reviews 807 books written prior to 1977. Estimated reading levels provided.

Building Bridges of Understanding. Charlotte Matthews Keating. Palo Verde, 1967. An annotated bibliography of books about blacks, Indians, Spanish-speaking ethnic groups, Chinese-Americans, Japanese-Americans, Jews, and other minority groups.

Building Bridges of Understanding between Cultures. Charlotte Matthews Keating, Palo Verde, 1971. Companion to the title above. Includes annotations by age level within each minority group.

Folklore of the American Indians: An Annotated Bibliography. Judith C. Ullom. Library of Congress, 1969. Selected bibliography arranged by culture areas.

Literature by and about the American Indian: An Annotated Bibliography, for Junior and Senior High School Students. Anna Lee Stensland. National Council of Teachers of English, 1979, 2nd ed. In addition to bibliography, provides biographies about American Indian authors and study guides.

Negro Literature for High School Students. Barbara Dodds. National Council of Teachers of English, 1968. Extensive annotated list of works about blacks. Also includes biographies of black authors and suggested classroom uses of black literature.

Starting Out Right: Choosing Books About Black People for Young Children. Bettye Lattimer. Wisconsin Department of Public Instruction, 1972. Bibliography and discussion of integration in children's books.

We Build Together: A Reader's Guide to Negro Life and Literature for Elementary and High School Use. Charlemae Rollins. National Council of Teachers of English, 3rd ed., 1967. Annotated bibliography of picture books, fiction, history, biography, poetry, folklore, music, science, and sports.

See Also List 83, Elementary Hi/Lo Books; and List 84, Secondary Hi/Lo Books.

SECTION X
Reference

90. STATE ABBREVIATIONS

The official postal abbreviations and the traditional abbreviations are listed for each state. Some of them are easy to remember, such as NY and FL. Others will take a bit of concentration to get straight, such as MI, MO, MS, MA, MT, and ME. The new postal abbreviations generally are not followed by periods.

Full Name	New	Old	Full Name	New	Old
Alabama	AL	Ala.	Montana	MT	Mont.
Alaska	AK	Alaska	Nebraska	NE	Nebr.
Arizona	AZ	Ariz.	Nevada	NV	Nev.
Arkansas	AR	Ark.	New Hampshire	NH	N.H.
California	CA	Calif.	New Jersey	NJ	N.J.
Colorado	CO	Colo.	New Mexico	NM	N.Mex.
Connecticut	CT	Conn.	New York	NY	N.Y.
Delaware	DE	Del.	North Carolina	NC	N.C.
Florida	FL	Fla.	North Dakota	ND	N.Dak.
Georgia	GA	Ga.	Ohio	OH	Ohio
Hawaii	HI	Hawaii	Oklahoma	OK	Okla.
Idaho	ID	Idaho	Oregon	OR	Oreg.
Illinois	IL	Ill.	Pennsylvania	PA	Pa.
Indiana	IN	Ind.	Rhode Island	RI	R.I.
Iowa	IA	Iowa	South Carolina	SC	S.C.
Kansas	KS	Kans.	South Dakota	SD	S.D.
Kentucky	KY	Ky.	Tennessee	TN	Tenn.
Louisiana	LA	La.	Texas	TX	Tex.
Maine	ME	Me.	Utah	UT	Utah
Maryland	MD	Md.	Vermont	VT	Vt.
Massachusetts	MA	Mass.	Virginia	VA	Va.
Michigan	MI	Mich.	Washington	WA	Wash.
Minnesota	MN	Minn.	West Virginia	WV	W.Va.
Mississippi	MS	Miss.	Wisconsin	WI	Wisc.
Missouri	MO	Mo.	Wyoming	WY	Wyo.

See Also List 34, Acronyms and Initialization;
and List 91, Common Abbreviations.

The NEW Reading Teacher's Book of Lists, © 1985 Prentice-Hall, Inc., Englewood Cliffs, NJ 07632. By E. Fry, D. Fountoukidis, and J. Polk.

91. COMMON ABBREVIATIONS

Abbreviations are so widely used that it is important to know what the common ones stand for. In addition to being an advantage in reading comprehension, knowing and using abbreviations saves time, space, and energy when we write.

acct.	account	dept.	department
A.D.	Anno Domini (in the year of our Lord)	diam.	diameter
adj.	adjective	div.	division
ad lib	ad libitum (improvise)	doz.	dozen
adv.	adverb	Dr.	Doctor, drive
AKA	also known as		
a.m.	ante meridiem (morning)	ea.	each
amt	amount	ed.	edition
anon.	anonymous	e.g.	exempli gratia (for example)
ans.	answer	elec.	electric
Apr.	April	Esq.	Esquire
arith.	arithmetic	et al.	et alii (and others)
assn.	association	etc.	et cetera (and others)
assoc.	association	ex.	example
asst.	assistant		
atty.	attorney	F	Fahrenheit
Aug.	August	Feb.	February
ave.	avenue	fem.	feminine
		fig.	figure
B.A.	Bachelor of Arts	freq.	frequency
bib.	bibliography	Fri.	Friday
biog.	biography	ft.	foot
B.C.	before Christ		
bldg.	building	g	gram
B.S.	Bachelor of Science	gal.	gallon
Blvd.	boulevard	Gen.	General
		govt.	government
c	centimeter, centigrade		
cap.	capital	H.M.S.	His (Her) Majesty's Ship
Capt.	Captain	Hon.	Honorable
cc	cubic centimeter	hosp.	hospital
cert.	certificate	hr	hour
chap.	chapter	H.R.H.	His (Her) Royal Highness
Chas.	Charles	ht	height
Col.	Colonel		
conj.	conjunction	ibid.	ibidem (in the same place)
corp.	corporation	id.	idem (the same)
cu	cubic	i.e.	id est (that is)
		illus.	illustration
D.C.	District of Columbia	in.	inch
D.D.	Doctor of Divinity	inc.	incorporated
D.D.S.	Doctor of Dental Surgery	incl.	including
Dec.	December	intro	introduction

The NEW Reading Teacher's Book of Lists, © 1985 Prentice-Hall, Inc., Englewood Cliffs, NJ 07632. By E. Fry, D. Fountoukidis, and J. Polk.

The NEW Reading Teacher's Book of Lists, © 1985 Prentice-Hall, Inc., Englewood Cliffs, NJ 07632. By E. Fry, D. Fountoukidis, and J. Polk.

Jan.	January		pres.	president
Jour.	Journal		prin.	principal
Jr.	junior		pron.	pronoun
			pt.	pint
kg	kilogram			
			qt.	quart
lat.	latitude		recd.	received
lb.	pound		ref.	referee; reference
lieut.	lieutenant		rev.	reverend
long.	longitude		R.N.	Registered Nurse
lt.	lieutenant			
			Sat.	Saturday
M.A.	Master of Arts		sci.	science
mag.	magazine		sec.	second
masc.	masculine		Sept.	September
math	mathematics		sgt.	sergeant
M.D.	Doctor of Medicine		sing.	singular
mdse.	merchandise		sq.	square
med.	medium		Sr.	Senior; Sister
mgr.	manager		St.	Street; Saint
min.	minute		subj.	subject
misc.	miscellaneous		Sun	Sunday
ml	milliliter		supt.	superintendent
mo.	month			
mph	miles per hour		tel.	telephone
Mr.	mister		Thurs.	Thursday
Mrs.	mistress		Tues.	Tuesday
neg.	negative		univ.	university
neut.	neuter		USA	United States of America
no.	number			
Nov.	November		vet.	veterinarian; veteran
			vocab.	vocabulary
Oct.	October		vol.	volume
opp.	opposite		vs.	versus
oz.	ounce			
			Wed.	Wednesday
p.	page		wk.	week
pd.	paid		Wm.	William
Ph.D.	Doctor of Philosophy		wt.	weight
pkg.	package			
pl.	plural		yd.	yard
p.m.	post meridiem (afternoon)		yr.	year
pop.	populaton			
pp.	pages			

See Also List 34, Acronyms and Initializations;
and List 90, State Abbreviations.

92. DICTIONARY PHONETIC SYMBOLS

Dictionaries tell you how to pronounce words by using phonetic symbols. These are based on the Roman alphabet but add diacritical marks and special letter combinations. Although all dictionaries use similar phonetic symbols, they are not all identical. This list shows four of the more widely used sets of symbols.

Common and Uncommon Spellings for Phonemes	Thorndike Barnhart (Scott Foresman)	Webster-Merriam (American Book Co.)	American Heritage (Houghton Mifflin)	Random House
hat, plaid	a	a	ă	a
age, aid, gaol, gauge, say, break, vain, they	ā	ā	ā	ā
care, air, where, pear, their	ã, er, ar	eər	âr	â(r)
father, heart, sergeant	ä	ä	ä	ä
bad, rabbit	b	b	b	b
child, watch, righteous, question, virtuous	ch	ch	ch	ch
did, add, filled	d	d	d	d
many, aesthetic, said, says, let, bread, heifer, leopard, friend, bury	ē	ē	ĕ	ē
Caesar, quay, equal, team, bee, receive, people, key, machine, believe, phoenix	ē	ē	ē	ē
stern, pearl, first, word, journey, turn, myrtle	ėr	ər	ûr	û(r)
fat, effort, laugh, phrase	f	f	f	f
go, egg, ghost, guest, catalogue	g	g	g	g
he, who	h	h	h	h
wheat	hw	hw	hw	hw
England, been, bit, sieve, women, busy, build, hymn	i	i	ĭ	i
aisle, aye, height, eye, ice, lie, buy, sky	ī	ī	ī	ī
bridge, gradual, soldier, tragic, exaggerate, jam	j	j	j	j
coat, account, chemistry, back, acquire, sacque, kind, liquor	k	k	k	k
land, tell	l	l	l	l
drachm, paradigm, calm, me, climb, common, solemn	m	m	m	m
gnaw, knife, no, manner, pneumonia	n	n	n	n

The NEW Reading Teacher's Book of Lists, © 1985 Prentice-Hall, Inc., Englewood Cliffs, NJ 07632. By E. Fry, D. Fountoukidis, and J. Polk.

The NEW Reading Teacher's Book of Lists, © 1985 Prentice-Hall, Inc., Englewood Cliffs, NJ 07632. By E. Fry, D. Fountoukidis, and J. Polk.

ink, long, tongue	ng	ng	ng	n͡g
watch, hot	o	ä	ŏ	o
beau, yeoman, sew, open, boat, toe, oh, brooch, soul, low	ō	ō	ō	ō
all, Utah, taught, law, order, broad, bought	ô	ȯ	ô	ô
boil, boy	oi	ȯi	oi	oi
house, bough, now	ou	aͧ	ou	ou
cup, happy	p	p	p	p
run, rhythm, carry	r	r	r	r
cent, say, scent, schism, miss	s	s	s	s
ocean, machine, special, sure, schist, conscience, nauseous, pshaw, she, tension, issue, mission, nation	sh	sh	sh	sͪh
stopped, bought, tell, Thomas, button	t	t	t	t
thin	th	th	th	tͪh
then, breathe	ŦH	th	*th*	tͪh
come, does, flood, trouble, cup	u	ə	ŭ	u
beauty, feud, queue, few, adieu, view, use	ū	yü	yo͞o	yo͞o
wolf, good, should, full	u̇	u	o͝o	o͝o
maneuver, threw, move, shoe, food, you, rule, fruit	ü	ü	o͞o	o͞o
of, Stephen, very, flivver	v	v	v	v
choir, quick, will	w	w	w	w
opinion, hallelujah, you	y	y	y	y
has, discern, scissors, Xerxes, zero, buzz	z	z	z	z
garage, measure, division, azure, brazier	zh	zh	zh	zͪh

See Also List 48, Phonics Example Words.

93. INITIAL TEACHING ALPHABET

The Initial Teaching Alphabet (ITA) is a special modification of the alphabet designed to make beginning reading easier by creating a one-to-one relationship between sounds and letters. The sample text shows how beginning reading material is rewritten using ITA spelling.

æ	b	c	d	ee
f<u>a</u>ce	<u>b</u>ed	<u>c</u>at	<u>d</u>og	ke<u>y</u>
f	g	h	ie	j	k
<u>f</u>eet	<u>l</u>eg	<u>h</u>at	<u>fly</u>	<u>j</u>ug	<u>k</u>ey
l	m	n	œ	p	ɹ
<u>l</u>etter	<u>m</u>an	<u>n</u>est	<u>o</u>ver	<u>p</u>en	gi<u>r</u>l
r	s	t	ue	v	w
<u>r</u>ed	<u>s</u>poon	<u>t</u>ree	<u>u</u>se	<u>v</u>oice	<u>w</u>indow
y	z	ʒ	wh	ch
<u>y</u>es	<u>z</u>ebra	dai<u>s</u>y	<u>wh</u>en	<u>ch</u>air
th	th	ʃh	ʒ	ŋ
<u>th</u>ree	<u>the</u>	<u>sh</u>op	televi<u>s</u>ion	ri<u>ng</u>
a	au	a	e	i	o
<u>fa</u>ther	b<u>a</u>ll	c<u>a</u>p	<u>e</u>gg	m<u>i</u>lk	b<u>o</u>x
u	ω	ω	ou	oi
<u>u</u>p	b<u>oo</u>k	sp<u>oo</u>n	<u>ou</u>t	<u>oi</u>l

"ie nœ!" sed polly.

"mee, too!" sed molly.

"tæk them too the sircus!" cried jack.

and that's just whot happend.

See Also List 92, Dictionary Phonetic Symbols; and List 94, Diacritical Marking System.

The NEW Reading Teacher's Book of Lists, © 1985 Prentice-Hall, Inc., Englewood Cliffs, NJ 07632. By E. Fry, D. Fountoukidis, and J. Polk.

The NEW Reading Teacher's Book of Lists, © 1985 Prentice-Hall, Inc., Englewood Cliffs, NJ 07632. By E. Fry, D. Fountoukidis, and J. Polk.

94. DIACRITICAL MARKING SYSTEM

The Diacritical Marking System was designed to help beginning readers pronounce words. Diacritical marks are added to the text without altering the words' traditional spellings.

SHORT	A	apple	F	fish	K	kitten	P	penny	U	umbrella
VOWELS &	B	Bill	G	girl	L	Linda	Q	queen (qu)	V	valentine
REGULAR	C	cookies	H	hat	M	midnight	R	Rickey	W	window
CONSONANTS	D	Daddy	I	Indian	N	nest	S	saw	X	box (ks)
(no marks)	E	egg	J	jar	O	ox	T	table	Y	baby
									Z	zebra

LONG VOWELS (bar over)	Ā	āpron	Ē	ēar	Ī	ice crēam	Ō	Ōcēan	Ū	Ūnited States

SCHWA (comma over)	À	àgo	=	È	ènough	=	'O	'other

LETTER Y

y in yes (consonant)   ȳ in mȳ (long vowel)   funny (Note y = E not marked)

DIPHTHONGS (underline both)	OI	boil	=	OY	boy	OU	out	=	OW	owl

BROAD O(A) (circumflex)

Â   âll   âwful   âuto   =   Ô   lông   ôr

LONG AND SHORT OO

One Dot U or Short OO   U̇ = Ȯ
                        pu̇t   goȯd

(one and two dots)

Two Dot U or Long OO   Ü = Ö = Ë
                       Jüne   roöm   nëw

R-CONTROLLED VOWELS

far   vāry   fir   her   fur (r acts as vowel)

DIGRAPHS (underline)	SH	shoe	CH	chair	WH	which	TH	that (voiced)
	TH	thing (unvoiced)	NG	sing	PH	=f phone		

SECOND SOUNDS OF CONSONANTS (underline)

C   c   (s)   cent
S   s   (z)   is
G   g   (j)   gem

SILENT (slash)

come   right   her

EXCEPTIONS (+ over)

+women   +action

Here is a sample of a text marked with the DMS:

"Look at our fish," said Bill.

"Hē wânts something.

But look at this box!"

See Also List 92, Dictionary Phonetic Symbols; and List 93, Initial Teaching Alphabet.

95. FOREIGN ALPHABETS

The table of alphabets shows how some other languages are written. Your students will enjoy writing their names and other messages using the different alphabets.

Hebrew
Vowels are not represented in normal Hebrew writing, but for educational purposes they are indicated by a system of subscript and superscript dots.
The transliterations shown in parentheses apply when the letter falls at the end of a word. The transliterations with subscript dots are pharyngeal consonants, as in Arabic.
The second forms shown are used when the letter falls at the end of a word.

Greek
The superscript ' on an initial vowel or *rhō*, called the "rough breathing," represents an aspirate. Lack of aspiration on an initial vowel is indicated by the superscript ', called the "smooth breathing."
When *gamma* precedes *kappa, xi, khi,* or another *gamma*, it has the value *n* and is so transliterated. The second lower-case form of *sigma* is used only in final position.

Russian
[1] This letter, called *tvordiǐ znak,* "hard sign," is very rare in modern Russian. It indicates that the previous consonant remains hard even though followed by a front vowel.
[2] This letter, called *myakiǐ znak,* "soft sign," indicates that the previous consonant is palatalized even when a front vowel does not follow.

HEBREW

Forms	Name	Sound
א	'aleph	
ב	bēth	b (bh)
ג	gimel	g (gh)
ד	dāleth	d (dh)
ה	hē	h
ו	waw	w
ז	zayin	z
ח	beth	ḥ
ט	ṭeth	ṭ
י	yodh	y
כ ך	kāph	k (kh)
ל	lāmedh	l
מ ם	mēm	m
נ ן	nūn	n
ס	samekh	s
ע	'ayin	'
פ ף	pē	p (ph)
צ ץ	ṣadhe	ṣ
ק	qōph	q
ר	rēsh	r
שׂ	sin	s
שׁ	shin	sh
ת	tāw	t (th)

GREEK

Forms	Name	Sound
A α	alpha	a
B β	beta	b
Γ γ	gamma	g (n)
Δ δ	delta	d
E ε	epsilon	e
Z ζ	zēta	z
H η	ēta	ē
Θ θ	thēta	th
I ι	iota	i
K κ	kappa	k
Λ λ	lambda	l
M μ	mu	m
N ν	nu	n
Ξ ξ	xi	x
O ο	omicron	o
Π π	pi	p
P ρ	rhō	r (rh)
Σ σ ς	sigma	s
T τ	tau	t
Υ υ	upsilon	u
Φ φ	phi	ph
X χ	khi	kh
Ψ ψ	psi	ps
Ω ω	ōmega	ō

RUSSIAN

Forms	Sound
А а	a
Б б	b
В в	v
Г г	g
Д д	d
Е е	e
Ж ж	zh
З з	z
И и Й й	i, ĭ
К к	k
Л л	l
М м	m
Н н	n
О о	o
П п	p
Р р	r
С с	s
Т т	t
У у	u
Ф ф	f
Х х	kh
Ц ц	ts
Ч ч	ch
Ш ш	sh
Щ щ	shch
Ъ ъ	"[1]
Ы ы	y
Ь ь	'[2]
Э э	e
Ю ю	yu
Я я	ya

The NEW Reading Teacher's Book of Lists, © 1985 Prentice-Hall, Inc., Englewood Cliffs, NJ 07632. By E. Fry, D. Fountoukidis, and J. Polk.

96. MANUAL ALPHABET

The NEW Reading Teacher's Book of Lists, © 1985 Prentice-Hall, Inc., Englewood Cliffs, NJ 07632. By E. Fry, D. Fountoukidis, and J. Polk.

The manual alphabet shows one way in which deaf persons communicate. They also use a signing language that uses hand positions for whole words or concepts, and most can read lips to some extent.

Manual Alphabet

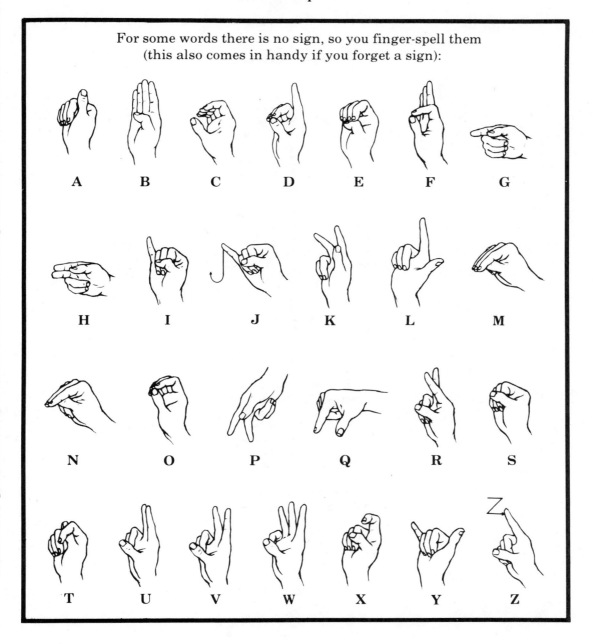

For some words there is no sign, so you finger-spell them
(this also comes in handy if you forget a sign):

A B C D E F G

H I J K L M

N O P Q R S

T U V W X Y Z

97. MORSE CODE

The Morse Code is still used by some radio hams. With practice, it is possible for amateurs to use it to send flashlight messages.

Morse Code

A	· —	V	· · · —
B	— · · ·	W	· — —
C	— · — ·	X	— · · —
D	— · ·	Y	— · — —
E	·	Z	— — · ·
F	· · — ·	Á	· — — · —
G	— — ·	Ä	· — · —
H	· · · ·	É	· · — · ·
I	· ·	Ñ	— — · — —
J	· — — —	Ö	— — — ·
K	— · —	Ü	· · — —
L	· — · ·	1	· — — — —
M	— —	2	· · — — —
N	— ·	3	· · · — —
O	— — —	4	· · · · —
P	· — — ·	5	· · · · ·
Q	— — · —	6	— · · · ·
R	· — ·	7	— — · · ·
S	· · ·	8	— — — · ·
T	—	9	— — — — ·
U	· · —	0	— — — — —
, (comma)	— — · · — —		
. (period)	· — · — · —		
?	· · — — · ·		
:	— · — · — ·		
;	— · — · — ·		
/	— · · — ·		
- (hyphen)	— · · · · —		
apostrophe	· — — — — ·		
parenthesis	— · — — · —		
underline	· · — — · —		

The NEW Reading Teacher's Book of Lists, © 1985 Prentice-Hall, Inc., Englewood Cliffs, NJ 07632. By E. Fry, D. Fountoukidis, and J. Polk.

98. GENERAL SIGNS AND SYMBOLS

Many specialized fields have sets of symbols or abbreviations, such as computer science, mathematics, and chemistry, which are needed to understand and work with concepts in those fields. In addition, there are many general use symbols that we need in everyday life.

+ plus	∟ right angle	≦ or ≤ less than or equal to	∴ therefore
− minus	△ triangle	absolute value	∵ because
± plus or minus	□ square	∪ logical sum or union	— vinculum (above letter)
∓ minus or plus	▭ rectangle	∩ logical product or intersection	( ) parentheses
× multiplied by	▱ parallelogram		[ ] brackets
÷ divided by	◡ circle	⊂ is contained in	ǀ ǀ braces
= equal to	⌢ arc of circle	∈ is a member of; permittivity; mean error	° degree
≠ or ≠ not equal to	⊥ equilateral	: is to; ratio	′ minute
≈ or ≒ nearly equal to	≜ equiangular	∷ as; proportion	″ second
≡ identical with	√ radical; root; square root	≐ approaches	△ increment
≢ not identical with	∛ cube root	⟶ approaches limit of	ω angular frequency; solid angle
⇌ equivalent	∜ fourth root	∝ varies as	Ω ohm
∼ difference	Σ sum	‖ parallel	μΩ microhm
≅ congruent to	! or ∟ factorial product	⊥ perpendicular	MΩ megohm
> greater than	∞ infinity	∠ angle	Φ magnetic flux
≯ not greater than	∫ integral		
< less than	ƒ function		
≮ not less than	∂ or δ differential; variation		
≧ or ≥ greater than or equal to	π pi		

℥ ounce	@ at	℈ per	‵ grave
ʒ dram	* asterisk	# number	˜ tilde
℈ scruple	† dagger	/ virgule; slash; solidus; shilling	ˆ circumflex
ƒ℥ fluid ounce	‡ double dagger	© copyright	¯ macron
ƒʒ fluid dram	§ section	% per cent	˘ breve
ℳ minim	☞ index	℅ care of	¨ dieresis
& or ℰ and; ampersand	´ acute	℀ account of	¸ cedilla
			ʌ caret
Ψ dielectric flux; electrostatic flux	♓ Pisces	♀ Venus	∞ haze; dust haze
ρ resistivity	☌ conjunction	⊖ or ⊕ Earth	T thunder
Λ equivalent conductivity	☍ opposition	♂ Mars	< sheet lightning
ℛ reluctance	△ trine	♃ Jupiter	☉ solar corona
⟶ direction of flow	□ quadrature	♄ Saturn	⊕ solar halo
⇌ electric current	✳ sextile	♅ Uranus	⎰ thunderstorm
◯ benzene ring	☊ dragon's head, ascending node	Ψ Neptune	＼ direction
⟶ yields	☋ dragon's tail, descending node	♇ Pluto	O or ⊙ or ① annual
⇌ reversible reaction		♈ Aries	◯◯ or ② biennial
↓ precipitate	● rain	♉ Taurus	♃ perennial
↑ gas	＊ snow	♊ Gemini	♂ or δ male
‰ salinity	⊠ snow on ground	♋ Cancer	♀ female
⊙ or ☼ sun	⟵ floating ice crystals	♌ Leo	□ male (in charts)
● or ⬤ new moon	▲ hail	♍ Virgo	◯ female (in charts)
☽ first quarter	△ sleet	♎ Libra	℞ take (from Latin *Recipe*)
◯ or ⊗ full moon	∨ frostwork	♏ Scorpius	ĀĀ or Ā or āā of each (doctor's prescription)
☾ last quarter	⊔ hoarfrost	♐ Sagittarius	℔ pound
☿ Mercury	≡ fog	♑ Capricornus	
		♒ Aquarius	

See Also List 56, Taxonomy of Graphs;
List 90, State Abbreviations; and List 91, Common Abbreviations.

99. PROOFREADING SYMBOLS

Helping students develop essays, short stories, term papers, or other writing goes more smoothly when you use proofreading symbols. Introduce these early in the school year and use them throughout. The time and space saved may be devoted to comments on content and encouragement.

Notation in Margin	How Indicated in Copy	Explanation
¶	true. The best rule to follow	New paragraph
⌒	living room	Close up
#	Mary hada	Insert space
⁀	Mary had a lamb little	Transpose
sp	There were ⑤ children	Spell out
cap	mary had a little lamb.	Capitalize
lc	Mary had a little Lamb.	Lower case
ℐ	The correct procedure	Delete or take out
stet	Mary had a little lamb.	Restore crossed-out word (s)
little	Mary had a lamb.	Insert word (s) in margin

The NEW Reading Teacher's Book of Lists, © 1985 Prentice-Hall, Inc., Englewood Cliffs, NJ 07632. By E. Fry, D. Fountoukidis, and J. Polk.

100. ROMAN NUMERALS

We might have taken our alphabet from the Romans but, thankfully, we did not take their number system. Roman numerals are used for formal or decorative purposes such as on clocks and cornerstones.

Roman	Arabic	Roman	Arabic
I	1	XX	20
II	2	XXI	21
III	3	XXIX	29
IV	4	XXX	30
V	5	XL	40
VI	6	XLVIII	48
VII	7	IL	49
VIII	8	L	50
IX	9	LX	60
X	10	XC	90
XI	11	XCVIII	98
XII	12	IC	99
XIII	13	C	100
XIV	14	CI	101
XV	15	CC	200
XVI	16	D	500
XVII	17	DC	600
XVIII	18	CM	900
XIX	19	M	1,000
		MCMLXXXVI	1986

The NEW Reading Teacher's Book of Lists, © 1985 Prentice-Hall, Inc., Englewood Cliffs, NJ 07632. By E. Fry, D. Fountoukidis, and J. Polk.

101. TRAFFIC SIGNS

As international travel has become more common, the United States has adopted traffic signs that use pictures and symbols. These help overcome language barriers. Understanding traffic signs is important for safety for drivers and pedestrians.

Shapes have meaning. Diamond-shaped signs signify a warning; rectangular signs with the longer dimension vertical provide a traffic regulation; and rectangular signs with the longer dimension horizontal contain guidance information. An octagon means stop; an inverted triangle means yield; a pennant means no passing; a pentagon shows the presence of a school; and a circle warns of a railroad crossing.

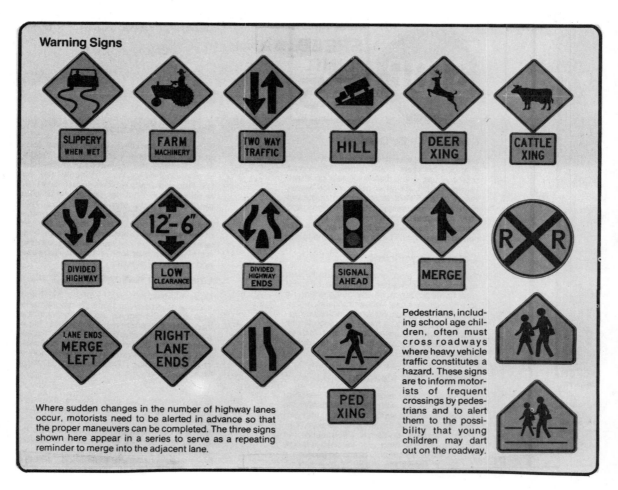

The NEW Reading Teacher's Book of Lists, © 1985 Prentice-Hall, Inc., Englewood Cliffs, NJ 07632. By E. Fry, D. Fountoukidis, and J. Polk.

Regulatory Signs

Black and white signs are for posting regulations. Red signifies stop, yield or prohibition. The red circle with a diagonal slash always indicates a prohibited movement.

NO U TURN

NO LEFT TURN

NO RIGHT TURN

NO TRUCKS

KEEP RIGHT

CENTER LANE — LEFT TURN ONLY

Left turns may be allowed for traffic coming from opposing directions in the center lane of a highway. There are two types of signs used to identify these locations. One a word message and the other a symbol sign showing opposing left turn arrows with the word "Only."

ONLY

SPEED LIMIT 55

NO TURN ON RED

RIGHT TURN ON RED AFTER STOP

Turns are permitted in many States at traffic signals when the red traffic signal is on. There are two types of laws which permit this movement. One permits the turn only with posting of the sign "Right Turn on Red After Stop." The other law allows turns at any intersection unless specifically prohibited by displaying the sign "No Turn on Red."

The pennant-shaped warning sign supplements the rectangular regulatory, "Do Not Pass" sign. The pennant is located on the left side of the road at the beginning of the no-passing pavement marking.

NO PASSING ZONE

YIELD

WRONG WAY

A "Restricted Lane Ahead" sign provides advance notice of a preferential lane which has been established in many cases to conserve energy by the use of high occupancy vehicles such as buses and carpools. The diamond symbol displayed on the sign is also marked on the pavement to further identify the controlled lane.

STOP

DO NOT ENTER

DO NOT PASS

RESTRICTED LANE AHEAD

Guide Signs

Green background signs provide directional information. Diagrams on some signs are being introduced to help motorists find the correct path through complicated interchange ramp networks. Roadside mileage markers will assist in trip planning and provide locational information. In addition mileage numbers (mile post numbers) are used to identify interchanges and exits. The number for an exit is determined from the nearest roadside mileage marker preceding the crossroad. Green signs also point the way of such items as trails for hiking and places for parking.

The brown background sign provides information pertaining to access routes for public parks and recreation areas.

ROCKY MOUNTAIN NATIONAL PARK 6 MILES

Signs for Bicycles

Bicycles are used by many persons on portions of heavily traveled roadways. This mixing of bicycles and motor vehicles is extremely dangerous and wherever possible, separate facilities are being provided for the bicycles. The green guide sign points out the bike route. The other two signs shown here appear where bicycles are restricted from use of the roadways and where separate roadway crossings for bicycles are provided.

The NEW Reading Teacher's Book of Lists, © 1985 Prentice-Hall, Inc., Englewood Cliffs, NJ 07632. By E. Fry, D. Fountoukidis, and J. Polk.

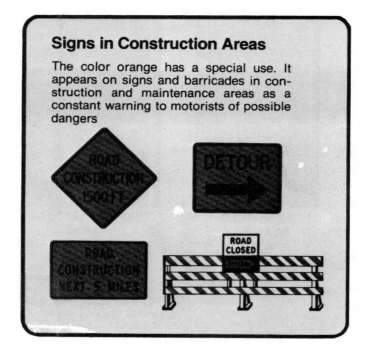

See Also List 9, Transportation Words;
List 56, Taxonomy of Graphs; and
List 98, General Signs and Symbols.

102. LIBRARY CLASSIFICATIONS

Most universities, research organizations, large public libraries, and of course, the Library of Congress, use the Library of Congress classifications for organizing their book collections. Most school libraries and smaller public libraries use the Dewey Decimal System. Students should have at least a modest acquaintance with both systems.

Library of Congress Classification

A — General Works
B — Philosophy and Religion
C — History of Civilization
D — General History
E-F — History-Americas
G — Geography and Anthropology
H — Social Sciences
J — Political Science
K — Law
L — Education
M — Music
N — Fine Arts
P — Language and Literature
    PA — Classical Language and Literature
    PB-PH — Modern European Languages
    PJ-PL — Oriental Language and Literature
    PN — General Literature
    PQ — French, Italian, Spanish, Portuguese Literature
    PR — English Literature
    PS — American Literature
    PT — German, Dutch, Scandinavian Literature
Q — Science
R — Medicine
S — Agriculture
T — Technology
U — Military Science
V — Naval Science
Z — Bibliography

Simplified Dewey Decimal System

000 — General Works
100 — Philosophy and Psychology
200 — Religion
300 — Social Sciences
    310 — Statistics
    320 — Political Science
    330 — Economics
    331 — Labor Economics
    331.3 — Labor by Age Groups
    331.39 — Employed Middle-aged and Aged
    340 — Law
    350 — Administration
    360 — Welfare and Social Institutions
    370 — Education
    380 — Public Services and Utilities
    390 — Customs and Folklore
400 — Philology
500 — Pure Science
600 — Applied Science
700 — Fine Arts
800 — Literature
900 — History

The NEW Reading Teacher's Book of Lists, © 1985 Prentice-Hall, Inc., Englewood Cliffs, NJ 07632. By E. Fry, D. Fountoukidis, and J. Polk.

103. NONSEXIST LANGUAGE GUIDELINES

Nonsexist language has had an impact in areas beyond the ERA, the women's movement, and activist associations. Texts and other materials are being written that show an increasing awareness and sensitivity to bias and sexism. These guides can help you and your students.

Slanted	Unbiased	Comment
The student chooses his assignments in this class.	The student chooses the assignments in this class.	omit *his*
	Students choose their assignments in this class.	change to plural
	The assignments in this class are chosen by the students.	rephrase
Man's search for knowledge has led him	The search for knowledge has led us	rephrased using first person
into areas unknown fifty years ago.	into areas unknown fifty years ago.	
man, mankind	people, humanity, human beings, humankind, the human species, the average person	use inclusive group
manpower	workers, personnel, staff, employees	use inclusive group
Each participant is to bring his own equipment.	Each participant is to bring his or her own equipment.	use *his* or *her*
The boys finally let Amy play on their team.	The boys finally "let" Amy play on their team.	shows bias of the team, not the author
The teacher should be on time for her class.	Teachers should be on time for their classes.	omit stereotype and make plural
This child suffers from lack of mothering.	This child suffers from lack of nurturing. This child suffers from lack of parenting.	inclusive noun substituted
The chairman of the committee recommends this book.	The chairperson recommends this book.	use nonspecific noun
chairman of the meeting	moderator, leader, discussion leader	use nonspecific noun
Dear Sir	Dear Editor	use nonspecific noun
	Dear Sir or Madam	use both or inclusive noun

104. GAMES AND METHODS

The games and methods for instruction listed here are suggestions for class activities that will help students learn many of the lists or words presented in this book.

Use these games or activities, or others that you like, for teaching the word lists in this book.

1. **Pairs.** A card game for two to five players. Five cards are dealt to each player, and the remainder of the deck is placed in the center of the table. The object of the game is to get as many pairs as possible. There are only two cards alike in each deck. To play, the player to the right of the dealer may ask any other player if he or she has a specific card. For example, "Do you have *and*?" The player asking must hold the mate in his or her hand. The player who is asked must give up the card if he or she holds it. If the first player does not get the card asked for, he or she draws one card from the pile. Then the next player has a turn at asking for a card.

   If the player succeeds in getting the card asked for, either from another player or from the pile, he or she gets another turn. As soon as the player gets a pair, he or she puts the pair down in front of him or her. The player with the most pairs at the end of the game wins. *Note:* A deck of 50 cards (25 pairs) is good for two to five players.

   you

   you

2. **Bingo.** Played like regular Bingo except that the players' boards have 25 words in place of numbers. Children can use bits of paper for markers and the caller can randomly call off words from a list. Be certain when making the boards that the words are arranged in a different order on each card.

the	of	it	with	at
a	can	on	are	this
is	will	you	to	and
your	that	we	as	but
be	in	not	for	have

The NEW Reading Teacher's Book of Lists, © 1985 Prentice-Hall, Inc., Englewood Cliffs, NJ 07632. By E. Fry, D. Fountoukidis, and J. Polk.

The NEW Reading Teacher's Book of Lists, © 1985 Prentice-Hall, Inc., Englewood Cliffs, NJ 07632. By E. Fry, D. Fountoukidis, and J. Polk.

3. **Board Games.** Trace a path on posterboard. Mark off one-inch spaces. Write a word in each space. Students advance from start by tossing dice, until one reaches the finish line. Students must correctly pronounce (or give the meaning or sample use) of the word in the square. Use three pennies if you don't have dice; shake and advance number of squares for heads up.

4. **Contests.** Students, individually or as teams, try to get more words in a category than anyone else. For example the teacher may start the contest by giving three homographs. The students try to amass the longest list of homographs. There may be a time limit.

5. **Spelling.** Use the list words in spelling lessons or have an old-fashioned spelling bee. See List 19, Spelling Demons—Elementary and List 20, Spelling Demons—Secondary.

6. **Use Words in a Sentence.** Either orally or written. Award points for the longest, funniest, saddest, or most believable sentence.

7. **Word Wheels.** To make a word wheel, attach an inner circle to a larger circle with a paper fastener. Turn the inner wheel to match outer parts. This is great for compound words, phonograms, or matching a word to a picture clue. Sliding strips do the same thing.

8. **Matching.** Make worksheets with two columns of words or word parts. Students draw a line from an item in column A to the item in column B that matches (*prefix* and *root*, *word* and *meaning*, two synonyms, etc.). Matching also can be done by matching two halves of a card that has been cut to form puzzle pieces.

9. **Flash Cards.** The word or word part is written on one side of a card. The teacher or tutor flashes the cards for the student to read instantly. Cards also can be shuffled and read by the student. Cards also can be used in sentence building, finding synonyms and antonyms, and so on.

10. **Hidden Words.** (or Word Search Puzzle). To make a word search puzzle, write words horizontally, vertically, or diagonally on a grid (graph paper is fine), one letter per box. Fill in all the other boxes with letters at random. Students try to locate all of the target words. When they find one they circle it.

C	E	Z	O
B	A	M	D
R	S	T	O
F	M	X	G

11. **Concentration.** To play Concentration, use one-sided flashcards or any card with a word or symbol written on one side. Cards must be in pairs such as two identical cards or an association pair. Shuffle four or more pairs (more for older or brighter students) and place cards face down spread out randomly over a table surface. The player may pick up any two cards and look at them. If they are a pair, he or she keeps them; if they are not, the cards must be put back in exactly the same place from which they came. The trick is to remember where different cards are located while they are sitting on the table face down so that when you pick up one card you remember where its pair is located. Players take turns and the object is to accumulate the most cards. Learning is needed to know what cards are pairs, for example, which definition matches which card.

12. **Association Cards.** For students who don't want to fool around with games, a useful learning device is to develop a set of association pair cards with the word on one side and the thing to be learned on the other side; for example, a word on one side and its definition on the other side. The student first studies both sides of a set of cards, then the student goes through a stack of cards reading the words and attempting to recall the definition. If correct, he or she puts the card into the "know pile"; if incorrect or the student can't remember, the card is studied and put into the "don't-know pile." Next, the "don't-know pile" is sorted once more into "know" and "don't-know." This process is complete when all cards are in the "know pile"; however, unfortunately there is also something called forgetting, so the stack of cards should be reviewed at later intervals, such as a few days later and a few weeks later. Students should not attempt to learn (associate) too many new (unknown) cards at one time, or learning will become boring. But as long as motivation is high and learning is occurring, this is an excellent learning and study technique.

13. **Tutoring.** A teacher and a student, or a tutor and a student, or even two students can use these double-sided association pair cards in many ways. The teacher holds up one card and the student calls off the associated definition. Students can take turns, have contests, win prizes, and so on.

14. **Testing.** Although it is often overused, testing is also a powerful learning motivator and teaching device. Done kindly and thoughtfully, testing can cause a lot of learning to occur in a classroom or tutoring situation. A technique of testing is to assign a set of association pairs to be learned (using any game or technique) and then test the results. Some teachers assign short daily tests that accumulate points or cause movement on a big chart. Other teachers give weekly tests and assign numeral or percent grades; these are shown to parents or the five best papers are posted on a bulletin board. Part of the learning occurs because the students are motivated to study and because the students get feedback or knowledge of the results as to whether they know or don't know something. Hence, the corrected papers should be returned or the students should trade papers and correct for more immediate and sometimes better knowledge of results.

The NEW Reading Teacher's Book of Lists, © 1985 Prentice-Hall, Inc., Englewood Cliffs, NJ 07632. By E. Fry, D. Fountoukidis, and J. Polk.

The NEW Reading Teacher's Book of Lists, © 1985 Prentice-Hall, Inc., Englewood Cliffs, NJ 07632. By E. Fry, D. Fountoukidis, and J. Polk.

Testing also gives feedback to the teacher or tutor so that the teacher can regulate the amount of new learning (number of words) to be learned next or the amount needing review. It also can help the teacher to individualize and to give some students more and other students less to be learned.

15. **Computer-Aided Instruction (CAI).** One of the newer methods of teaching is to use computers to provide instruction, drills, and tests. An example is the Fry Word Drills Program (Jamestown Publishers), which uses a vanishing technique in which the student gradually replaces missing letters. This program is repeated and students are given more practice if any errors are made. The program also teaches spelling and word recognition. Some lists are included on the disk, but the teacher can add any list of words to this program. Other CAI programs teach vocabulary both in and out of context, different types of comprehension, and subject content reading. CAI uses many elements of programmed instruction, such as small steps (limited from content), clear objectives, careful sequencing, active student response, immediate feedback on correctness, and often branching and recordkeeping. Most teachers buy programs already made, but it is possible to develop your own on a blank disk with the aid of a utility program in which the teacher only inserts desired content. This *Reading Teachers' Book of Lists* has much excellent content for CAI programs.

16. **Association Pairs.** This is a table of items to be associated or learned together. We are calling them association pairs because they are often taught by association learning. The following association pairs can be used in developing games such as Concentration and Association, and in creating programs for computer-aided instruction.

List Number	Association Pair
1	Word–Homophone
2	Homograph—Definition
3	Word—Look-alike or sound-alike word
10	Measurement term—Abbreviation
10	Measurement term—Numerical relation (for example, kilometer—1000 meters)
10	Measurement term—Conversion
23	Word—Synonym
23	Word—Antonym
24	First three words in analogy—Last word
28	Idiom root word—three or four usages
30	Clipped word—Full word
31	Portmanteau word—Full words
33	Contraction—Full words
34	Acronym—Full words
35	Borrowed word—Origin
36	Foreign word—Translation (origin)
38	-Ology word—Definition

39	Phobia word—Definition
40	Greek root—Meaning
41	Latin root—Meaning
42	Prefix—Meaning
43	Suffix—Meaning
43 and 44	Suffix—Grammar (part of speech, plural, etc.)
48	Illustrating word or example word—Phoneme (for example, at—short A)
51	Propaganda technique—Example
56	Graph term—Example
61	Key object—Number
68	Part of speech—Definition (example)
69	Irregular verb present—Past
69	Irregular verb present—Past participle
75	Literary term—Definition
90	State abbreviation—Full name
91	Common abbreviation—Full term
95	Latin alphabet—Hebrew or Greek or Russian alphabet
96 and 97	Alphabet—Manual alphabet or Morse Code
98	Symbol—Verbal equivalent
99	Proofreading symbol—Explanation
100	Roman numeral—Arabic numeral
102	Library classification symbol—Area description

The NEW Reading Teacher's Book of Lists, © 1985 Prentice-Hall, Inc., Englewood Cliffs, NJ 07632. By E. Fry, D. Fountoukidis, and J. Polk.

105. ONE HUNDRED WAYS TO PRAISE

Be free with praise for even minor successes; it will encourage larger successes. Be careful, however, never to be phony and praise when it isn't deserved; you will lose your credibility and the value of future praise.

Fantastic!
That's really nice.
That's clever.
You're right on target.
Thank you!
Wow!
That's great!
Very creative.
Very interesting.
I like the way you're working.
Good thinking.
That's an interesting way of looking at it.
It's a pleasure to teach you when you
    work like this.
Now you've figured it out.
Keep up the good work.
You've made my day.
Purrrfect!
You're on the ball today.
This is something special.
Everyone's working so hard.
That's quite an improvement.
Much better.
Keep it up.
That's the right answer.
Exactly right!
You're on the right track now.
This is quite an accomplishment.
I like how you've tackled this assignment.
A powerful argument!
That's coming along nicely.
I like the way you've settled down
    to work.
You've shown a lot of patience with this.
I noticed that you got right down
    to work.
You've really been paying attention.
It looks like you've put a lot of work
    into this.
You've put in a full day today.
This is prize-winning work.
An A-1 paper!
I like your style.
Pulitzer-prize-winner in training.

Your style has spark.
Your work has such personality.
That's very perceptive.
This is a moving scene.
Your remark shows a lot of sensitivity.
This really has flair.
Clear, concise, and complete!
A well-developed theme!
You are really in touch with the feeling here.
This piece has pizzazz!
A splendid job!
You're right on the mark.
Good reasoning.
Very fine work.
You really scored here.
Outstanding!
This is a winner!
Go to the head of the class.
Superb!
Super!
Superior work.
Great going!
Where have you been hiding all this talent?
I knew you could do it!
You're really moving.
Good job.
What neat work!
You really outdid yourself today.
That's a good point.
That's a very good observation.
That's certainly one way of looking at it.
This kind of work pleases me very much.
Congratulations! You got _____ more
    correct today.
That's right. Good for you.
Terrific!
I bet your parents will be proud to see the
    job you did on this.
That's an interesting point of view.
You're really going to town.
You've got it now.
Nice going.
You make it look so easy.
This shows you've been thinking.

271

You're becoming an expert at this.
Topnotch work!
This gets a four-star rating.
Beautiful.
I'm very proud of the way you worked
    today.
Excellent work.
I appreciate your help.
Very good. Why don't you show the class?
The results were worth all your hard work.

You've come a long way with this one.
I appreciate your cooperation.
Thank you for getting right to work.
Marvelous.
I commend you for your quick thinking.
I like the way you've handled this.
That looks like it's going to be a good report.
I like the way you are working today.
My goodness, how impressive!

The NEW Reading Teacher's Book of Lists, © 1985 Prentice-Hall, Inc., Englewood Cliffs, NJ 07632. By E. Fry, D. Fountoukidis, and J. Polk.

See Also List 78, Book Report
Alternatives.

106. READABILITY GRAPH

The NEW Reading Teacher's Book of Lists, © 1985 Prentice-Hall, Inc., Englewood Cliffs, NJ 07632. By E. Fry, D. Fountoukidis, and J. Polk.

The Readability Graph is included on the next page so you will have it on hand when you need it. Use it to help judge the difficulty level of the materials your students use so that you can better match reading selections to students' reading abilities.

1. Randomly select three sample passages and count out exactly 100 words beginning with the beginning of a sentence. Count proper nouns, initializations, and numerals.

2. Count the number of sentences in the hundred words estimating length of the fraction of the last sentence to the nearest 1/10th.

3. Count the total number of syllables in the 100-word passage. If you don't have a hand counter available, an easy way is to put a mark above every syllable over one in each word, and then when you get to the end of the passage, count the number of marks and add 100. Small calculators also can be used as counters by pushing numeral "1", then push the "+" sign for each word or syllable when counting.

4. Enter graph with *average* sentence length and *average* number of syllables; plot a dot where the two lines intersect. The area where a dot is plotted will give you the approximate grade level.

5. If a great deal of variability is found in syllable count or sentence count, putting more samples into the average is desirable.

6. A word is defined as a group of symbols with a space on either side; thus, "Joe," "IRA," "1945," and "&" are each one word.

7. A *syllable* is defined as a phonetic syllable. Generally, there are as many syllables as vowel sounds. For example, *stopped* is one syllable and *wanted* is two syllables. When counting syllables for numerals and initializations, count one syllable for each symbol. For example, *1945* is four syllables, and *IRA* is three syllables, and & is one syllable.

EXAMPLE:

	Syllables	Sentences
1st Hundred Words	124	6.6
2nd Hundred Words	141	5.5
3rd Hundred Words	158	6.8
AVERAGE	141	6.3

READABILITY 7th GRADE (see dot plotted on graph)

See Also List 108, Writeability Checklist.

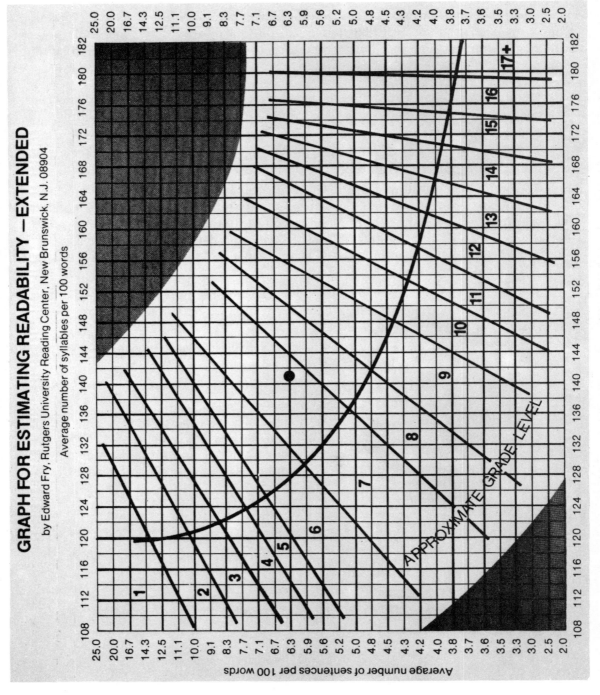

GRAPH FOR ESTIMATING READABILITY — EXTENDED

by Edward Fry, Rutgers University Reading Center, New Brunswick, N.J. 08904

Average number of syllables per 100 words

Average number of sentences per 100 words

APPROXIMATE GRADE LEVEL

The NEW Reading Teacher's Book of Lists, © 1985 Prentice-Hall, Inc., Englewood Cliffs, NJ 07632. By E. Fry, D. Fountoukidis, and J. Polk.

The NEW Reading Teacher's Book of Lists, © 1985 Prentice-Hall, Inc., Englewood Cliffs, NJ 07632. By E. Fry, D. Fountoukidis, and J. Polk.

107. HANDWRITING CHARTS

Have you ever needed a handwriting chart for a special student and couldn't quickly locate one? The Zaner-Bloser manuscript and cursive alphabet charts are here to help you out in just such a situation.

Zaner-Bloser MANUSCRIPT ALPHABET

Aa Bb Cc Dd Ee Ff
Gg Hh Ii Jj Kk Ll
Mm Nn Oo Pp Qq
Rr Ss Tt Uu Vv Ww
Xx Yy Zz 0123456789

2500 W. Fifth Ave. • P.O. Box 16764 • Columbus, Ohio 43216 • 614·486·0221

Zaner-Bloser CURSIVE ALPHABET

Aa Bb Cc Dd Ee
Ff Gg Hh Ii Jj
Kk Ll Mm Nn
Oo Pp Qq Rr Ss
Tt Uu Vv Ww Xx
Yy Zz 1234567890

c 1984 Zaner-Bloser   6008

Used with permission from *Handwriting: Basic Skills and Application.* Copyright © 1984, Zaner-Bloser, Inc., Columbus, Ohio.

108. WRITEABILITY CHECKLIST

The following is a list of suggestions for writing materials that are on an easy readability level.

VOCABULARY

    _____ Avoid large and/or infrequent words.
    _____ For high frequency words use lists such as the Carroll, Davies, Richman word list or 3000 Instant Words. (See List 4, Instant Words.)
    _____ For meaning lists, use *Living Word Vocabulary*.
    _____ Avoid words with Latin and Greek prefixes. (See List 42, Prefixes.)
    _____ Avoid jargon.
    _____ Okay to use technical words but make sure to define them and, if possible, give an example when you use them for the first time.

SENTENCES

    _____ Keep sentences short on the average.
    _____ For adults, keep average sentence below fifteen words.
    _____ Avoid splitting sentence kernel (embedding).
    _____ Keep verb active (avoid nominalizations).
    _____ Watch out for too many commas. (See List 71, Punctuation Guidelines.)
    _____ Semicolons and colons may indicate need for new sentence.

PARAGRAPHS

    _____ Keep paragraphs short on the average.
    _____ One-sentence paragraphs are permissible at times.
    _____ Indent and line up lists.

ORGANIZATION

    _____ Suit organization plan to topic and your purpose.
    _____ Try to use SER—Statement, Example, Restatement
    _____ Use subheads.
    _____ Use signal words. (See List 50, Signal Words.)
    _____ Use summaries.

PERSONAL WORDS

    _____ Use personal pronouns, but not too many.
    _____ Use personal sentences.

IMAGEABILITY

    _____ Use more concrete or high imagery words.
    _____ Avoid abstract or low imagery words.
    _____ Use vivid examples.
    _____ Use metaphors. (See List 26, Metaphors.)
    _____ Use graphs whenever appropriate. (See List 56, Taxonomy of Graphs.)

REFERENTS

    _____ Avoid too many referents (for example, *it*).
    _____ Replace some referents with nouns or verbs.
    _____ Avoid too much distance between noun and referent.
    _____ Don't use referent that could refer to two or more nouns or verbs.

MOTIVATION

    _____ Select interesting topics.
    _____ Select interesting examples.
    _____ Write at level that is a little below your audience. (See List 106, Readability Graph.)

The NEW Reading Teacher's Book of Lists, © 1985 Prentice-Hall, Inc., Englewood Cliffs, NJ 07632. By E. Fry, D. Fountoukidis, and J. Polk.

109. MAJOR READING JOURNALS

To stay abreast of happenings in the field of reading instruction, read one of the professional journals. Ask to have a subscription kept in your school library or better yet, in the teacher's room.

Journal of Reading (general and secondary orientation) International Reading Association. Eight issues yearly.

Journal of Reading Behavior (research orientation) National Reading Conference. Quarterly.

The Reading Teacher (elementary teacher orientation) International Reading Association. Eight issues yearly. (Formerly *Journal of Developmental Reading*.)

Reading Research Quarterly (research orientation) International Reading Association. Quarterly.

Reading World (general and college orientation) College Reading Association. Quarterly.

Language Arts (elementary teacher and language arts orientation) National Council of Teachers of English. Eight issues yearly. (Formerly *Elementary English*.)

110. READING ORGANIZATIONS

The four organizations listed below publish many useful journals, monographs and research reports. They also organize and sponsor many local and regional conferences. They are excellent sources of current information in the field.

International Reading Association (IRA)*
Box 8139
Newark, DE 19711
Annual meeting, late April or early May.

National Reading Conference (NRC)
1070 Silbey Tower
Rochester, NY 14604
Annual meeting, early December.

College Reading Association (CRA)
3340 South Danbury Avenue
Springfield, MO 65807
Annual meeting, October.

National Council of Teachers of English (NCTE)
1111 Kenyon Road
Urbana, IL 61801
Annual meeting, mid-November.

*Note: Many state and local councils and national affiliates of the International Reading Association hold regular meetings and publish either journals or newsletters on reading. A complete list of them can be obtained without charge from the IRA.

IRA Presidents				NRC Presidents
1955–56	William S. Gray	1971–72	Theodore L. Harris	Oscar Causey, 1952–59
1956–57	Nancy Larrick	1972–73	William K. Durr	William Eller, 1960–61
1957–58	Albert J. Harris	1973–74	Millard H. Black	George Spache, 1962–64
1958–59	George D. Spache	1974–75	Constance M. McCullough	Albert Kingston, 1964–65
1959–60	A. Sterl Artley	1975–76	Thomas C. Barrett	Paul Berg, 1967–68
1960–61	Mary C. Austin	1976–77	Walter H. MacGinitie	Alton Raygor, 1969–70
1961–62	William D. Sheldon	1977–78	William Eller	Wendell Weaver, 1971
1962–63	Morton Botel	1978–79	Dorothy Strickland	Earl Rankin, 1972–74
1963–64	Nila Banton Smith	1979–80	Roger Farr	Edward Fry, 1974–76
1964–65	Theodore Clymer	1980–81	Olive S. Niles	Jaap Tuinman, 1976–78
1965–66	Dorothy K. Bracken	1981–82	Kenneth S. Goodman	Harry Singer, 1978–80
1966–67	Mildred A. Dawson	1982–83	Jack Cassidy	Frank Greene, 1980–82
1967–68	H. Alan Robinson	1983–84	Ira E. Aaron	Irene Athey, 1982–84
1968–69	Leo Fay	1984–85	Bernice C. Cullinan	Lenore Ringler, 1985
1969–70	Helen Huus	1985–86	Joan C. Manning	David Pearson, 1986
1970–71	Donald L. Cleland	1986–87	Roselmina Indrisano	Jerome Harste, 1987

The NEW Reading Teacher's Book of Lists, © 1985 Prentice-Hall, Inc., Englewood Cliffs, NJ 07632. By E. Fry, D. Fountoukidis, and J. Polk.

111. PUBLISHERS OF CURRICULUM MATERIALS AND TESTS

The NEW Reading Teacher's Book of Lists, © 1985 Prentice-Hall, Inc., Englewood Cliffs, NJ 07632. By E. Fry, D. Fountoukidis, and J. Polk.

This list of publishers' addresses will come in handy in requesting current catalogues and in ordering curriculum materials.

Addison-Wesley Publishing Co., Inc.
Reading, MA 01867

Allyn & Bacon, Inc.
El-Hi Division
7 Wells Avenue
Newton, MA 02159

American Guidance Service
Publishers' Building
Circle Pines, MN 55014

Barnell Loft and Dexter Westbrook
Publications
958 Church Street
Baldwin, NY 11510

Borg-Warner Educational Systems
600 West University Drive
Arlington Heights, IL 60004

Bowmar/Noble
P.O. Box 25308
Oklahoma City, OK 73125

The Continental Press, Inc.
520 East Bainbridge Street
Elizabethtown, PA 17022

The College Board
888 Seventh Avenue
New York, NY 10106

Croft Educational Services
100 Garfield Avenue
New London, CT 06320

CTB/McGraw-Hill
(California Test Bureau)
Del Monte Research Park
Monterey, CA 93940

Curriculum Associates, Inc.
5 Esquire Road
North Billerica, MA 01862

Developmental Learning Materials
One DLM Park
Allen, TX 75002

Dreier Educational Systems
(see Jamestown Publishers)

The Economy Company
P.O. Box 25308
Oklahoma City, OK 73125

Educational Development Corporation
 (EDC)
P.O. Box 25308
Tulsa, OK 74145

Educators Publishing Service
75 Moulton Street
Cambridge, MA 02138

ERIC/RCS/NCTE
1111 Kenyon Road
Urbana, IL 61801

Fearon Publishers, Inc.
(Pitman Publishing Corporation)
6 Davis Drive
Belmont, CA 94002

Follett Publishing Company
1010 West Washington Boulevard
Chicago, IL 60607

Garrard Publishing Company
107 Cherry Street
New Canaan, CT 06840

Ginn and Company
191 Spring Street
Lexington, MA 02173

Globe Book Company, Inc.
175 Fifth Avenue
New York, NY 10010

Good Apple, Inc.
P.O. Box 299
Carthage, IL 62321

Harcourt Brace Jovanovich, Inc.
757 Third Avenue
New York, NY 10017

Harper & Row, Publishers, Inc.
10 East 53rd Street
New York, NY 10022

D. C. Heath and Company
125 Spring Street
Lexington, MA 02173

Holt, Rinehart and Winston
383 Madison Avenue
New York, NY 10017

Houghton Mifflin Company
1 Beacon Street
Boston, MA 02107

Ideal School Supply Company
11000 South Lavergne Avenue
Oak Lawn, IL 60453

Imperial International Learning
 Corporation
P.O. Box 548
Kankakee, IL 60901

Instructional Fair, Inc.
4158 Lake Michigan Drive
Grand Rapids, MI 49504

Instructional Objectives Exchange
11411 West Jefferson Boulevard
Culver City, CA 90230

The Instructor Publications, Inc.
757 Third Avenue
New York, NY 10017

International Reading Association
800 Barksdale Road
Newark, DE 19711

Jamestown Publishers
P.O. Box 6743
Providence, RI 02940

Laidlaw Brothers
Thatcher and Madison Streets
River Forest, IL 60305

Learn, Inc.
113 Gaither Drive
Mount Laurel, NJ 08057

J. B. Lippincott Company (see Harper &
 Row)
10 East 53rd Street
New York, NY 10022

Lyons and Carnahan (see Rand McNally)

Macmillan Publishing Company, Inc.
866 Third Avenue
New York, NY 10022

McGraw-Hill Book Company
1221 Avenue of the Americas
New York, NY 10020

Charles E. Merrill Publishing Company
1300 Alum Creek Drive
Columbus, OH 43216

Milliken Publishing Company
1100 Research Boulevard
St. Louis, MO 63132

Milton Bradley Company
Springfield, MA 01101

Modern Curriculum Press, Inc.
13900 Prospect Road
Cleveland, OH 44136

National Council of Teachers of English
1111 Kenyon Road
Urbana, IL 61801

National Textbook Co.
4255 W. Touhy Avenue
Lincolnwood, IL 60646

New Readers Press
Laubach Literacy, Inc.
Box 131
Syracuse, NY 13210

Oceana Educational Communications
40 Cedar Street
Dobbs Ferry, NY 10522

Open Court Publishing Company
P.O. Box 599
LaSalle, IL 61301

Parker Publishing Company, Inc.
(see Prentice-Hall, Inc.)

Prentice-Hall, Inc.
Englewood Cliffs, NJ 07632

The Psychological Corporation
304 East 45th Street
New York, NY 10017

Rand McNally and Company
P.O. Box 7600
Chicago, IL 60680

Random House, Inc.
201 East 50th Street
New York, NY 10022

Reader's Digest Services, Inc. (see
 Random House)

Regents Publishing Co., Inc.
2 Park Avenue
New York, NY 10016

The NEW Reading Teacher's Book of Lists, © 1985 Prentice-Hall, Inc., Englewood Cliffs, NJ 07632. By E. Fry, D. Fountoukidis, and J. Polk.

The Riverside Publishing Co.
8420 W. Bryn Mawr Avenue
Chicago, IL 60631

Frank Schaffer Publications
1926 Pacific Coast Highway
Redondo Beach, CA 90277

Scholastic Inc. (magazines and book
  services)
730 Broadway
New York, NY 10003

Science Research Associates, Inc. (SRA)
155 North Wacker Drive
Chicago, IL 60606

Scott, Foresman and Company
1900 East Lake Avenue
Glenview, IL 60025

Silver Burdett Co.
250 James Street
Morristown, NJ 07960

Steck-Vaughn Co.
P.O. Box 2028
Austin, TX 78768

Teachers College Press
1234 Amsterdam Avenue
New York, NY 10027

Webster/McGraw Hill (see McGraw-Hill)

Zaner-Bloser, Inc.
P.O. Box 16764
Columbus, OH 43216

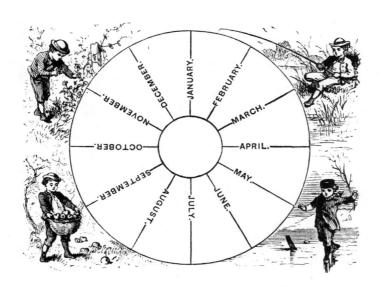

See Also Section IX, Books.

SECTION XI
Entertainment

112. MURPHY'S LAW AND OTHERS

The NEW Reading Teacher's Book of Lists, © 1985 Prentice-Hall, Inc., Englewood Cliffs, NJ 07632. By E. Fry, D. Fountoukidis, and J. Polk.

Murphy's Law and other principles might amuse or bemuse you. Some have a little jab of truth in them. Society is governed by certain immutable laws and principles. Murphy's Law, though, of somewhat doubtful authorship, is none the less real. Ask any engineer, mechanic, office manager, or computer programmer.

Both the Peter Principle and Parkinson's Law were developed by very real college professors and both are explained somewhat seriously in full books.

The other principles given here are sometimes original and sometimes borrowed from the common folklore. Use them and amuse with them as needed. Both you and your students might like to add to this important list of real-life observations for fun and profitable insight.

Murphy's Law: If anything can go wrong, it will, and at the worst possible moment.

Peter Principle: In a hierarchy every employee tends to rise to his or her level of incompetence.

Parkinson's Law: Work expands to fill time available for its completion.

Fry's Observation: The more obnoxious the kid, the less he or she will be absent.

Kling's Axiom: Any simple idea can be worded in a complicated way.

No matter how hard you teach a thing, some student is certain not to learn it.

Trouble never comes at a convenient time.

Everything takes longer than you think.

The other line always moves faster.

The greater the hurry, the slower the traffic.

No amount of careful planning will ever beat dumb luck.

A good theory might be worth a thousand words, but that won't make it any more practical.

School budgets are always cut in a manner so as to create the most disruption.

There are three kinds of lies: white lies, damned lies, and statistics.

A camel is a horse put together by committee.

Extracurricular activities sometimes are neither extra nor curricular.

One person's exuberance is the next person's annoyance.

Principals may come and principals may go, but the secretary will run the school regardless.

You can plan anything you like; just don't expect it to happen that way.

Things don't get lost, but they sometimes are carefully put away in some strange places.

People who ask for just a minute of your time don't have very accurate watches.

There's got to be a way to eliminate the last few days of school.

Just when you are sure kids are no good, one of them will do something nice for you.

Maybe a school could exist without heat, light, and water, but take away the duplicating machine and it would have to close down.

If Saint Peter uses multiple choice tests, we are all in for trouble.

Whoever said the worst students aren't creative? Look at their excuses.

113. EUPHEMISMS

These euphemisms might stand you in good stead at report card time or for parent interviews. They might also take some of the puffery out of some reports you may have to read. Students enjoy euphemisms; share some of these with your class and have them add to the list.

Blunt Truth	Euphemism
Lies	Shows difficulty in distinguishing between imaginary and factual material.
Is a klutz	Has difficulty with motor control and coordination.
Needs nagging	Accomplishes task when interest is constantly prodded.
Fights	Resorts to physical means of winning his or her point or attracting attention.
Smells bad	Needs guidance in development of good habits of hygiene.
Cheats	Needs help in learning to adhere to rules and standards of fair play.
Steals	Needs help in learning to respect the property rights of others.
Is a wise guy or gal	Needs guidance in learning to express himself or herself respectfully.
Is lazy	Requires ongoing supervision in order to work well.
Is rude	Lacks a respectful attitude toward others.
Is selfish	Needs help in learning to enjoy sharing with others.
Is gross	Needs guidance in developing the social graces.
Has big mouth	Needs to develop quieter habits of communication.
Eats like a pig	Needs to develop more refined table manners.
Bullies others	Has qualities of leadership but needs to use them more constructively.
Is babyish	Shows lack of maturity in relationships with others.
Hangs out	Seems to feel secure only in group situations; needs to develop sense of identity and independence.
Is disliked by others	Needs help in developing meaningful peer relationships.
Is often late	Needs guidance in developing habits of responsibility and punctuality.
Is truant	Needs to develop a sense of responsibility in regard to attendance.

The NEW Reading Teacher's Book of Lists, © 1985 Prentice-Hall, Inc., Englewood Cliffs, NJ 07632. By E. Fry, D. Fountoukidis, and J. Polk.

114. PALINDROMES

A palindrome is a word or sentence that reads the same way forward and backward. They are enjoyed by people of all ages who like to have some fun with words. Here is a starter list, your students will likely come up with several more.

Incidentally, many decades ago a physician named Samuel Orton coined the term *strepholsymbolia* to describe the error of reading or writing words backward, like *saw* for *was*.

Word Palindromes

Mom	noon	deed	did	Anna	tot	Hannah	kayak	nun
Dad	level	peep	eve	radar	dud	rotor	eye	
pop	Otto	ere	Bob	madam	toot	sees	deed	

Sentence Palindromes

Name no one man.	May a moody baby doom a yam?
Step on no pets.	Madam I'm Adam.
Never odd or even.	A man, a plan, a canal, Panama!
Able was I ere I saw Elba.	
Red root put up to order.	

Words That Read Differently Backward and Forward

Similar to palindromes are words that give different words when read backward. These words are often used in forming palindromes.

but	tub	now	won	top	pot	step	pets
no	on	net	ten	stop	pots	reward	drawer
not	ton	draw	ward	sleep	peels	cod	doc
saw	was	reed	deer	sinned	Dennis	emit	time
yam	may	leg	gel	stab	bats	sloop	pools
mood	doom	sleek	keels	star	rats	slap	pals
live	evil	strap	parts	spat	taps	keep	peek
Noel	Leon	tar	rat	span	naps		

115. WACKY WORDIES

The Wacky Wordies that follow are a rather new twist added by word afficionados. These rebuses represent a familiar phrase, saying, cliché, or name. They are a great pastime for a rainy or snowy day.

To add to students' interest in words and language, you might also keep a good assortment of commercial games on the shelves in your class that students can enjoy. Some favorites are *Scrabble, Boggle, Word Rummy, Spill-and-Spell, Facts-in-Fives,* and *Password.*

The object in solving is to discern a familiar phrase, saying, cliché, or name from each arrangement of letters and/or symbols. For example, box 1a depicts the phrase "Eggs over easy." Box 1b shows "Trafalgar Square." The puzzles get more diabolical as you go.

	a	b	c	d	e	f
1	eggs easy	T R A F A L G A R	told told tales	e t t r i k c i t p	new leaf	silky
2	price	L +O SS	swear bible bible bible bible	league	bridge water	school
3	-attitude	hoppin	century	E RC O T N U	orseman	D UC K
4	set one's teeth	or O or	bet one's dollar	tpmerhao	what must	way yield
5	t o 2 par n	dictnry	rifle rifle rifle rifle	pAINS	everything pizza	L Y I N G JOB
6	tr ial	prosperity	monkey O	busines	writer's	moon sonata
7	power	mesnackal	Wilson	pit	wheel wheel wheel wheel drive	✓✓ ✓ counter

black

1a Eggs over easy
1b Trafalgar Square
1c *Twice-Told Tales*
1d Round-trip ticket
1e Turn over a new leaf
1f Pie in the sky
2a *The Price Is Right*
2b Total loss
2c Swear on a stack of Bibles
2d Little League
2e Bridge over troubled water

2f High school
3a Negative attitude
3b Shopping center
3c Turn-of-the-century
3d Counterclockwise
3e Headless Horseman
3f Sitting duck
4a Set one's teeth on edge
4b Double or nothing
4c Bet one's bottom dollar
4d Mixed metaphor

4e What goes up must come down
4f Yield right of way
5a Not up to par
5b Abridged dictionary
5c Repeating rifle
5d Growing pains
5e Pizza with everything on it
5f Lying down on the job
6a Trial separation

6b Prosperity is just around the corner
6c Monkey around
6d Unfinished business
6e Writer's cramp
6f *Moonlight Sonata*
7a Power blackout
7b Between-meal snack
7c Flip Wilson
7d Bottomless pit
7e Four-wheel drive
7f Checkout counter

The NEW Reading Teacher's Book of Lists, © 1985 Prentice-Hall, Inc., Englewood Cliffs, NJ 07632. By E. Fry, D. Fountoukidis, and J. Polk.

The object in solving is to discern a familiar phrase, saying, cliché, or name from each arrangement of letters and/or symbols. For example, box 1a depicts "once over lightly." Box 1b shows "gossip column." Sounds easy, but wait until you see the others.

	a	b	c	d	e	f
1	once lightly	g o s s i p	˷ radio	c a p t a i n	noon good	bathing suit
2	ee ch sp	God nation ✄	✓ yearly	ses ame	d e e r	hold second
3	r−i×s+k	pox	strokes *strokes* **strokes**	n P y o c m a	law of returns	e a p s p u a l
4	hou se	age beauty	harm on y	encounters encounters encounters	breth	hearted
5	p a r t i c i p l e	**MAN** campus	momanon	˹ld block	"Duty!" and beyond	day day
6	sigh	ɓoqɾ	skating ice	inflat10n	g o s p e l	enemy enemy
7	to ngue ngue	gettingitall	e a v e s	c m ʳ e a ban ana	e e q u a l s m c	aluminum

Wacky Wordies

Names of contributors appear in parentheses following their answers:

1a Once over lightly (Karen Sayer, Ann Arbor, MI)

1b Gossip column (E. J. Ridler, Depew, NY)

1c Short-wave radio (Mary Sampley, St. Petersburg, FL)

1d Captain Hook (Karen Sayer, Ann Arbor, MI)

1e Good afternoon (Jim Tarolli, Rocky River, OH)

1f Topless bathing suit (Gifted class of Matteson School District 162, Matteson, IL)

2a Parts of speech (Ann Madura, Yonkers, NY)

2b One nation, under God, indivisible (Jamie Lubin, Randolph, NJ)

2c Yearly checkup (Richard Janssen, Churchville, PA)

2d Open sesame (David Reifer, Garden Grove, CA)

2e Deer crossing (Jamie Lubin, Randolph, NJ)

2f Hold on a second (The Imberts, Belcourt, ND)

3a Calculated risk (Barbara DePaoli, Brockton, MA)

3b Smallpox (Stephen Sundel, South Orange, NJ)

3c Different strokes (E. J. Ridler, Depew, NY)

3d Mixed company (Bradley W. Brunsell, Milton, MA)

3e Law of diminishing returns (Karen Sayer, Ann Arbor, MI)

3f Round of applause (Said Zeiba, Bellevue, WA)

4a Split-level house (Karen Sayer, Ann Arbor, MI)

4b Age before beauty (Colleen Brady, Malverne, NY)

4c Three-part harmony (Karen Sayer, Ann Arbor, MI)

4d *Close Encounters of the Third Kind* (Jamie Lubin, Randolph, NJ)

4e A little out of breath (Bradley W. Brunsell, Milton, MA)

4f Light-hearted (Ann Madura, Yonkers, NY)

5a Dangling participle (Karen Sayer, Ann Arbor, MI)

5b Big man on campus (Josh Tarnow, South Orange, NJ)

5c Man in the moon (Bradley W. Brunsell, Milton, MA)

5d Chip off the old block (Jim Galvez, Santa Maria, CA)

5e Above and beyond the call of duty (Rob McDonough, Hamilton, OH)

5f Day in and day out (Beth Eason, Atherton, CA)

6a No end in sight (Barbara DePaoli, Brockton, MA)

6b Shadow of a doubt (Karen Sayer, Ann Arbor, MI)

6c Skating on thin ice (Ann Madura, Yonkers, NY)

6d Double-digit inflation (Vicki Sheskin, Bethel, CT)

6e Spread the gospel (Virginia McLaughlin, Sherman Oaks, CA)

6f Archenemies (Karen Sayer, Ann Arbor, MI)

7a Forked tongue (Howie Orona, Grand Valley, CO)

7b Getting it all together (David Reifer, Garden Grove, CA)

7c Eavesdropping (Leonard M. Levine, New York, NY)

7d Banana split with whipped cream topping (Leonard M. Levine, New York, NY)

7e $E = mc^2$ (Danny McClelland, Carmichael, CA)

7f Aluminum siding (Evanne & Peter Kofman, Phoenix, AZ)

In cases where the same rebus was contributed by more than one person, we chose the entry with the earlier postmark.

If you enjoyed "Yet Wackier Wordies," we recommend the new Bantam book *WORDoodles* by Marvin Miller (paperback, $1.25).